If Gold Is Our Destiny

If Gold Is Our Destiny

How a Team of Mavericks Came Together for Olympic Glory

Sean P. Murray

ROWMAN & LITTLEFIELD
Lanham • Boulder • New York • London

Published by Rowman & Littlefield
An imprint of The Rowman & Littlefield Publishing Group, Inc.
4501 Forbes Boulevard, Suite 200, Lanham, Maryland 20706
www.rowman.com

86-90 Paul Street, London EC2A 4NE, United Kingdom

British Library Cataloguing in Publication Information Available

Library of Congress Cataloging-in-Publication Data
Names: Murray, Sean (Performance consultant), author.
Title: If gold is our destiny : the 1984 U.S. men's volleyball team and its quest for
   Olympic glory / Sean Murray.
Description: Lanham, Maryland : Rowman & Littlefield, [2022] | Includes bibliographical
   references and index. | Summary: "This book tells the inspiring story of the 1984
   U.S. men's Olympic volleyball team. After many years playing as underdogs, a maverick
   coach would take over and push the players to their physical and emotional limits.
   Their journey to the Olympics reveals the value of teamwork, never giving up, and
   trusting in an innovative style of leadership"—Provided by publisher.
Identifiers: LCCN 2021052270 (print) | LCCN 2021052271 (ebook) | ISBN
   9781538154854 (Cloth : acid-free paper) | ISBN 9781538192528 (pbk : alk. paper) |
   ISBN 9781538154861 (ePub)
Subjects: LCSH: Volleyball—United States—History. | Coaching (Athletics)—United
   States—Psychological aspects. | Olympic athletes—United States—Psychology. |
   Teamwork (Sports)—Psychological aspects. | Olympic Games (23rd : 1984 :
   Los Angeles, Calif.)
Classification: LCC GV1015.55 .M87 2022 (print) | LCC GV1015.55 (ebook) |
   DDC 796.3250973—dc23/eng/20220405
LC record available at https://lccn.loc.gov/2021052270
LC ebook record available at https://lccn.loc.gov/2021052271

To my father, who showed me the way

Contents

Acknowledgments

$\mathcal{I}$ could not have written this book without the unwavering support of my wife, Francine, who believed in me, and this project, from the very beginning. Writing the book was a five-year journey, and there were several times when I was ready to give up, but each time, it was her encouragement and confidence in me and the story that brought me back and kept me going.

The book would, of course, not be possible without my father and his decades-long involvement and dedication to U.S. men's volleyball. The friendships he formed and the incredible work he did with his partner, Chuck Johnson, and the coaches and administrators at USA Volleyball are a testament to the power of the team principles that ultimately played out in the gold medal victory of the 1984 team.

I would like to thank my mother, who is a gifted writer and showed me with her example how the power of words on a page can move the hearts and minds of others. Growing up, she encouraged me to write and follow my dreams. She always cherished the time she got to spend traveling with the team in Japan in 1982, and she became one of its biggest fans at the 1984 Olympics. When my father passed away in May 2021, she inspired me to finish the project and ensure the incredible story of the 1984 team would live on.

I couldn't have written the book without the help of Doug Beal. When I called him in June 2017 and briefed him on my intention to write a book about the 1984 team, he was supportive of the project, making himself available for countless phone interviews and email exchanges. He introduced me to the players, coaches, and just about anyone who had played even a minor role in helping the 1984 team be successful. He invited me into his home and opened his personal archives, over twenty boxes of articles, pictures, and clippings from his long and distinguished career. His generosity and enthusiasm for the project were instrumental in helping me overcome the many roadblocks and challenges along the way.

Bill Neville is one of the all-time great storytellers of volleyball, and he was a huge help. What came across most with Bill was how much he cared about the "boys" on the 1984 team and how proud he was of the men they became. He was very generous with his time, sitting for several long interviews and many follow-up conversations and emails.

Blaine Harden met with me over a beer one night—another aspiring writer asking advice—and very generously provided a roadmap for how to write a book and get it published. His support of my early drafts gave this project a jolt of energy when it almost didn't get off the ground.

Lisa Shannon helped me improve the book proposal and shop it to potential agents, and Scott Bedbury read an early chapter and encouraged me to keep going. Brent Snow was a sounding board throughout the project, helping me find my way when I got lost.

Amarjit Chopra read several early drafts of the book and provided detailed notes and feedback. His mentorship was invaluable.

I'm especially grateful for my agent, Leah Spiro, who took a chance on an unknown and unpublished writer. She had faith in me and the story and has been an unwavering champion for the book.

I'm forever indebted to Glenn Stout, who took a rough and unpolished draft of the book and worked with me, tirelessly, word by word and sentence by sentence, helping me transform the manuscript into something worthy of the subject. His professionalism and dedication to the craft of writing was both inspiring and motivating to a writer trying to navigate my way through my first book.

My editor, Christen Karniski, recognized the potential in the story and saw enough promise in my early drafts to back this project and run with it. Thank you to Erinn Slanina, for her detailed work and persistence and keeping the project moving, and to my publisher, Rowman & Littlefield, and everyone on the team there, for having faith in a first-time author creating a beautiful book.

And finally, I want to acknowledge and thank my children, Will and Annie. More than a few times, in the past five years, I missed out on spending time with them because of the book, but they understood and always kept a smile on their faces. As my parents passed down the lessons of life to me and my siblings, my wife and I try to do the same with our children, and I hope this story becomes a part of that knowledge—that their grandfather was part of something special and left the world a little better than he found it—something we can all aspire to achieve.

Foreword

One of the biggest regrets I have from my USA Men's National Team (MNT) playing days is that I lacked the discipline to keep a journal. My teammates and I lived, and regularly suffered, a mountain of unique experiences on our journey to becoming the best in the world. To read such a journal today and relive those moments would be a priceless treasure. This struck poignantly a few weeks ago, as several members of our 1984 team celebrated the life of our deceased teammate, Mike Blanchard. As we honored Mike, we struggled to recall some of those events, dates, and places.

The sad reality is that many of those MNT moments have now faded from memory. That's the void into which author Sean Murray has leaped. Sean's father, Don, and his partner Chuck Johnson, were our MNT sport psychologists during the years leading up to our first Olympics. Inspired by his dad, and by our USA coaches and players, Sean spent five arduous years writing our story leading up to L.A. 1984, and the result is . . . a joy.

First, I got refreshers on details of our long climb to the highest levels of volleyball play and teammateship. For example, we played a 1981 exhibition tour in Japan and came up short, match after match, including a particularly painful implosion. When both teams returned to America to complete the home and home series, I had forgotten what a strong response our team had formed, and how we did it: we beat the Japanese men for the first time in 13 years. And it's always fun to hear more details of our highly contentious Outward Bound project—read the book to find out why it was so controversial, and why I need so much memory refreshment.

Then there were the back stories I had never heard. Like how our Head Coach Doug Beal jumped out of a sailboat to further pursue his passion for volleyball. Or that Beal was only 29 years old when he first took the job, and how that youth led to internal struggle because he was capable of both playing and coaching. I learned how Assistant Coach Bill Neville got his start in volleyball: as teenagers, Nev and his friends fell for a simple "hustle" at summer camp.

And I knew our MNT history had some rough moments, but I had no idea that in the 1970 World Championships, we finished two places *behind* Mongolia. That's right, Mongolia, a team that is currently ranked 134th in the world. I now understand more deeply the inertia of mediocrity our players and coaches had to fight, so we could turn our ship toward a path of excellence.

I believe that Sean has honored his father, and certainly honored our quest for greatness. I invite you to hop in and let Sean be your tour guide, right through the final point of the Olympic tournament. Whether you're a fan of volleyball, of Olympic sports in general, or of the pursuit of excellence, you'll be glad you did.

Karch Kiraly is a three-time Olympic volleyball gold medalist and the head coach of the U.S. Women's National Team. Karch coached the U.S. women to their first gold medal at the 2021 Tokyo Olympics.

Introduction

$\mathcal{I}$n the summer of 1984, the Olympics were coming to Los Angeles. I was 13 years old and living in Eugene, Oregon, a sleepy college town 860 miles north of L.A. These Games, being relatively close to home, were much anticipated, and the long wait for their arrival was nearly over. Yet there was something beyond proximity that made these Olympics a big deal in my family—we were on a mission. Or more accurately, my father was on a mission, serving as the team psychologist to the U.S. men's national volleyball team. My mother and the rest of us were along for the ride.

When I mentioned to my friends that Dad was "helping the team," they were skeptical. Dad was 5'11" with a four-inch vertical jump on a good day. No one would ever mistake him for an Olympic athlete, especially on the volleyball court. Yet he had a role, and an important one: to help the team play at the highest level. He was traveling to L.A. in an official capacity. He'd been telling us for years that the goal was for the team to peak at the Olympics, and he was tasked with helping create the conditions to make it happen. I had no idea at the time that the men's volleyball team, "our team," would become the hottest ticket in town and go on to capture the heart of a nation.

To understand how someone with no volleyball experience, beyond the backyard barbeque variety, found himself in the role of team psychologist to the national team, you have to go back to Eugene in the late 1960s. My parents moved to Eugene at that time so my father, Don Murray, could enroll in a Ph.D. program at the University of Oregon. Their plan was always to move back to Montana when he graduated, but they fell in love with the town and decided to stay and raise a family.

While Dad worked on his thesis, Mom had her hands full taking care of my older sister and me, both toddlers at the time (my younger brother was born nine years later). Our family lived in the married housing complex for graduate students. A few units down, the McGown family, Carl and Sue and their two young boys, was roughly in the same situation. Carl was working toward a Ph.D. in motor learning, but his real passion was volleyball. He had served as an assistant coach to the U.S. men's national team in 1970, and he was intent on pursuing a career in coaching after graduate school.

A third family lived nearby, Chuck and Merrilee Johnson. Chuck studied in the same department as my father. He was working toward a Ph.D. in organizational psychology, and like my parents, the Johnsons had young children at the time.

When the weather warmed up in the spring and the sun dried out the rain-soaked grass outside our duplex unit, the coolers came out, cheap lawn chairs were unfolded, and my father fired up the barbeque. Raising a family on a grad student budget wasn't easy. These gatherings offered a rare chance for my parents and their friends to relax and forget about the stress of money and the pressure of writing a dissertation.

Throughout his life, my father loved to throw a party. He had the rare combination of being both a great listener and a great storyteller. At these outdoor gatherings, he mingled with his grad school buddies, inquiring about their latest line of research and always eager to make connections and share ideas.

McGown, Johnson, and my father often organized a volleyball game for the adults, complete with a net that sagged in the middle and shoes roughly placed on each corner to mark the boundary. It was the kind of game most of us have played at least once or twice in our lives at family reunions or summer gatherings.

Even in its most rudimentary form, volleyball demands a level of teamwork and coordination far beyond what we experience in many other sports. There is no ability to go one-on-one in volleyball like there is in basketball or soccer. Success requires players to work together.

The game was set in motion with the serve from the backline, usually an underhanded hit in my dad's case, launching the ball in a parabolic motion over the net. McGown would hold his arms together in the shape of a V to absorb the serve and bump the ball to Johnson. In volleyball lingo, they call this the pass.

The player who receives the pass is the setter, and Johnson, being the shortest of the three, would often take on that role. If all went well, Johnson would use his fingers and a flick of his wrist to loft the ball gracefully in the pocket of space near and above the net. The third touch is the hit, which starts with a player leaping in the air and ends with a forceful overhand swing of the arm, crushing the ball across the net. If the hitter and setter are in synch, the hitter times his or her jump so that the swinging arm intersects with the ball at the apex of the set. Less experienced players learned to stay out of the way when McGown went to the net.

When all three touches are executed perfectly, there is a grace and beauty to the sequence of movement. Coordination and communication are key. The satisfaction players derive from linking three well-executed touches is something special to volleyball, and many who experience it can't get enough of it. They keep coming back for more.

McGown was one of those rare backyard volleyball players who also understood and experienced the game at the international elite level. For my dad and Johnson, volleyball was a playful diversion on Saturday afternoons, but for McGown, volleyball was a lifelong obsession.

After the game, the three grad students would update each other on their respective lines of research, and a certain amount of cross-pollination of ideas was inevitable. My father and Chuck were studying how to make organizations and teams more effective. They were pioneers in a field that would come to be known as organization development.

The central question that organization development seeks to answer is this: *what makes an organization or team perform at its highest level?*

The answer is complicated, but in a formal sense it involves elements of trust, communication, role clarification, accountability, goals, purpose, leadership, and vision. As a coach, McGown was ahead of his time. He was curious about applying the ideas of organization development to volleyball.

In 1973 McGown was offered the head coaching job of the U.S. men's national team. He immediately invited his two graduate school pals to join him in Los Angeles that spring at the tryouts to serve as team psychologists. Although players would be evaluated primarily on their individual volleyball skill, McGown, influenced by the team psychologists, introduced a new element to the selection criteria: a player's willingness to buy in to his team philosophy.

McGown believed that success at the elite international level was not just about skill—the national teams from volleyball-crazed countries like Russia, Cuba, Poland, and Japan were packed with players with lightning-quick reflexes, natural jumping ability, and freakish body coordination. When each side of the net fields elite talent, the key differentiator—the X factor—is how the players work together. McGown wanted to find the best players in America who could also play together as a team.

Sports psychology was just getting started as a formal field of study when McGown became coach of the national team. Bruce Ogilvie and Thomas Tutko wrote a seminal book in 1966 titled *Problem Athletes and How to Handle Them*, where they applied the principles of psychology, especially motivation and incentives, to athletics. Ogilvie and Tutko went on to develop a popular written assessment, a personality test that was widely administered to Olympic athletes, called the Athletic Motivation Inventory. Athletes would answer a series of questions that measured personality traits, such as mental toughness and leadership, that are conducive to achieving success in sports.

When McGown assessed his own squad, he was shocked to learn that some of the players scored so poorly he felt their results warranted a new personality type: "uncoachable."[1] That was a problem.

It probably didn't help that many of the players on the national team learned volleyball on the beaches of Southern California, where they figured out the game as they went along, without the benefit of a coach. If a player didn't mesh with a teammate on the beach, there was no need to work out their differences and figure out how to play as a team; they simply found a new teammate. While this kind of unstructured development environment fostered creativity and a wide variety of techniques and approaches to the game, it didn't prepare the players to work in the structured team environment of the indoor game, under the guidance of a coach.

McGown tasked my dad and Johnson with improving the national team's culture and creating the conditions for the team to flourish. The goal was to get the players to work together and commit to the success of the team. My dad and Johnson, working together, facilitated meetings for players and coaches to set both individual and team goals, define roles, and discuss how to improve communication both on and off the court. The players and coaches even agreed to a process for each group to provide feedback to the other. The players would anonymously write down comments on note cards, and then later, in a separate room, the team psychologists would go through the feedback with the coaches, card by card. Some of it was petty, but other comments were valid and, although they weren't always easy for the coaches to hear, surfaced issues that needed to be dealt with to make the team better.

These types of exercises, although common in the world of professional sports today, were at the vanguard of team sports psychology at the time. Some players recognized the merit in team building, while others considered such activities a waste of time. To the skeptics, it seemed pretty obvious that you get better at volleyball by playing volleyball, not sitting in a room talking about your feelings to some "team shrinks," the nickname the players gave my father and Johnson.

As the sports psychologists worked with the team, one player stood out from the others. Doug Beal, an intellectually curious Midwesterner who had played for Ohio State, was cerebral and serious. He grew up playing the indoor game—six-on-six volleyball at various YMCAs in and around Cleveland.

Northeast Ohio was home to a large immigrant population from Eastern Europe. In Cleveland there was a thriving club league among the YMCAs and Turner Clubs—a sort of German version of the YMCA that was imported to America. Each ethnic community—Czech, Slovakian, Russian, Polish, Hungarian, and others—fielded its own team. Beal's family was Jewish, emigrating from Poland to America in the early twentieth century. All four of his grandparents came from Bialystok, a small town near the Russian border. Beal and his brother competed against many different ethnic teams through the years, and each team played its own style of indoor volleyball imported from their home country. Beal had noticed how the strong ethnic identity of each team, along with its sense of community, helped foster the teamwork that is so important to volleyball.

Beal's approach to the game differed from his Southern California teammates, many of whom were first introduced to the sport through the two-on-two beach game that afforded players more touches and celebrated individual achievement. In many ways, Beal was an outsider.

Still, like all the players on the national team at that time, Beal had dreams of qualifying for the 1976 Olympics in Montreal. He desperately hoped that the work of the team psychologists, and McGown's emphasis on teamwork, would bring the team together and lead the U.S. team to qualify for the 1976 Olympics.

It didn't happen.

The U.S. men's national volleyball program had so many problems in the 1970s it's hard to point to just one, but it was obvious to the coaches and players alike that the practice of hastily assembling a new team each spring and selecting a new coach each year contributed to its failure. The team would invite a group of "all-star" players to try out. The selected players would then practice together for a few months before traveling to international tournaments to face opponents who had played together for years. Although immensely talented as individuals, the Americans couldn't compete at the elite level against opponents playing and training together year-round. There simply wasn't enough time for the U.S. players to adjust to a new coach, learn a new system, and gel as a team. McGown may have had the right philosophy, but he didn't have enough time or resources to see it through.

When McGown stepped down as coach in 1976, Beal became his unlikely successor, taking over the reins as head coach in 1977. He began laying the foundation for the program's future success, but it didn't happen overnight.

Fast-forward to July 1984. As team psychologist to the men's national volleyball team, my father was invited to join them at the Olympics. Early that month we visited the team in Pullman, Washington, a remote college town where they were conducting pre-Olympic training. Then, later in the month, a few days before the opening ceremony, we loaded up my parent's custom Ford Econo-line van (my father's love for custom vans was only slightly less intense than his love for my mother) and drove down Interstate 5. As we approached Los Angeles and I gazed out the windows of the van, signs of the Olympics were everywhere. The iconic Olympic rings were prominently displayed on banners and venues; the logo for the Games, the "Stars in Motion," was ubiquitous; and in the newspapers and on the TV pre-Olympic coverage dominated the media. The sense of anticipation for the Games electrified the city.

The author standing next to the team manager and statistician, Mark Miller, in Pullman, Washington, a few weeks before the 1984 summer Olympics. PHOTO BY DON MURRAY

I was swept away with excitement. As an adolescent, the biggest event I had ever witnessed was the Fourth of July parade. This seemed a lot bigger.

Los Angeles buzzed throughout the Games. Carl Lewis won four gold medals in track and field and the Coliseum erupted. American Joan Benoit won gold in the first ever women's marathon, while the Swiss runner Gaby Andersen-Schweiss stumbled from heat exhaustion on the last lap as she entered the stadium. To this day, the image of her collapsing a few hundred yards from the finish line is startling. It provided my first inkling of just how far athletes will push themselves, the suffering and sacrifice they are willing to endure, in pursuit of greatness.

Naturally, due to my father's involvement, the team that most captured my attention was men's volleyball, and I wasn't alone. They were local heroes. Many of the players grew up learning the game on the beaches of Los Angeles—Manhattan, Huntington, Corona Del Mar, Venice, Zuma, Santa Monica, East Beach. Nine of the twelve players on the U.S. Olympic squad were from Southern California: Karch Kiraly, Steve Timmons, Dusty Dvorak, Pat Powers, Craig Buck, Steve Salmons, Paul Sunderland, Dave Saunders, and Chris Marlowe. Most of the country had no idea who these players were, but in volleyball-crazed Southern California, they were not only recognized but revered. Some had won major beach tournaments, while others led their local collegiate team (UCLA, USC, Pepperdine, and San Diego State) to a national championship, and a few had done both. They were the hometown boys, and the top teams in the world had shown up to take them on. They didn't plan on losing

My father wasn't on the court, nor was he on the bench with the coaches, but he was part of a wider "team around the team" that head coach Doug Beal had assembled to support the players. This included nutritionists, physical trainers, business managers to raise corporate sponsors, and business partners who hired the players part-time as part of the Olympic Jobs Opportunity Program. Even Tom Selleck, the actor famous for playing Magnum P.I. at the time, signed on to help the team. Selleck was an accomplished volleyball player who played for the Outrigger Club in Hawaii and was named the honorary team captain. He participated in exhibition matches and granted permission to print two very lucrative posters featuring his image, raising critical funds for the program.

At the time I was unaware that the U.S. national team had never won a medal at an Olympics. I didn't know about the long history of mediocrity and frustration that for well over a decade had defined U.S. men's volleyball. Before this team, U.S. men's volleyball were perennial underachievers. They might play a great match or two, but in the end, they would always come up short. Beal took over a program with a long history of losing and turned it into a winner. He guided the players on a journey where they learned to commit to something bigger than themselves—the success of the team. When everyone in the world doubted them, Beal and the coaching staff got the players not only to believe they could win, but to trust and believe in one another, and to work in harmony toward the same goal.

If you've been on a team before—any team—you know how rare it is for a group of people to come together and achieve their highest potential. My

My father, Don Murray, at the 1984 Los Angeles Olympics in a photo that appeared in our local paper, the *Eugene Register-Guard*, alongside an article about his involvement with the U.S. men's volleyball team.
SOURCE: DAVE KAYFES

varsity high school basketball team in Eugene was talented and on our way to the state tournament. The only remaining obstacle was a game against the weakest team in our league, a team we had beaten twice before with a healthy margin. As we approached the game, a serious, personal rift developed between two of our best players. What we needed at that moment was honest communication to repair trust. Instead, what we got from our young coach was more diagrammed plays and fancy defenses. We didn't need more *x*'s and *o*'s on a whiteboard; we needed to learn to trust each other again.

We went down in flames, losing a game we should have won and missing out on the state tournament. I can still remember how much it hurt. In fact, it still does.

I eventually followed a similar path as that of my father. For the past twenty years, I've been working with leaders and teams in corporate America, helping them come together and collaborate to achieve something that no one individual could do on their own. I've learned how challenging it can be to create a winning team culture. For a team to succeed in business, or in any organization, a thousand little things have to go right. If just one of those things goes wrong—poor communication, vague goals, misaligned incentives, absence of trust, weak leadership, lack of standards, or unclear roles, just to name a few—the team will fail.

When I set out to relive the experience and uncover the dynamic of the 1984 men's national team, I'm not sure precisely what I expected to learn. I knew they had spent three weeks in the mountains of Utah in the middle of winter, as part of an Outward Bound experience, but I didn't know how controversial the trip was, or how that unique experience impacted the team. I knew there had been hardships and challenges on the journey to the Olympics, but I was surprised to learn of the depth of discord at times between the players and their head coach, the persistence of cliques that emerged like weeds and divided one group of players from another, the clash of cultures between beach volleyball and the indoor game, the intensity of the internal competition, and the depth of emotion, heartbreak, and redemption experienced by individual players based on good fortune or bad luck.

But I really shouldn't have been surprised. I know now that all great teams become great by pushing through adversity and using setbacks and failure as a means to grow stronger and become better at what they do. It's a lesson I first learned from the 1984 Olympic volleyball team.

I still remember the evening of August 11, the last night of the 1984 Olympics. The following day would be the closing ceremony, but there were still a few pieces of hardware to hand out. The U.S. men's volleyball team was playing for the gold medal in front of 13,000 fans in sold-out Long Beach Arena while millions more watched on television. Although my family enjoyed four tickets to most of the Olympic volleyball tournament, for the gold medal match our allotment was pared back to two, so my parents cheered the team on in the arena while I huddled around the television with my sister and younger brother. Men's volleyball was, surprisingly, pulling in the highest ratings among all team sports at these Olympics. The city of Los Angeles was watching. The country was watching. The world was watching. As I watched the team play that night, I felt a part of something bigger. I felt that their challenge was in some way my own.

Looking back at the Los Angeles Olympics from a distance of 37 years, I realize now that I had a front-row seat to something special that summer. It's something you might see once or twice in your life if you're lucky, and something that you never forget, an experience that continues to resonate in my life. I got to watch a group of individuals become a team—and in the process, become the best in the world at what they did.

• 1 •

Argentina 1982

$\mathcal{I}$n the fall of 1982, the U.S. men's national volleyball team boarded a military transport plane in Buenos Aires. As they walked across the tarmac and ascended the stairs into the cabin, they got a good look at the well-worn fuselage and prop engines. The plane looked to the players to be something right out of a World War II movie. With baggage piled up in the aisles, the already tight quarters became cramped. All of this might not have been so concerning for the players if they weren't so tired. They had been traveling for over twenty-four hours, with almost no sleep, and they were still 700 miles from their destination.

Their first match was in Catamarca, a regional agricultural town nestled near the foothills of the Andes, one of several cities across Argentina hosting matches for the Volleyball World Championships that year. For reasons that were never clearly explained to the coaches, the plane landed well-short of the final destination. Blurry-eyed and jetlagged, the players disembarked and were promptly ushered into a dusty old, converted school bus. They took one look at the bus and shook their heads in disbelief. Assistant coach Bill Neville verbalized what they were all thinking. "Complaining is not going to do any good here boys. Just get in and get some sleep."[1]

Again, the luggage was piled in the aisles and the players, most of whom were well over six feet tall, squeezed into their seats for what became a seven-hour drive, over dirt roads and through the mountains, to Catamarca.

Their coach, Doug Beal, liked to claim one of the strengths of this team was "the ability to sleep in any condition, under any situation, in any cramped quarters."[2] True to form, the players shifted luggage and twisted their frames until the conditions were just comfortable enough to find sleep.

The bumpy road to Catamarca was rough, but these players had endured worse, much worse. The previous summer they had left their home base in San

Diego on June 22, flew to Asia, and didn't return to the United States until August 2. During those six weeks, spanning the hottest days of summer, they endured planes, trains, and buses from Shanghai to Seoul and all over Japan.

Beal, on the other hand, never could sleep on buses, so he found a seat in the front with the local interpreter on one side and the bus driver on the other. The interpreter offered Beal yerba mate tea, a traditional indigenous drink of Argentina. Having nothing else to drink, Beal took him up on the offer. First one cup, then another; before long he had downed five cups. Drinking tea from the caffeine-rich yerba mate plant, it has been written, "raises morale, sustains the muscular system, augments strength and allows one to endure privations. In a word, it is a valiant aid."[3] Beal was going to need every ounce of valiant aid he could get over the next two weeks. His team of young Americans would soon face off against the Soviet Union men's volleyball team, the biggest, baddest, most dominant volleyball players on the planet.

In addition to the yerba mate coursing through his veins, Beal had a lot on his mind. The U.S. men's national volleyball team traveling to Argentina to compete in the World Championship in 1982 was by far the most talented group of volleyball players the United States had ever assembled for international competition. Many of the younger players were from Southern California and had developed their skills on the beach and then learned the indoor game in high school and college, and the World Championship was their first big test.

The emerging star of the team was also its youngest player, Karch Kiraly (pronounced *Kee-Rye*), a volleyball prodigy who from 1979 to 1982 had led UCLA to three national championships in four years. Not yet twenty-two years old, Karch was already becoming a leader on the court for the National Team. A versatile talent, he was one of the best hitters on the team, and he could also set, pass, and play defense at an elite level. Karch played with a determination and focus that stood out even among the best players in the world. "He's a demon, going full out all the time," said Beal. "He has the ability to lift a team's performance level by sheer will power and ability."[4]

Karch was special. Beal knew it and his teammates knew it too. "The chance to coach someone like that doesn't happen very often," Beal said.

While many of the players came from Southern California, head coach Doug Beal most definitely did not. The thirty-five-year-old former National Team player with a Ph.D. in exercise physiology grew up in Cleveland and played for Ohio State in the late 1960s. He learned volleyball in the musty gyms of a YMCA, not at the beach.

The 1982 World Championships consisted of six pools of four teams. The U.S. team was placed in a four-team pool that included the Soviet Union, Bulgaria, and Chile. After a round of pool play, the top two teams from each pool then advanced to the championship round.

It was a tough draw. While Chile did not pose much of a threat, the Soviet Union was the defending Olympic champion, world champion, and number-one ranked team in the world, heavily favored to win the pool and the tournament. If the U.S. team could handle Chile and lost, as expected, to the Soviet Union, that left Bulgaria as the team to defeat in order to advance to the medal round. Bulgaria, Beal knew, was talented, but beatable. The United States drew Bulgaria for their first match in Catamarca.

For Beal and the team, the first challenge was just getting to the match. The vintage school bus rolled into Catamarca at 2 a.m. covered with a thick layer of dust and dirt. The players unloaded, along with their luggage, at the team hotel where they enjoyed their first full night of sleep in two days. They needed every minute.

The next day the players visited the stadium for practice. The arena had a capacity of six thousand with good lighting, but it was semi-open-air and far from ideal. At night, wind blew dust inside, where it settled on the court. Despite multiple attempts to remove it, a thin layer persisted, producing a slick surface and disrupting the balance and timing of the players. During the first practice, Marc Waldie, one of the veterans on the team, leapt into the air and, thrown off by the dust, came down awkwardly on the foot of a teammate, badly twisting his ankle and knocking him from the tournament. Several other players developed stomach ailments, and their ability to compete at full strength was in jeopardy.

Still, Beal remained confident. He and his staff had scouted Bulgaria extensively, watching film of the team and studying their tendencies. Volleyball was extremely popular in Eastern European countries, and although not on the same level as the Soviet Union, Bulgaria consistently fielded teams that competed for medals at the World Championships and Olympics. Yet Beal felt there was an opportunity to surprise the Bulgarians. The United States knew the Bulgarians were a strong team, but Bulgaria didn't know how much the United States had improved since the two teams last met. The Americans had changed both players and tactics, and Beal hoped to use this to his advantage.

In addition to Karch, the U.S. team featured another young star, Dusty Dvorak, a six-foot-two athlete from Laguna Beach who was rapidly becoming one of the best setters in the world. As a four-time NCAA All-American at USC, Dvorak led the Trojans to a national championship in 1980, defeating Karch Kiraly and his UCLA teammates, the only year the Bruins didn't win a national championship during Karch's four years at UCLA.

Dvorak was a master tactician on the court with a feel and understanding for the game that set him apart from any National Team setter who came before him. To this day, Beal calls him "the best setter I ever coached,"[5] and many believe he is the best pure setter the United States has ever produced.

A setter in volleyball must make split-second decisions based on the location and movement of teammates, the ball, and even the other team. Dvorak knew who to set and when—a skill that's difficult to coach. "As good as he is," wrote Beal in his memoir, "he presented special, and at times, seemingly insurmountable problems."

Supremely confident in his abilities, Dvorak thought he knew best about how to win and he wasn't shy in sharing his opinion with his coaches. While Beal respected Dvorak's talent and recognized his value to the team, Dvorak's vision often conflicted with Beal's, and the tension sometimes spilled over into practices and games.

The setter is much like the quarterback on a football team, responsible for starting the offense and delivering the ball to another player and giving him or her the opportunity to score. In football, the coach and quarterback must adhere to the same strategy and work from the same playbook, and the same is true of a volleyball coach and the setter.

That wasn't always the case with Beal and Dvorak. From time to time, they would disagree on tactics, dig their heels in, and both player and coach would refuse to back down. Dvorak thought Beal was stubborn, while Beal thought Dvorak was "thin-skinned, high strung and temperamental."[6]

Once, while playing against China in Hershey, Pennsylvania, Beal watched as Dvorak consistently set the outside hitters. This drew the Chinese blockers toward the outside, leaving a big opportunity down the middle that Beal hoped to capitalize on. Beal called Dvorak over to the bench and explained the situation: "Dusty, I need you to set the middle more."[7] It wasn't Dvorak's favorite set. He preferred the outside. Beal could see the resistance on Dvorak's face, so he tried to come at it from another angle. "We're scoring well. You're doing a good job, but I need you to set the middle." When Dvorak got back on the court, he proceeded to set five straight balls in the middle, placing each one directly in front of a Chinese blocker. The U.S. hitters got stuffed five times in a row. Dvorak turned to Beal and gave him a look that said, "Is that what you mean? You want me to set the middle more?"

Beal was livid. He turned to his assistant, Bill Neville, and said, "I'm not coaching this guy anymore, Nev. He's yours."

"Gee, thanks,"[8] responded Neville, who had grown accustomed to defusing the clashes between the head coach and his players. Beal and Neville made a good pair in that sense. Beal cared for his players, but he wasn't there to be their friend. He had high standards for himself and his players, and he could be brutally honest and direct in his communication. But as head coach he also maintained an emotional distance from his players because he knew he would have to cut some of them before the Olympics, and he didn't want emotions to cloud his decisions. Beal's approach sometimes led to disagreements and bruised egos. Neville, who had a great relationship with all the players, was tasked with smoothing over such disagreements.

With Dvorak and Karch, the United States had two premier players, a setter and an outside hitter, on the court at the same time. When they were in sync, they created havoc for opposing teams and made everyone around them better. Beal hoped this lethal combo would take the Bulgarians by surprise

The night of their first match in Catamarca, it became apparent the crowd in Argentina was hostile toward the United States. This was something the coaching staff had anticipated. The brief ten-week Falklands War between Argentina and the United Kingdom in 1982 had just ended the previous June. Although the English team hadn't qualified for the World Championships, the Argentinians decided to take their frustration and anger out on two British allies who were competing, the American and Canadian teams.

In Argentina, crowds don't boo to voice their displeasure, they whistle. As the U.S. team stepped on the court for their match with Bulgaria, the arena erupted with an ear-piercing, high-pitched shrill. "Welcome to Argentina boys," Neville told his players.

To defuse the crowd, Neville had an idea. In the prematch meeting, he handed out two roses to each player and told them, "Okay, boys, we need to get the crowd on our side. When they announce your name, go up into the stands, find two ladies, and give them each a rose. At least we'll have twenty-four people rooting for us."[9] Neville knew his players well, so he added, "And don't just give them to some young beauty. If you see a grandmother, give one to her too." The pregame gesture won tepid applause, but once the match began the crowd turned decisively against the United States.

In volleyball, matches are decided in best-of-five formats, so the first team to win three games or "sets" wins the match. Under the rules at the time, the first team to reach fifteen points won the game, but, similar to today, teams had to win by two points. When two sides were evenly matched, games went beyond fifteen points, sometimes far beyond. In addition, volleyball during this era operated under side-out scoring, meaning a team could only score a point if it held serve. If the team receiving serve won a rally, no point was awarded, the service simply returned to that team. Under side-out scoring, volleyball matches lasted much longer than they do under the rally scoring system used today, whereby it is possible for a team to score regardless of whether they are serving or not.

Early on, in the match against Bulgaria, both teams were evenly matched, trading games back and forth. After four games, each team had won two. The match would be decided by a fifth and final game.

The U.S. jumped to a 12–5 lead in the decisive fifth game and seemed to be on their way to an easy win. With side-out scoring, it would take a miracle for Bulgaria to come back and win. The format made comebacks from so far behind rare.

Then the miracle started. Slowly at first, the momentum shifted away from the Americans. A mental mistake here, a bit of bad luck there, and Bulgaria clawed back into the game, breaking the Americans' serve time and time again and putting themselves in position to score and make the plays they needed. As Bulgaria gained confidence with each point, the cohesion and trust between the U.S. players eroded. The Americans' mind-set shifted from winning to trying not to lose, and the players tightened up, leading to unforced errors.

It was a complete meltdown. The teamwork Beal worked so hard to foster came apart, and the U.S. team folded as Bulgaria scored eleven of the next thirteen points to beat the United States 16–14. The loss was devastating—not so much because they lost the game but because of how they lost. They had a commanding lead, and they blew it.

Viacheslav Platonov, the Soviet coach, was scouting from the stands that evening. Over the years he had befriended Beal, and he watched in disbelief as his friend's team unraveled. After the match, he tracked down Beal and simply asked, "How?"[10] Beal didn't have an answer. He just shrugged and asked Platonov, "How?" Platonov shrugged and they both walked away, struggling to make sense of what had happened.

Something was missing. This U.S. team was stacked with talent, but when the pressure turned up and the game was on the line, they had a tendency to choke. Lines of communication broke down, trust eroded, and confidence vanished. They were like a puzzle that had all the pieces, but they just didn't fit together.

Beal and his assistants didn't have the luxury of time to dissect the loss. The following evening they were scheduled to play the Soviet Union. Volleyball was a popular sport in Russia, and an extensive club system evolved identifying and cultivating talent from a young age. While the United States had perhaps twenty-five players with the skills to compete at the elite international level, the Soviets had hundreds to choose from.

Only one day after the disappointing loss to Bulgaria, the United States managed to regroup and played hard against the Soviets, challenging them at a time when they were rarely tested. The United States almost took the third game of the match, losing 16–14, but in the end, they still lost in three straight games (15–11, 15–12, 16–14). They had played better against the Soviets than they had against Bulgaria, but it hadn't mattered. The United States would not be advancing to the medal round in the World Championships.

The blunt-spoken Beal didn't like meeting with the press, particularly after the two losses. This was during the height of the Cold War, and every match of any kind between the Soviet Union and the United States was ripe with symbolism. The room was packed with press from all over the world expecting some fireworks from Beal, whom they hoped to bait into making some headlines. Emotionally drained, Beal decided not to attend the postgame press conference and sent Neville out to field questions alongside Platonov.

While Beal usually managed to control his emotions, Neville was fiery and passionate. Still stinging from the defeat, Neville defiantly declared to the press that the United States would beat the Soviets the next time they played.

Sensing Neville was on the edge, a reporter made an attempt to push him off the cliff altogether. "Why do you have such an unathletic player on your team?"[11]

"Excuse me," Neville snapped back. "What did you just ask me?"

"Number ten. Why is he even on the team?"

The reporter was referring to Chris Marlowe, the backup setter and oldest player on the team.

"Excuse me, but are you a heart surgeon?" Neville replied.

"No, I'm not a heart surgeon. I'm a reporter."

Neville's voice rose and his face flushed with anger. "Okay, so you don't understand what's in his heart, but if you knew what was in his heart, you would know why he is on this team. The player you're referring to has more heart, more character, and more guts than any player I've ever coached. If you think you can judge a man by his physical appearance, you are sorely mistaken. You have no idea what the hell you're talking about! And by the way, he's a hell of an athlete!"

Platonov looked on from the seat next to Neville and seemed to nod in agreement with his American counterpart. The members of the organizing committee, seeing the press conference heading off the rails, jumped in to bring it to a close.

The Soviets went on to win the tournament and continue their run of international dominance in men's volleyball. The Soviets had now won gold at every major international tournament going back to the World Cup of 1977.

Bulgaria, the team the United States came so close to beating in the preliminary round, came in fifth. The United States could take some solace in scoring more points against the Soviets than any other team at the tournament, and then breezing through the consolation bracket to finish thirteenth out of twenty-four teams. It was the highest possible finish given the failure to advance to the championship round, but finishing thirteenth was not why they had traveled to Argentina.

The United States, despite playing a game invented in their own country, finished behind not only Bulgaria but Canada and Cuba as well. Forget the world; the United States wasn't even the best team in North America.

With the Olympics in Los Angeles less than two years away, something had to change.

· 2 ·

A Friendship

*I*n the 1890s, William Morgan, an undergraduate student at the Springfield College of the YMCA in Springfield, Massachusetts, met James Naismith, who had recently invented the game of basketball. It was a golden era of innovation for athletics in America, with physical education directors, particularly in the YMCA network, inventing new activities and sports for the emerging leisure class of "businessmen" who frequented their facilities. Like Naismith, after graduation, Morgan pursued a career in physical education, taking a job at the YMCA in Holyoke, Massachusetts, where he established exercise programs and sports classes for adults.

Morgan noticed basketball, which required running up and down the court as well as a great deal of contact, was physically demanding of his older, less athletic students. He sought to create a new sport suitable for a wider variety of ages and athletic abilities, one that could be played in gymnasiums as well as the outdoors. He combed through the features of a number of sports, including basketball, baseball, badminton, tennis, and handball and designed a sport that combined elements of each of these games. He called the game "mintonette," a nod to its close association to badminton.

Describing his early experimentation, Morgan said, "In search of an appropriate game, tennis occurred to me, but this required rackets, balls, a net and other equipment, so it was eliminated, but the idea of a net seemed a good one. We raised it to a height of about 6 feet, 6 inches from the ground, just above the head of an average man. We needed a ball and among those we tried was a basketball bladder, but this was too light and too slow. We therefore tried the basketball itself, which was too big and too heavy."[1]

Following further experimentation, Morgan asked the sporting goods firm A.G. Spalding & Bros. to make a smaller, lighter ball more suited to his game. When Morgan introduced the game to his fellow YMCA athletic directors in 1896, they loved it, but it was suggested he change the name to "volley" ball since the main object was to volley the ball back and forth across the net. The name stuck, and thus volleyball and basketball were invented within five years of each other in two towns in Massachusetts just eight miles apart. Today, according to most sources, as measured by participation, both sports are among the most popular in the world.

The sport's popularity quickly spread through the YMCA network, which carried the game to Japan, China, and the Philippines in the early 1900s. Soon after it made its way to Europe, and by the 1920s the level of play in Eastern Europe reached a higher standard than the recreational version played in the United States. In 1928, the sport's governing body, the United States Volleyball Association (USVBA), was formed at the Yale Club in New York City, with the purpose of representing the sport internationally and organizing an annual open national championship among club teams.

U.S. soldiers in World War II played the game wherever they were stationed, further expanding its popularity. By 1949, the first World Championships were held in Prague, Czechoslovakia. The Soviet Union won gold. The United States didn't even send a team.

In a move reminiscent of a volley, immigrants from Eastern Europe brought their style of play across the Atlantic when they immigrated to the United States in the 1930s, and again after World War II. Many of these immigrants made their way to industrial jobs in the Midwest, settling in places like Detroit and Cleveland.

Doug Beal grew up in just such an immigrant community. Both of Beal's grandparents had immigrated to New York City from the same village in Poland near the Russian border. Beal's father grew up across the street from Yankee Stadium, but for him sport always remained only a game, not something to be taken seriously. He eventually embarked on a successful career in publishing that took him and his family to Cleveland, where Beal came of age amid a hotbed of volleyball activity.

As a fourth grader at Malvern Elementary, Doug Beal first encountered the game in the school gymnasium one day when physical education teacher Ken Zorge introduced volleyball to the students. Beal's classmates found it interesting, but were already enamored with baseball, basketball, and football. Beal, on the other hand, was immediately taken by the game. The challenge of keeping the ball alive and the joy of scoring points appealed to him, and he was good at it. Zorge recognized Beal's natural ability and enthusiasm for the game, so as soon as Beal and his younger brother were old enough, Zorge took them to the Central Y in Cleveland to practice with adult teams. In those days, there was no high school volleyball in Cleveland, but by the time Beal was in high school, he was traveling around the Midwest on the weekends playing for a competitive club team.

Although Beal's father never discouraged his son's enthusiasm for the sport, he also didn't consider it a serious pursuit. He didn't attend his son's games and instead took his boys sailing on Lake Erie, hoping they would share his love for the water, but Doug Beal suffered from motion sickness and hated sailing. Once, while the family was sailing not far from shore, Beal was overcome with sea sickness. Finding no relief on the boat, he found a creative solution to his misery. Without warning his family or asking permission, he simply jumped overboard and swam to shore. Beal's willingness to find creative solutions and pursue them, regardless of what other's might think, is a trait that would later set him apart in his career as a player, a coach, and eventually the president and CEO of USA Volleyball.

Upon graduating high school, Beal attended Hobart College in Upstate New York for two years, where he played both basketball and volleyball, but at Hobart volleyball increasingly became a bigger part of his world. On the weekends, he traveled to tournaments, sometimes, to his father's dismay, neglecting his studies. After his sophomore year, he transferred to Ohio State because it had a more serious volleyball program.

At Ohio State Beal became the starting setter, and his skills continued to improve. Beal played well in several national tournaments, where he caught the attention of the National Team coaches. At a time when the selection process for the National Team was much less formal and the roster was more fluid, they told him that if he was ever in California, he would be welcome to practice with the National Team.

Beal decided to take the coaches up on their offer. During spring break his senior year, he joined two teammates from the volleyball team in an epic road trip from Columbus, Ohio, to Los Angeles and back in ten days. The three college buddies took turns driving and sleeping to cover the distance as quickly as possible, eager to get to L.A. and determine how their volleyball skills stacked up against the best players in the country, most of whom lived and played in that area.

The experience lit a fire under Beal. He discovered that although he was good enough to scrimmage with the National Team players, he didn't quite have the skills to make the team, at least not yet. He returned to Ohio State to finish his senior season, more determined than ever to improve and earn a spot on the National Team that summer. After graduating in 1970, he was officially invited to try out.

This time Beal made the trip alone. Yet as one of the few players not from California, Beal noticed for the first time that there was a huge divide between the California players and everyone else, differences not only in playing style but in culture and attitude. Beal was an outsider and not quite as gifted physically as some of the other players trying out. He was disciplined, adept at making decisions, and a natural leader, but he soon realized he needed to work harder than others to make the team. In the end, he made it, one of the few members of the squad not native to California.

There was no designated national training center in those days. The National Team trained wherever gym space could be secured in various facilities throughout Los Angeles. That first summer on the National Team, Beal moved into an apartment with two teammates in Inglewood, near the Los Angeles airport. Just when Beal and his teammates figured out how to drive to one location, practices would be relocated to another and they would have to learn a whole new route. To make matters worse, the three men moved three times that summer. They spent so much time driving and getting lost that they joked they were learning more about how to navigate the L.A. freeways than they were about volleyball.

One of the assistant coaches on the National Team that summer was Bill Neville. Just a few years older than Beal, Neville was younger than some of the players he was coaching. Beal knew Neville; they had competed against each other when they were both in college.

Neville grew up near Seattle, Washington, where competitive volleyball was still virtually unknown. However, every summer he attended a YMCA camp on Puget Sound, where recreational volleyball was a regular activity. One day in his junior year of high school, Neville was hanging out with his group of friends and the conversation turned to the question of what is the toughest sport? Neville and his pals, all athletes, played all the sports, but by "all" they meant football, basketball, and baseball.

Neville jumped in and said, "Football, hands down."[2]

Another friend defended basketball as the toughest sport, while a third friend disagreed completely with the first two, making the case for baseball.

Joining the group that day was Larry Sears, a camp counselor.

"Let me throw in another one," Sears interjected. "I know you guys might laugh at this one, but I'm going to say it's volleyball."

Neville and his pals doubled over, thinking it was a joke, but Sears was serious. A few years older than Neville, Sears was admired by all the boys, not only because he was an excellent athlete and a respected leader, but because he was going to college, something they all aspired to themselves. What they didn't know was that in 1962 Sears, a student at George Williams College, had been named to the first team of the Midwestern Intercollegiate Volleyball Association, the volleyball near equivalent of an All-American team.[3]

"Now, I can understand why you would think that," he said. "I know you guys are fabulous athletes, so I can see why you'd think it's football or basketball or baseball."[4]

To Neville and his friends, volleyball was a soft game, not even in the same ballpark as the big three. They learned the basics of the game in middle school, but it was perceived more as a "girls sport," and not something to take seriously.

"I'll tell you what," Sears proposed, "let's have a little competition. I'll take you on. I'll be on one side of the net, all by myself, and you can have as many as you want on your side. I'll spot you thirteen points and the serve."

"Sure! Let's do it!" Neville shouted. "You're on."

"Of course, we got to put something on it," Sears said.

"Like what?"

"Okay, if you guys can beat me, then I'll concede volleyball is not the toughest sport, but if you lose, you have to join me on a team this fall."

"*Oh, sure*,"[5] Neville said, thinking that would never happen.

Sears immediately went around the camp, going from cabin to cabin, announcing the time and place for the game and encouraging everyone to come and watch. Soon the entire camp gathered around the grass court to witness what most thought would be a one-sided showdown.

Neville and his friends walked out on the grass court, filling in two rows of three players, just as they had learned in middle school. When Sears walked out to his side of the net, he tried to look as forlorn and pathetic as possible, playing it up to the camp crowd, and he quickly won them over, appealing to their natural instinct to root for the underdog.

"Okay, ready to serve. Send it over," Sears yelled across the net. Neville was situated right in the middle of the pack. As the serve soared over his head toward the lone player on the other side, he saw Sears do three things he had never seen before.

He first bumped it to himself, passing it perfectly in the air, directly above his head. Then he set it to himself, lofting the ball near and above the net. And then he rushed forward and pounded the ball toward the opposing court, spiking it on a trajectory toward Neville.

The ball struck Neville directly between the eyes. He didn't know what had hit him.

Neville staggered backward, stunned both by the jolt to his head and by Sears's skills. The sport Sears was playing didn't appear to be the same game Neville learned in middle school. The campers erupted with cheers, yelling wildly for Sears.

Suddenly Sears didn't look so forlorn and pathetic. He took the ball and jump served, throwing the ball above his head, leaping in the air and hitting it on a low trajectory with overhand spin, scoring an ace. Sears went on to win the game despite spotting Neville's team thirteen points.

Sears approached the losing side with a wry smile. "Well, boys, looks like you are joining me on a team this fall."

Neville tried to object, stammering, "You used three hits for yourself," but there was no way to win that argument—one player, all by himself, had handily beaten a team of six. Neville and his friends were won over and kept their promise, joining Sears on a team that fall. With Sears as their coach, they took on men's teams at YMCAs all over the Pacific Northwest, and Neville became enamored with the sport.

When Neville graduated from high school the following summer, he only applied to one college: George Williams. If it was good enough for Sears, it was good enough for him, and he wanted to learn from the best.

The most prominent volleyball coach in America at the time was Jim Coleman, a professor at George Williams College. In the early 1960s, Coleman had traveled to Poland to study why the Poles and other Eastern European teams were so dominant in volleyball, bringing this knowledge back to the United States and applying it to his teams at George Williams. While Neville was a good player and he enjoyed the game, he had already decided that his goal was to coach. Eventually he took an independent study course in international coaching from Coleman, who saw potential in Neville and took him under his wing.

When Neville graduated, he was drafted into the army. Coleman, who knew everyone in the volleyball world, rang up his good friend George Wilson at the Pentagon, a civilian in charge of all army sports. "You've got someone I trained to be a coach," Coleman told his friend. Within days Wilson called Neville and offered him a new assignment. "You have a choice," he said. "You can be coach or you can be a player-coach."[6] Neville didn't hesitate. At age twenty-two, he became the head coach of Army, and his coaching career was launched.

In 1968, Coleman was tapped to coach the U.S. National Team at the Olympics in Mexico City and brought Neville along as an assistant. Their first game was against the Soviet Union, the number-one ranked team in the world. The Soviets had won gold at the Tokyo Games of 1964, the first time volleyball was included in the Olympics. The Soviets underestimated the U.S. team, which was led by Larry Rundle, a native of Los Angeles who learned the game on the beach. The American squad stunned the volleyball world by beating the Soviets. It was the biggest win in the history of the U.S. program. In the next game Rundle went down with a bad ankle sprain and Coleman's team lost most of their remaining matches, finishing seventh. The United States had no backup plan if Rundle went down, so when he did, it was all over. The experience taught Neville a valuable lesson; always ask "what if?" and be ready for every conceivable scenario.

When Beal first showed up on the National Team, Neville immediately recognized that as a Midwesterner and an Ohio State grad, the others considered

Beal an outsider, and he was not fully accepted by the team. The beach-bred California athletes were skeptical of players from outside the state, and Beal had to earn his teammate's respect. And he was different in other ways too. An intellectual with aspirations for graduate school, maybe even a Ph.D., he stood out among his teammates. Sporting a Fu Manchu and glasses, Beal even looked different.

Doug Beal and his signature Fu Manchu mustache, in a picture from the late 1970s, a time when the National Team training center was in Dayton, Ohio, and at times Beal was both a player and a coach.
SOURCE: DOUG BEAL ARCHIVES

Neville already had a keen sense for team dynamics and player relationships. If there was a whiff of discord on his team, he was on the scent. He quickly noticed that other players didn't seem to appreciate Beal's talent and work ethic, so Neville sought a way to make sure the other players on the team could see what he saw in Beal.

The opportunity came in the midst of practice one day when Carl McGown, the head coach, said to Neville, "Take Beal down to the other side of the court and teach him to play defense."

"I can do that," said Neville. He believed that although Beal was a setter, who was not known for defense, he could meet the challenge. It was time for Beal to prove himself to the rest of the team.

For the next hour, Neville blasted Beal, belting him with ball after ball, asking him to dig this and block that, berating him to jump higher, extend his arms, work on his form.

Beal didn't complain or slack off. Neville waited for Beal to say, "Enough!," but he never did. The rest of the team couldn't help but notice how hard Neville was pushing Beal, and how committed the sweat-soaked Beal was to improving as a player. Although not as talented a defender as many of his teammates, his work ethic and stamina made up for his shortcomings.

After an hour of nonstop work, Neville called it quits and reported back to McGown, speaking loud enough for everyone to hear. "Coach, I guess you probably want to fire me because I tried everything I can to teach Beal how to play some reasonable defense, and I don't think there's a chance."[7] Everyone laughed, including Beal, but the message came through loud and clear. Now the entire team recognized that Beal was willing to push himself to the limit and do whatever it took to make the team and help his teammates. Over the course of one short hour, he won their respect. He was no longer an outsider, but an integral part of the team.

• 3 •

Pepperdine 1974

$\mathcal{A}$lthough Beal was improving as a player, his addition to the team was not near enough to make the Americans a world championship team. That would require a complete makeover of the way the team was put together, and that was out of any individual player's control.

One of the challenges facing American volleyball at that time was the amateur status rule: all Olympic athletes were required to maintain their amateur status. The International Olympic Committee placed strict limits on an amateur athlete's ability to make money from their designated sport. Larry Rundle, for example, should have had a long run on the national team, but when he got married and started a family, he quit because it was just too difficult to support a family and put in the time required for practice and traveling to tournaments. The Soviets and other Eastern European teams got around this by placing their best players in the military, where they essentially got paid to play volleyball while still maintaining their amateur status. That option wasn't available to the Americans.

In the United States, volleyball was still considered a marginal sport, and the National Team simply didn't have access to the resources available to the U.S. track squad or basketball team. In the early 1970s, there was little money or resources for National Team players. The athletes, even if they didn't have a family to provide for, still had to find a way to support themselves while pursuing their dreams.

The players worked various jobs, some as waiters, others in real estate. It was impossible for any of them to concentrate entirely on volleyball, or even to make every practice. And even when they did make practices, they were often exhausted. Despite spending three months training for the 1970 World Championships, to be held in Bulgaria, the practice schedule was erratic. Due

27

to everyone's work schedules, it was rare to have the whole team together at one time—even the coaches sometimes had to miss practice.

Meanwhile, the best teams in the world, many of them from Eastern Europe, trained together almost year-round. The Americans didn't have a chance and finished a disappointing eighteenth out of twenty-four teams, two spots below Mongolia,[1] a third-world country with a population of only one and a half million. The sport was dominated by Eastern European countries: East Germany, Bulgaria, the Soviet Union, Poland, Czechoslovakia, and Romania. Of the top seven teams that year, the only non–Eastern European country was Japan, which finished in third place. Soon afterward a *Sports Illustrated* article accurately described volleyball as "just another American invention, like the assembly line, that the rest of the world was doing a little better."[2]

Throughout the remainder of the early 1970s, America's volleyball fortunes continued to wallow. Each spring or early summer, the United States Volleyball Association (USVBA), the governing body for the sport, would hire a new coach. The coach would hold tryouts for the National Team in a designated city, usually Los Angeles, and select a talented group of players from the best college teams and clubs in the country. But few of the players had ever played together before, and for those who had it was often on the beach. The National Team would practice for several months and play a few exhibition games before traveling to international tournaments, and then fall apart and lose in every way possible.

The problems were obvious, and the gap between the U.S. National Team and other elite international teams grew ever wider. The best volleyball teams in the world were simply better organized, better trained, and better funded—they practiced and played together all the time. While the United States had elite-level talent, the players simply didn't have enough time together to learn a system and play their best volleyball as a *team*.

Qualifying for the Olympics, much less medaling, was a distant dream. The American coaches were knowledgeable and well meaning, but, like the players, they were only part-timers too, holding full-time positions coaching collegiately. Lacking corporate sponsorship, the program was continually underfunded, and without sufficient resources, the National Team couldn't establish its own training facility or properly pay a full-time staff. Without an Olympic jobs program for the amateur athletes, the players struggled financially and were forced to make trade-offs between work and practice.

Beal and his teammates were competitive by nature and found the situation both disheartening and frustrating. The men's national program was foundering, and the players were losing hope.

When Beal and his teammates lost to Cuba in the North American qualifiers for the 1972 Olympics, the USVBA finally realized that if the National

Team was to be competitive the USBVA would have to get more serious about the program. They decided to make a change.

The first step in that direction was the hiring of Carl McGown to be the head coach for a four-year term starting in 1973, providing a consistent philosophy and approach. McGown's charge was clear: prepare a U.S. team to qualify for and compete in the 1976 Olympics in Montreal.

When McGown took over, he had recently graduated from the University of Oregon with a Ph.D. in motor learning. That's where he befriended two graduate students from the Educational Psychology Department who were studying the new field of organizational development—my father, Don Murray, and his colleague Chuck Johnson. Although neither of the two academics was by any measure a gifted athlete, Murray and Johnson were particularly interested in the elements and conditions that lead to team success—things like building trust, clarifying a team's mission, helping people understand and accept their role, and getting everyone to place the success of the team above their individual goals.

In June 1974, McGown invited his graduate school buddies to join the National Team as volunteer advisors and sports psychologists for a weeklong training camp held at Pepperdine University, where McGown would select twelve players from thirty competing for a spot on the team. McGown tasked them with applying what they were learning about the conditions and principles that lead to team success to his volleyball team. That simple directive and awareness of its importance would eventually prove critical.

McGown wasn't interested in following in the steps of his predecessors by simply selecting the twelve best individual volleyball players to represent the country. He wanted to find the twelve players who, together, would make up the best team. Murray and Johnson would then help his staff take those twelve great athletes and mold them into great teammates, turning individual talents into a successful unit on the court.

The morning of Saturday, June 22, 1974, marked the final day of tryouts for the National Team. Beal was selected, making the team as a backup to starting setter Danny Patterson.

That afternoon, McGown brought the players and coaches together, congratulated the young athletes who had made the team, and then got down to business. He expressed his desire for the players to support and openly communicate with one another and the coaches. McGown informed the athletes that their first official meeting together would be focused entirely on team building, and with that he turned the meeting over to Murray and Johnson.

At first, the players weren't sure what to think of the team psychologists and were skeptical of their presence, calling them collectively "the shrinks." Just as elite athletes today hire sports psychologists to strengthen their mental game, McGown essentially tasked Murray and Johnson with strengthening the collective mental game of the team. Murray and Johnson stood in front of the team that Saturday and introduced the players and coaches to a theory for how teams come together to perform at the highest possible level. They explained that team building was made up of four main elements.

First, Murray gave a kind of lecture to describe the basics of team dynamics, something the young athletes had probably never given much thought to. He told them that teams are composed of individuals, and those individuals are organized into subsystems based on the various tasks they perform. The two primary subsystems are players and coaches. The idea that the coaches were part of the "team" was news to some of the players and maybe even a few of the coaches. "Primarily a team meets its goals through collaborative effort," said Murray. "No one person can meet the team's goals single-handed."[3]

The second element Murray emphasized was that teams are goal directed. High-performing teams have clarity around both the mission and the ultimate outcome they are striving to achieve. They want to win, sure, but what, specifically, did that *really* mean and how could it be accomplished? Clearly, talent isn't always enough. Up to this point, the National Team had not explicitly written down its goals, nor had the coaching staff demanded individual players set goals.

This was all about to change. Murray explained that "team-building interventions should uncover the discrepancy between goal-striving and actual goal achievement. If the goal is to give 100% in practice for three hours solid and some players are not totally involved for three hours, we have a discrepancy."

The third element, offered Murray, was that "great teams embody a degree of openness and adaptability." He used the example of a coach introducing a new training technique, a situation in which the players must be open to trying out the technique and adopting it in a way that moves the team toward its goal. "The team should be an open system," Murray explained. "It should be responsive to input from outside the player group." In other words, the players must be willing to experiment with new ideas and new approaches. If the team is not willing to innovate and evolve, it will not improve.

Lastly, Murray emphasized that teams are made up of people with a wide variety of skills, experiences, and expertise. "For example," Murray explained, "a particularly charismatic player may be the team's best resource for handling an interpersonal conflict. The team captain may be the best person for providing feedback to players who aren't pulling their share of the load." This was fairly obvious to everyone, but Murray then provided the reason why it was so important. "For organizations to be truly effective," he said, "they must make maximum use of the resources and skills within the team."

He went on to tell the team that it would undergo team-building sessions designed to help the team identify its "variety pool" of resources and figure out how to leverage those unique resources to achieve collective success. "If one coach has a particular knack for teaching a method of playing, his skills should be uncovered and made known." Although Murray's example spoke to coaching, the natural extension of this concept would eventually lead the team to favor more specialization of player skills on the court and using that specialization to its advantage.

With these four elements serving as a foundation, Murray and Johnson explained that over the following week they would meet with the players and coaches. Sometimes they would work only with the players, at other times they would work only with the coaches, but eventually both groups would come together to address issues, build cohesion, and set goals.

After a rigorous practice the following day, Murray and Johnson held a players-only meeting to work on becoming a better team. The players were greeted by the team psychologists as they filed into a small conference room with chairs forming a half circle around a flip chart. Murray approached the flip chart, pen in hand, and addressed the team. "Look, you've all been on winning teams," he said. "You wouldn't be here if you hadn't, but Chuck and I are guessing you've also been on some losing teams. So let's talk about the characteristics of the best and worst teams you have ever played on."

A long pause followed. This was unfamiliar territory for many of the players.

Finally, one of the players spoke up. "On good teams, the players back and support the coaching staff."

"Good," Murray said, keeping eye contact with the players, while Johnson wrote the characteristic on the flip chart under the heading "Good Teams."

Murray and Johnson made a good team themselves. As one man asked questions, the other wrote down the players' answers on the flip chart, and then, after a short time, they would switch roles. And they both liked to use humor, often at their own expense, to disarm the players.

"Sameness of goals," another player added.

"What do you mean by that?" Murray asked.

"When individual goals and team goals are aligned, that helps the team win."

"That's good," Murray said, adding to the growing list. "Can you give me an example?"

"Sometimes," the player said, "a player has to sacrifice for the team, which could mean less playing time, or switching to a position that isn't their first choice."

"That's great," Murray confirmed, as Johnson added another bullet point to the growing list.

"What else?" Murray asked.

"Punctuality," another player added, "Being on time for events with our mind in gear."

"Okay, why is that so important?"

"It sounds like a minor thing, but it's not. Being on time shows respect. On good teams, I've noticed players are prepared and ready to give their best at practices and games."

"What else?"

"Knowledge of our strengths and the strengths of others, and how we contribute to the team," a player added.

Johnson wrote it down while Murray asked for more comments.

"Players are clear about their role on the team and what's expected of them."

It was a solid list, so Murray and Johnson then inverted the question. Now they asked the players to identify the characteristics of the worst teams they have ever played on. The players found this easier, and the answers came fast.

"Everyone plays as individuals," one player suggested.

"Players bad-mouth other players, and cliques develop," another player chimed in.

"Players don't agree and support coaches, and that coaches don't back and support fellow coaches," said a third player.

Both Murray and Johnson wrote furiously to keep up with the players.

"Not getting everyone to work for the team goal first," a player threw out.

As the exercise ended, Murray and Johnson posted the two lists on the wall and invited the team to reflect. "What is this telling us?" Murray asked.

There it was, on the flip chart, all their problems as a team and all the solutions. For the first time, Beal and his teammates collectively voiced the characteristics of the team they wanted to be, and, just as significant, they acknowledged to one another the kind of team they didn't want to be.

Murray and Johnson then introduced the concept of "norms," behaviors that are accepted as appropriate in a given setting. They emphasized that norms can be a positive force, helping a team meet its goals, or they can be destructive. "When a group of individuals get together, norms will emerge," Murray explained. "One norm might be that players give 100% effort during practice. Another norm might suggest it's okay to bad-mouth another player behind their back. The crux of the norm issue is that norms exist anyway, so why not uncover them and talk about them?"

Murray and Johnson figured the players had covered enough ground for their first meeting, although some of the players were still skeptical of spending so much time talking about team building instead of working on their volleyball skills. Before the meeting ended, Murray and Johnson asked them to rate the session on a scale of 1 to 10. "The range overall was between 5–8, with the bulk of the scores in the 5–6 category," wrote Murray in a report he assembled for USA Volleyball. Then the consultants challenged the players, asking them how much effort they put into the session. Did they give a 2 and receive a 6 from the session? Or did they give a 10 and get back a 5? "The overall positive impact of these sessions is really up to you and how much you put into it," Murray told the players. Of all the players, Beal was most excited to see where this was leading. Like McGown, he recognized the importance of investing in team cohesion.[4]

The following day, after another strenuous morning practice, Beal and his teammates gathered in a conference room for their third team-building session. This time the goal was to zero in on the most important expectation of the players: to get to know, enjoy, and trust one another.

Murray and Johnson had the players pair up and interview one another, not just about who they were as a volleyball player but who they were as a person. What hobbies do they enjoy? What's important to them in their lives? What's something about them that might surprise others on this team? Each player then introduced their partner to the team. The personal stories they shared created opportunities for connection and helped the players view each other as real people, not just competitors for playing time. The goal was to start building trust and strengthening bonds as quickly as possible.

Next, Johnson and Murray organized an exercise where half the team wore blindfolds while the other half guided the blindfolded players on a walk outside. The roles were then reversed. When the players finished and returned to the conference room, they described the unsettling feeling of being dependent on a teammate for something as critical as their sight. Shuffling around in the dark, they felt vulnerable at first, but gradually they came to trust their partners. And when they did, moving around became much easier than they imagined it could be.

At the end of the session, the consultants reinforced the importance of trust and cohesion. "The player on a volleyball team cannot accomplish a successful season unless each player recognizes his virtual dependence upon others for team success," they told the players.

As the meeting was ending, the players were again invited to rate the session, and the scores improved to between 8 and 10, with the overwhelming majority in the top end of the scale. "This was, in the consultant's eyes, the turning point for the players. They were 'on board,'" wrote Murray in a report about the session.[5]

The following day Murray and Johnson held a team-building session with McGown and his staff. "The coaching staff is also a team," Murray first reminded them. They focused the session on communication and decision making, two skills the coaching staff would have to master if they wanted the team to succeed. This involved becoming more comfortable with feedback, both from players and from coaches. The coaches also worked out a system of group norms, rules of behavior the staff collectively agreed to follow. These included "speaking up when there is a problem" and "agreeing to go directly to another staff member to work out disagreements."

"If you can commit to these behaviors," Murray assured them, "you'll improve as a team." When planning a practice or designing a drill, they agreed to work together to find creative solutions to address the team's challenges and find the best solution. Ever so slowly, they began to look at themselves as a problem-solving group, drawing on the collective wisdom and experience of the entire staff.

The staff generated a set of potential team goals, and the coaches worked together as a team to rank them in order of importance. Their top three goals were the following:

1. Beat Cuba in 1975.
2. Require individual players to set goals.
3. Help players grow as humans and individuals.

The coaches also developed the process by which players could provide feedback to the coaching staff by writing down their feedback on note cards. Although some of the feedback was difficult for the coaches to hear, the consultants pointed out that it served to surface important issues that needed to be addressed if the team was going to succeed.[6]

In the final meeting that week at Pepperdine, the team psychologists met with the players and the coaches together, in one room, to develop a shared set of written and agreed-upon individual and team goals and group norms. To facilitate this, Murray and Johnson distributed a stack of blank four-by-six-inch note cards. They asked each player to write down five individual goals, one per note card, and present them to the group. After each goal was read aloud, the note card was taped to the wall, clearly visible to all players and coaches.

When Murray finished the instructions, he sat down and waited for the players to start. The players looked around the room to see who among them would speak up. Would it be perceived as "cool" to go first? Would they be ridiculed later? McGown scanned his players, curious to see who would step up. Finally, Beal rose, walked to the front of the room and read each of his cards. Just as importantly, he did so with no ironic tone in his voice, no smirky smile; he was all business.

With a voice that was both serious and determined, he shared what he wrote on each card and then turned to pin them to the wall for all his team-mates to see:

1. Be setting errorlessly by return from Japan.
2. Improve my defensive stand. Dig more balls.
3. Contribute to team cohesion by not coaching on the floor.
4. Be a starter on the team that beats Cuba in 1975.
5. See an upward curve in strength and fitness through 1976.

Danny Patterson, the starting setter and one of the leaders on the team, stood up and read each of his cards:

1. To be a helpful blocker on this team.
2. To increase my defensive mobility.
3. To run a smoother offense.
4. To make continuous improvement on my running, lifting, and conditioning.
5. To win a medal in 1976.

That last goal was a big one and something of a surprise. The United States had never medaled in Olympic men's volleyball. Most of the players that day shared the more modest goal of simply qualifying for the Olympics. Beal's goal of beating Cuba in 1975 was effectively equivalent to qualifying for the Olympics. Players and coaches alike knew that Cuba alone stood between the United States and the Olympics. To qualify for the 1976 Olympics in Montreal, they had to beat Cuba in 1975. And if they could do that, well, why not medal?

One after another, the remaining players stood and announced their goals, each adding to the list of goals:

Gus Mee: "Make the right setting decision."

Jim Iams: "Pass the ball better."

Byron Shewman: "Improve blocking and cross-court hitting."

Tom Read: "Be a better student of the game."

Miles Pabst: "Become an excellent team player."

Jon Roberts: "Get to know players better in hopes of forming lasting and meaningful relationships."

The last to stand up was Kirk Kilgour, a team leader and someone the players respected. He had won two national championships for UCLA in 1970 and 1971, establishing the Bruins as a powerhouse in men's volleyball. In addition to "winning a medal at the Olympics," Kilgour cited "improve communication with all players."

Next, Murray handed out note cards to all the players and coaches while Johnson invited them to write down a proposed team goal, one per note card, share the goal with the team, and post it on the wall. The note cards started flying:

"Become a total team."

"Become a family."

"Be happy."

"Become a better team by learning from the mistakes made in the past."

"To leave the court knowing we didn't hold anything back."

"Every player gives everything they have to the team."

"Improve every match."

"Become the Honolulu Roofing Company"—a term Hawaiian players used to describe a team that was excellent at blocking, effectively forming a "roof" over their opponents. The term made its way to the mainland and the beaches of California.

"Play up to our potential."

A montage of cards covered the wall, over twenty in all. The last goal presented was the perfect capstone to the weeklong training: "Beat Cuba!" The room erupted with applause and cheers.

Beal had just participated in his first volleyball team-building activity. He admired McGown for taking the time off the court to work on culture and team cohesion, but he still left the meeting a little uncertain what the overall impact might be. It all *sounded* good, but would it really make a difference? He didn't know the answer to that question.

Even Murray and Johnson had their misgivings. In a report Murray later wrote up about the event, his optimism was tepid. "To say the team building session will have a lasting and positive effect would perhaps be premature at this time. However, if the results we heard expressed on the last day of the training were any indication of their [players and coaches'] spirit, the original goals of moving them towards becoming a closer, more cohesive team were successfully met."[7]

It was a start.

McGown already understood that success on the volleyball court was about more than just getting the x's and o's right. He knew that even the best offensive and defensive strategies fail if players can't work together as a team or don't buy into the system. Now Beal began to take notice of McGown's emphasis on team cohesion and the "team psychology" exercises facilitated by Murray and Johnson. Beal was already coaching Ohio State during his breaks from playing on the National Team, and McGown could see that Beal had the raw talent to be a great coach, so he took Beal on as a mentee, sharing with him what he could of the art of coaching. They soon became friends.

McGown understood that building a world-class team culture required more than a weeklong team-building intervention, but he also knew the National Team lacked the resources to fund more such meetings. McGown teamed with Murray and Johnson, and together they developed a comprehensive proposal to incorporate periodic team-building sessions into the National Team's training schedule, one they hoped to present to various foundations seeking the funds needed to support such a program. They even dreamed of creating some kind of shared experience for the team, maybe something outside of volleyball that would serve to bring the team even closer together.

The idea was ahead of its time, and there weren't many foundations that considered giving money to an amateur athletic team to help them "build trust and cohesion" a worthy expenditure. It became apparent that, at least for now, it would be up to the players and coaches to take what they learned in the team-building session and keep it alive.

What McGown really needed at that moment was an internal leader who could bring the team together and maintain team dynamics. Baseball has a term for this kind of player; they call him the "glue guy." The glue guy's greatest contribution to a baseball team is not on the diamond, although he can typically hold his own; rather, it's his ability to build relationships, motivate teammates, and set high standards on the field and in the clubhouse. A glue guy may not be the best athlete on a team, but he elevates the play of everyone around him.

Beal was an intelligent player and a capable leader on the court, but he didn't have the rare combination of social skills and relationship-building tools that make a "glue guy." Fortunately, a player who would one day develop into just such a world-class glue guy joined the team that summer of 1974.

He was only twenty-two years old, but he had already led his Palisades high school basketball team to an improbable LA city championship and his San Diego State volleyball team to an even more improbable NCAA championship. He was known up and down the beaches of California for his tenacious play on the court and his fun-loving personality off. He had that rare but coveted ability to somehow get a team to play better than the sum of its parts.

He also happened to be charismatic and funny, with movie-star looks, an enduring smile, an infectious laugh, and a name that would make Shakespeare jealous.

Chris Marlowe, the "Big Cy."

• *4* •

The Big Cy

$\mathcal{C}$hris Marlowe grew up in Pacific Palisades, California, in the 1960s, in a family with a rich background in Hollywood. Marlowe's grandfather on his mother's side, the acclaimed Hollywood director Sam Wood, got his start as an assistant to Cecil B. DeMille in 1916 and directed a string of box office hits and critically acclaimed movies in the 1930s and 1940s, including *Kitty Foyle*, starring Ginger Rodgers, and *For Whom the Bell Tolls*, starring Gary Cooper and Ingrid Bergman. Nominated for Best Director three times,[1] he earned his own star on the Hollywood Walk of Fame. The Marx brothers, Clark Gable, and DeMille even served as pallbearers at his funeral.

Marlowe's mother, actor K. T. Stevens, appeared in a number of films and television shows, including *Kitty Foyle*. His father, Hugh Marlowe, appeared in over thirty movies, mostly as the secondary lead or supporting actor. Hugh and K. T. married in 1946 and eventually settled in Pacific Palisades to raise their two sons.

Marlowe loved movies, and his favorite, the 1942 film *The Pride of the Yankees*, starring Gary Cooper, was also directed by his grandfather. It follows the story of Lou Gehrig's rise to baseball stardom with the Yankees and his shocking diagnosis of ALS, which cut his career and life short. The movie culminates with Gehrig's famous speech at Yankee Stadium: "Today I consider myself the luckiest man on the face of the earth."

Gehrig, the captain of the Yankees from 1935 to 1939, was beloved by teammates and fans alike. In the film's seminal scene, Gehrig visits a young invalid in a hospital who hopes to one day walk again. "If you want to do something hard enough, you can do it," Gehrig tells the boy. Gehrig's confidence and character must have made an impression on young Marlowe.

In the summers, Marlowe's mother would pile her son and his gaggle of neighborhood friends into her Chevy station wagon and drive to Santa Monica State Beach. At midday, after playing in the ocean for hours, they would break for lunch. That's when Chris first noticed the older boys playing beach volleyball. Intrigued, he wandered over to the nets to get a closer look. Soon he was playing in matches and gaining confidence in his skills. He competed in his first tournament as a teenager in 1967 and placed fifth.

On a family vacation to Hawaii when Chris was young, his older brother, Jeff, teased him relentlessly. "Did you know you're a cyclops?" Jeff would say to him over and over. "You're a cy."

Jeff wouldn't give up, and the nickname soon caught on with his brother's friends in the neighborhood. Young Chris didn't like being called "Cy" and rebelled against it, at least until he figured out how to turn it into a positive.

"I would kid people and tell them it's short for 'Psycho,'" said Marlowe. "I get what I want."

As he grew older and women would ask about the name, he had a ready-made response. "I'm the big Sigh, S-I-G-H. I make the women sigh," he'd say with a smile.

At Pacific Palisades High School, "Cy" Marlowe joined the volleyball team. He discovered that the skills he picked up on the beach translated to the indoor game and he led his high school team to three straight L.A. city championships.

Marlowe's other love was basketball. His senior season, in 1969, his high school basketball team, coached by legendary L.A. prep basketball coach Jerry Marvin, also won the city championship. Although a number of talented players later came through his program at Palisades, including future NBA stars Kiki VanDeWeghe and Steve Kerr, Marvin's subsequent teams never won another city championship.

The coach credits the 1969 championship to the unique camaraderie on Marlowe's team. "What matters," Marvin said, "is working to bring out the chemistry in a team, getting players to know each other's moves, getting them to resist taking a bad shot and pass to the open man instead."[2] Marvin said the chemistry on Marlowe's 1969 city championship team was relatively easy to achieve because the players had all grown up in Pacific Palisades and had known each other their entire lives. Marvin recognized that their trust and shared experiences off the court helped them play better basketball.

Although Marlowe was a fine athlete, what made him special were those hard-to-measure "intangibles." His passion, charisma, and leadership elevated the play of his teammates. Effort is contagious, and whenever Marlowe showed up on the court the team's level of effort went up a notch.

Recruited by the San Diego State Aztecs to play basketball and volleyball, Marlowe started on the basketball team, but volleyball was his true passion. Jack Henn, the volleyball coach at San Diego State, was a former setter on the 1968 U.S. Olympic team that upset the Soviets. Henn was eccentric and a bit of a maverick, and he built the team in his own image. The star of the Aztecs was Duncan McFarland, but the captain, and the heart of the team, was Marlowe.

The group of players that coalesced around McFarland and Marlowe were fun-loving guys who, although extremely competitive, didn't take themselves too seriously. Even at a time when most students dressed formally for class, the San Diego State volleyball players wore shorts, sandals, and puka shell necklaces. The players grew beards and long hair, earning the nickname "the freaks."

As "the freaks" won game after game, word got around on campus that there was something special about this team, and they started attracting crowds unheard of for collegiate volleyball. For one memorable match, they crammed 6,600 fans into the 3,668-person Peterson Gymnasium.[3] Before the game, a line a half mile long formed outside the arena, and once inside, people sat in the aisles, hung off the rails, and crowded around the edge of the court. When the local fire marshal arrived, appalled by the overcrowding, he walked directly to the public address announcer and told him, "This is over capacity. It's a fire hazard. I'm shutting this down."

The announcer refused to pass along his message. "With all due respect," he said, "if we shut this down now, we'll have a riot and people will get hurt."

The fire marshal thought about it for moment and nodded. "I was never here," he said, then disappeared into the crowd himself.[4]

It became a lovefest for volleyball. At least at San Diego State, suddenly volleyball was "cool." In a sports town dominated by the Chargers and the Padres, the Aztec men's volleyball team was the hottest ticket in the city. Marlowe later reflected on the team and the movement they started, saying, "There was a unique bond between the students and the team. They fell in love with us, and we played better because of them."[5]

In 1972, Marlowe, McFarland, and the other Aztecs made it all the way to the NCAA championship game against defending champion UCLA. San Diego State jumped out to a 2–0 lead, but then "the freaks" inexplicably lost their mojo. UCLA swept the remaining three games to win their third straight NCAA championship.

One year later, in 1973, Marlowe's senior year, the Aztecs met the Bruins again in the national semifinals, and it was the Bruins who jumped out to a two-game lead. But Coach Henn wasn't rattled, telling his team, "We have them right where we want them."[6] This time Marlowe and the Aztecs recovered their mojo, winning three straight games to secure the victory.

Chris Marlowe (#10) goes up for the block for San Diego State in a match against Long Beach State at Peterson Gymnasium in 1973. Aztec men's volleyball drew huge crowds, and the team was popular with the student body. To Marlowe's left is Mike Cote (#7), and to Marlowe's right is Milo Bekins (#4).
SOURCE: SAN DIEGO STATE ATHLETICS

After the match, team captain Marlowe told a *Sports Illustrated* writer, "It was like it was willed to be. It was like God came down from the mountain and was rooting for the Aztecs."[7] That's simply the way things often went for a team that included Marlowe; victory appeared inevitable. The Aztecs went on to defeat Long Beach State for the 1973 NCAA Championship at the San Diego Sports Arena in front of 8,412 fans, the largest crowd ever assembled for a volleyball match up to that point, to collect the first and only Division I NCAA team title ever won by any San Diego State's sports team. Marlowe was voted first-team All-American, and his stellar performance caught the attention of National Team coach Carl McGown, earning Marlowe a place on the 1974 National Team.

Later in 1974, *Sports Illustrated* sent acclaimed writer Joe Jares to Hilo, Hawaii, to cover the U.S. Volleyball Open Championship, where the best club teams in America faced off annually to crown a champion. Encouraging his club team with positive talk while snarling at his opponents under the net, Marlowe's presence on the court could not be ignored. Just who is this Cy, people wondered?

The article, titled "The Big Cy Wasn't One Bit Shy,"[8] ended up devoted largely to Marlowe.

"He's just the Big Cy," one of Marlowe's teammates said of him in the story. "It's short for Cyclops and I don't know how it came about, but it doesn't matter because everyone thinks it's 'Psy' for psycho. Cy does things his own way, like nobody else on a volleyball court. He's also completely obnoxious out there."

Dick Davis, Marlowe's basketball coach at San Diego State, also weighed in, saying, "The guy has got a special kind of leadership ability."

"Marlowe," concluded Jares, "has charisma in a sport that badly needs it."

The legend of the Big Cy continued to grow after Marlowe joined the National Team. At 6'3" Marlowe, one of the taller players at San Diego State, generally played outside hitter, but the increased height of players at the international level forced Marlowe to become a setter. The National Team already had a starting setter in Danny Patterson, so Marlowe found himself competing with the other backup setter on the team, Doug Beal.

Another player arriving on the National Team at this time was a teammate from Marlowe's club team, Paul Sunderland of Malibu. Like Marlowe, Sunderland grew up playing volleyball on the beach and excelled at both basketball and volleyball. He was awarded a scholarship to play basketball at the University of Oregon, but after two seasons playing for the Ducks in Eugene, he transferred to Loyola Marymount to be closer to home and concentrate on volleyball.

Beal, Marlowe, and Sunderland shared the common goal of competing at the 1976 Olympics, yet for Beal, a few years older, the Olympic dream was running out of time. Beset with injuries, there was no guarantee his body would hold out for a chance at the 1980 Games in Moscow. His dream rested heavily on the National Team qualifying for the 1976 Olympics.

In international volleyball, the United States competes in the North American, Central American, and Caribbean Region (NORCECA). The team that won the 1975 NORCECA Zone Championships in Los Angeles would receive an automatic bid to the 1976 Olympics. The tournament was the Americans' best opportunity to qualify, and the biggest obstacle was their regional nemesis, Cuba. Yet despite the Americans' home-court advantage, Cuba dominated the United States in three straight games. Demoralized, they also lost to Mexico.

After the losses, team stalwart Danny Patterson and a number of other veteran players had had enough and quit, ready to move on with their lives. Kirk Kilgour, the team leader who stood up at the team-building session with Murray in 1974, pledging to win an Olympic medal, chose to accept an offer to play professionally in Italy, becoming the first U.S. player to play for money overseas.

Yet there was still hope for Beal, Marlowe, Sunderland, and the players who remained. The best teams in the world who hadn't qualified in their regional tournament were invited to a tournament in Rome in January 1976. The winner would claim a spot at the Olympics as a "world qualifier."

Just before leaving, the U.S. National Team was rocked by tragic news. While training with his professional team in Italy, Kirk Kilgour injured his spinal cord. When in Rome for the qualifying tournament, the team visited Kilgour in an attempt to comfort their former teammate, but the scene was heartbreaking. The former star was immobilized in a hospital bed. The doctors gave him a very slim chance of walking or moving his arms again, a tough blow to Kilgour, whose life, up to this point, was largely defined by his athleticism.

Inspired by Kilgour, the U.S. team battled courageously in Rome but still fell in the semifinals to Yugoslavia 3–1. Marlowe, Beal, Sunderland, and the other players were crushed. Their dream to play volleyball at the 1976 Olympic Games had come to an end. Beal had no medals or championships to show for his six years of hard work and sacrifice on the National Team, only frustration and disappointment.

The USVBA recognized it was time for a change and made two momentous decisions that would have a dramatic impact on the National Team. First, a search was initiated to locate a permanent year-round national training center for men's volleyball. There was no rush from communities eager to serve in that role as host. The only city that offered a real option was Dayton, Ohio, where a small group of volleyball enthusiasts convinced the chamber of commerce to get involved, and Dayton was eventually selected as the new home for the men's National Team.

Dayton, Ohio? The sport was closely tied to California, and many of the best players found the choice perplexing. The pipeline of talent largely flowed from the beaches through the powerhouse programs at UCLA, USC, and Pepperdine. Los Angeles was all sunshine, palm trees, beaches, convertibles, movie stars, and near perfect weather. But Dayton? Not only was Dayton a long way from home for most players, but it was everything L.A. was not: midwestern, industrial, economically struggling, and with frigid winters, humid summers . . . and no beaches.

The second decision involved coaching, as the USVBA finally chose to make the National Team coach a full-time, paid position. Doug Beal was invited to apply. The interview was in Los Angeles, and it lasted until late into the night. Beal returned to his hotel room exhausted and fell asleep, only to be woken up shortly after midnight with a call from a member of the hiring committee: "You were lucky to be selected since you gave such a lousy interview."[9]

Beal was still a bit dazed and confused, but once he figured out he got the job, he was excited. It wasn't exactly a vote of confidence in their new young coach, but "I gleefully accepted," said Beal.

Although Beal was only twenty-nine years old, he had gained valuable experience as the head coach at Ohio State University from 1972 to 1974. While his experience as a player had sometimes been frustrating, it also gave him insight into what needed to change. Beal envisioned a program with more consistency, more structure, and more long-term investment in players and facilities.

Still, he was not a popular choice among the West Coast players. They had hoped that UCLA coach Al Scates would apply, but the position was not highly coveted by the best collegiate coaches. A combination of low pay, the team's history of failure, and the requirement to relocate to Dayton led Scates and several other high-profile coaches to turn down the opportunity. None of these impediments was an issue for Beal.

Beal took over the program in Dayton in the winter of 1977, one of the coldest winters on record in Ohio. The Ohio River froze for the first time since 1958, and there were 26 consecutive days below freezing.[10] The knee-deep snow and frigid air didn't bother Cleveland native Beal, yet for many of the players on the National Team it was a shock, and although Beal was a great salesman, one of the best in the game, even he admitted that convincing players to move to Dayton was a hard sell.

The experience of two of his players was emblematic of the culture shock Beal's recruits had to overcome. In early February that winter, Joe Battalia and Ralph Smith, two Southern California players Beal convinced to join the program, packed up Smith's 1965 Volkswagen bug and started the long drive from California to Ohio. Smith wore the warmest pair of shoes he owned—Adidas Smash—a shoe built for playing indoor volleyball, not trudging in the snow.

They entered Indiana to rapidly falling temperatures and snow drifts building up on the highways and pulled up at a motel to spend the night. When they went to start the Volkswagen the next morning, the motor was frozen and wouldn't turn over, so they rolled the car up to the door of their motel room and directed a hair dryer at the engine to thaw it out. When word got back to California about Battalia and Smith's winter adventure, it put a chill on Beal's player recruiting effort.

The one advantage of Dayton was its proximity to Ohio State, and Beal soon realized it was a lot easier to convince players to move from Columbus, only a little more than an hours' drive away, than from California. As an alumnus and the former head coach, Beal's ties to the school were strong, and he eventually recruited three OSU players to join the team.

Rich Duwelius was perhaps the most unlikely player to arrive at the National Team training center. He was tall but hadn't even played volleyball or any other team sport in high school. When he arrived at Ohio State, he tried out for the freshman basketball team on a lark, with the goal of walking onto the court at St. John Arena at least once in his life while wearing an Ohio State jersey. He made the team by an utter fluke. Injured during tryouts, he returned just as the coach discovered that, in his haste, he had cut too many players. He gave the one remaining spot to Duwelius, the last man standing. It was a miracle.

As a sophomore, he was cut from the basketball team but told that someone wanted to talk with him: Doug Beal.

"Look," said Beal, "the volleyball team is looking for athletes. Tall athletes. I understand you got cut from the basketball team. Come try out for volleyball."[11] Duwelius did, working his way onto the varsity team as a junior and becoming a starter his senior year, but he was far from a star. By his own estimation, he was no better than the fourth best player on the Ohio State volleyball team that season.

Desperate for players, and with a tournament coming up in Canada, Beal called him up and invited him to train in Dayton. When Duwelius arrived, he looked around and realized he was the only middle blocker in camp. "This is the opportunity of a lifetime," he said to himself. "I have a good coach. We're practicing four hours per day. I have a chance to get a lot better and make an Olympic team."[12]

Another former Buckeye who joined the National Team in Dayton during this period was Marc Waldie. Waldie learned volleyball from his dad, who was introduced to the game as a soldier during World War II. When his father returned from the war to Wichita, Kansas, he joined a club team. Young Waldie would go to his dad's games and shag balls and even traveled with him to tournaments. Like many boys who enjoyed volleyball in the 1970s, it wasn't easy to find opportunities to compete against players his age, but he eventually was picked up by a junior club team based out of Kansas City, where he caught the attention of Beal, who recruited him to play at Ohio State.

Following Waldie's freshman year, Beal left Ohio State and was replaced by Terry Liskevych, a Ukrainian American whose parents immigrated to the United States after World War II, settling in Chicago. Volleyball was a popular sport among the Ukrainian diaspora, and Liskevych honed his skills as a player-coach for the Chicago Ukrainians team. Like Neville, he, too, was a graduate of George Williams College and protégé of Jim Colemen, and he later coached the U.S. Women's National Team from 1985 to 1996.

Under the guidance of Liskevych, Waldie's volleyball skills improved, and the Ohio State program continued to win. In 1977, Waldie's senior year, the Buckeyes went all the way to the NCAA championship game before falling to USC.

After Waldie graduated, Beal invited him to join the National Team training program in Dayton. The travel schedule for the National Team was demanding, especially in the summer, when the team typically traveled to tournaments overseas, and Waldie and his girlfriend, who lived in Wichita, wanted to get married. That left a very small window to hold a wedding. In September, Waldie returned from a trip on a Thursday and drove from Dayton to Wichita, arriving on Saturday just in time for the ceremony. The couple's honeymoon then consisted of a three-day drive back to Dayton.

When the newlyweds arrived in Dayton, Waldie moved his bride into his apartment, pointed out the Kmart and a restaurant or two, and then said, as he rushed out the door to join the National Team on another trip, "I love you. Good luck. I'll see you in three weeks."[13] He wasn't sure what to expect when he returned, but fortunately, his wife was still in Dayton, and they are still married today.

A third Ohio State recruit, Aldis Berzins, was Latvian American. His family left the Baltic country of Latvia during World War II after it was first invaded by the Russians, then "liberated" by the Germans, and finally reinvaded by the Soviet army. Aldis Berzins's father, like many Latvians, fled the country and by the end of the war was living in a displaced persons camp run by the Allies. He completed his degree at a camp university and then was awarded a scholarship to LSU, sponsored by the Lutheran Church. After arriving, he married a Latvian woman in 1953, and Aldis was born in 1956. The family settled in Wilmington, Delaware, where Berzins's father worked at the DuPont global headquarters.

Many members of the Latvian diaspora in the United States, worried about losing their connection with their culture, taught their children to speak Latvian and sent them to Latvian summer camps. Berzins attended these camps, where in addition to singing Latvian songs and participating in outdoor activities, there was a lot of time to play volleyball, one of the most popular sports in Latvia. In high school he returned as a camp counselor, logging even more hours on the volleyball court.

In the summer of 1976, Berzins and another counselor were excited for the Olympic tournament in Montreal, and they followed the results in the newspaper. When Berzins's friend scored two tickets to the Olympic volleyball final, they drove to Montreal to attend the epic five-game gold medal match between the Soviet Union and Poland. Many consider that battle, which the underdog Poles eventually won after being down 2–1, the greatest volleyball match of all time. In the volleyball world, it was an instant classic, but it hardly registered a blip in the American sports media of that time.

After graduating high school, Berzins was set to attend Penn State to play soccer when he got a call from Liskevych. Through the network of Eastern European volleyball players in the United States, Liskevych heard that there was a talented Latvian player headed to Penn State. He convinced Berzins to change course and play volleyball for Ohio State, where he teamed with Waldie and Duwelius. At 6'2" Berzins was small for a volleyball player, but he had quick hands and great footwork from his days playing soccer. Berzins also had an instinct for the ball on defense, something you just can't coach, making him a natural passer.

In 1978, Berzins's senior year, the Buckeyes lost in the NCAA semifinals to the eventual national champions, Pepperdine, coached by Marv Dunphy and led by two rising volleyball stars, Mike Blanchard and Ron Wilde. It was OSU's fourth consecutive appearance in the NCAA final four and a sign that the talent gap between midwestern players and those from California was beginning to narrow.

Still, the draw for the National Team was strong, and a few California players made the move to Dayton. Paul Sunderland, a member of the National Team since 1975, still harbored Olympic dreams and followed Beal to Dayton.

So did Chris Marlowe—for a while. Marlowe had visited Dayton with the National Team the previous summer to train and play in exhibition games as part of a trial run. Rising early in the morning to do wind sprints, he found himself running through a cloud of gnats. They were everywhere—in his mouth, in his eyes, buzzing his ears. Marlowe dubbed Dayton the "Gnat Capital of the World" and hated every hot and humid minute of it. After only one week, he packed his bag and headed back to L.A., apparently letting go of his Olympic dream and, like his parents, taking aim at Hollywood stardom.

Marlowe, however, couldn't quite give up on volleyball entirely. He continued to play for a club team in Los Angeles and entered beach tournaments on the weekend, where he made a name for himself and earned another nickname, "The Lion," on account of his unruly tuft of blond hair that blew in the wind like a mane, and his ferocious intensity on the court. He was always hungry to win.

The chemistry between teammates in two-on-two beach volleyball is critical. A bad teammate, even if highly talented, can send the duo into a downward spiral of negativity. A good teammate, on the other hand, brings the best out in a partner so that the sum is often greater than the individual parts. The most prestigious tournament at the time was the Manhattan Beach Open, and Marlowe, in between casting appointments, won back-to-back titles in 1976 and 1977. Incredibly, he did so with two different partners, a rare feat in beach volleyball, first with Steve Obradovich and then Jim Menges.[14]

While Marlowe was winning tournaments on the beach and making a name for himself as an up-and-coming actor, he remained on Beal's radar as the coach worked in Dayton to build a team and a national training center almost from scratch. He had no blueprint to follow. In addition to coaching, Beal hired staff, recruited players, arranged for gym time, made travel arrangements for international tournaments, interfaced with the community, and even helped find jobs for his players.

"We wanted players to make the team because they were good enough," Beal said. "Not because they were available, and we didn't want to lose the best players because they couldn't afford to be members of the team."[15]

The national training center in Dayton initiated an Olympic Job Opportunities Program, the first of its kind in any sport, but Beal would later admit that the program "met with minimal success," at least in its initial form. One problem was that although the jobs helped pay the rent, they often made training difficult. Waldie, for instance, landed a job working for a storage company, picking up furniture and moving it all day long, then, after taking a bus to the end of the line, walked the final two miles home, sometimes in snow. After a quick dinner with his wife, he would run out the door for a grueling three-and-a-half-hour practice, collapse in bed, and do it all again the next day.

However, the Olympic Job Opportunities Program, despite its humble beginning in Dayton, allowed players to continue to develop and learn as they played volleyball, and that was important to Beal. "We wanted to prepare them for the future and give them job opportunities," wrote Beal. "We wanted them to grow in a number of directions and thought our philosophy would culminate in better, more dedicated, and mature athletes."[16]

Building a team from scratch took time, and everything took longer than Beal wanted. Through extensive trial and error, he learned what worked and what didn't. Nevertheless, Beal could sense the development of a team culture slowly evolving. As more players took up residence in Dayton and devoted themselves full-time to the National Team, a level of professionalism emerged.

The National Team was no longer a seasonal occupation but the central focus of their lives.

Although the gap between the U.S. National Team and the best teams in the world was narrowing, it was still considerable. Their biggest problem was a lack of consistency. In 1978 the team traveled to Ancona, Italy, for the World Championships, and there were games and matches where the Americans were competitive, notching victories over Hungary and Argentina, two very good teams, but they also played poorly at times and ultimately finished in what Beal characterized as "inglorious 19th place."[17]

For Beal, "success over time is the most relevant measure of quality and achievement." And the team that most epitomized consistency and greatness for Beal was the Boston Celtics dynasty of the 1960s. Although the Celtics didn't win the NBA championship every season, they consistently fielded competitive teams, always giving themselves opportunities to win. "To defeat the Celtics, the opposition had to play a great game, and due to their consistency, the Celtics rarely defeated themselves," Beal said.[18]

What the Boston Celtics dynasty of the 1960s had was something the national volleyball team in Dayton didn't have: a player like Bill Russell. Never a big scorer, Russell focused on defense and rebounding. He had the unique ability to coax superior performance out of his teammates, and he led by example, setting a tone of excellence through his actions on and off the court.

The volleyball team that most defined greatness at the time was the Soviet Union men's team. After losing to the Poles in Montreal at the Olympics in 1976 in the famous five-game match, the Soviets went on a tear, winning the World Cup in 1977, the World Championships in 1978, the gold medal at the 1980 Olympics, the World Cup again in 1981, and the World Championships again in 1982, an unprecedented period of domination not just in volleyball but across all team sports.

The Soviet team was a hallmark of consistency, almost militaristic in its planning and approach. Year in and year out, the Soviet volleyball juggernaut produced exceptional athletes who played together as a team, in a system designed to take advantage of their strengths. They were mentally tough, and they rarely lost, especially at home. And like the Celtics teams that Beal admired, they almost never beat themselves. If the Americans stepped on the court to play the Soviets, they knew they would have to play their very best to expect even a chance of winning.

Beal and his American players were up against not just one of the best volleyball teams in the world but one of the best teams in any sport. For the Americans to beat the Soviets at Olympic volleyball would take a miracle, something akin to the Americans' improbable victory over the Soviets in hockey at the 1980 Winter Olympics—the "Miracle on Ice."

Beal also recognized that he couldn't try to duplicate the Soviet system. Their disciplined program was the product of a totalitarian regime—utterly hierarchical, with a top-down command-and-control structure. Motivated by the opportunity to enjoy a higher standard of living and perks like traveling abroad that were unavailable to most, Soviet coaches had little trouble recruiting the best players—players who followed orders, obeyed their coaches, and adjusted to the system. Personal freedom was discouraged, and insubordination was nonexistent. That wouldn't work in the United States.

Among the very best volleyball teams in the world, only two were not products of a communist sports system, Brazil and Japan. The difference in approach was telling. Each of these national teams had found success by developing a system that specifically worked for their national culture and the skill sets of their players.

For Beal, the question soon became clear: how could the Americans develop their own system for success? Many of the best American players learned the game on the beaches of California, attracting mavericks, surfers, and free spirits, embodying the essence of youth and independence. Teams like "the freaks" had won championships by bucking the trends and following their own inner sprit. When it worked, the players had more fun and their game displayed a unique creativity. Beal's players weren't afraid to voice their opinions about what they wanted and how things should be run, and, as Marlowe did with his flirtation with an acting career, even left the team when they felt constricted by the lifestyle.

If Beal was going to beat the Soviets, he was going to have to create an entirely new way of building a team by developing a system that leveraged the best of American culture and somehow enabled the team to play at its best. And the talent for this team would come from two disparate talent pools—those bred on the beaches of California, and those schooled in the more disciplined style of play brought over by Eastern European immigrants.

At the 1978 Open National Championships, Beal first noticed an extraordinary young talent—the one player who combined both the free-wheeling, athletic California style of play with the more methodical and orderly style of play Beal himself favored.

They would call him "Karch," and he would become the greatest volleyball player in the world.

• 5 •

Karch

On October 23, 1956, 20,000 students gathered in Budapest, the capital of Hungary, for a peaceful demonstration against the Soviet-backed communist government. The youthful crowd chanted, sang songs, and read manifestos. Their chief demands included a free and democratic Hungarian government independent of Soviet influence and for the people of Hungary to have the rights and protections enjoyed by the citizens of Western democracies.

One protestor was twenty-one-year-old Laszlo Kiraly, a university student and former member of the junior national Hungarian volleyball team who went by Las for short. Like his countrymen, he longed for Hungary to be free. At one point, the crowd started chanting "The National Song," a patriotic poem banned by the communist government, which includes the refrain: "This we swear, this we swear, that we will no longer be slaves."

As the afternoon wore on, the spirited yet peaceful crowd swelled, and the demonstrators made their way across the Danube to join a growing crowd outside the parliament building. By that evening, the multitude grew to 200,000 and the demonstrators toppled a thirty-foot-high bronze statue of former Soviet dictator Josef Stalin. The only vestige of the statue that remained were two bronze boots still firmly affixed to the pedestal. A protestor placed a Hungarian flag in the boots.

Eager to broadcast their demands, a group of students gathered outside the Radio Hungary building, which was heavily guarded by the Hungarian secret police. As the crowd became increasingly unruly, tensions began to rise. Eventually, the secret police deployed tear gas on the demonstrators and fired on the unarmed crowd. The Hungarian Uprising was underway, putting in motion a series of events that would change Las Kiraly's life forever.

By the next morning, Soviet tanks had entered Budapest, guarding the parliament building and main roads and bridges. The Hungarian secret police targeted the student leaders of the revolution, and many, including Las, went into hiding. Between October 23 and November 4, the authorities faced sporadic resistance, but with the help of Soviet troops and tanks the revolution was eventually crushed.

By some estimates, more than 200,000 refugees fled Hungary in the aftermath of the failed revolution, and Las Kiraly was one of them. Las's son later described his father's situation as dire, explaining, "His choices were stay, get tortured and executed, or leave and escape."[1] Saying goodbye to his family and younger sister, Las took his rifle and navigated the dangerous trek to the border, traveling mostly at night, being careful to avoid military patrols searching for fleeing student leaders. He crossed over into Austria, where he handed in his rifle before making his way to Germany, and eventually immigrating to the United States.

Intelligent and driven, Las wasted no time in applying to American universities to continue his studies in mechanical engineering. He was accepted at Wayne State University outside Detroit and studied there for a time before transferring to the University of Michigan. In Ann Arbor, he met a young woman, Toni, and the couple soon married.

After a short stint working as a mechanical engineer, Las decided to go back to Michigan to study medicine, eventually graduating from medical school. On November 3, 1960, the Kiralys' son was born. Although his name was Charles, they referred to him as "Karcsi" (pronounced *Kar-chee*), the Hungarian version of "Charlie." The young boy soon became known to family and friends as simply "Karch."

Soon the Kiraly family moved to Santa Barbara, where Las interned at a hospital, working long hours. Young Karch treasured what little time he could get with his father. They often spent their few free moments playing beach volleyball at East Beach in Santa Barbara, one of Southern California's premier venues for the sport. Although Las had primarily played six-on-six indoor volleyball in Hungary, he was attracted to the speed and intensity of the two-on-two beach game.

During their time together at the beach, Karch and his father played "pepper," volleying back and forth with no net, and when Las joined a pickup game, his son watched and shagged stray balls.

"He virtually had no choice," said Las. "This was my sport in Hungary and so he started bumping the ball around with me on the beach. The bug bit him at that point, and it was my bug." Given volleyball's relative obscurity in the 1970s, it wasn't unusual for American players, even those on the National Team, to have picked up the game in high school or even college. Having a volleyball-obsessed father accelerated Karch's development as a player, giving him an advantage over his contemporaries. "My wife keeps telling me," Las said, "that I never took no for an answer when I said, 'Karch, let's bump the ball around.'"[2]

Due to Las's Hungarian upbringing, he realized in the United States he had to seize the opportunities unavailable to him before. "I think what I imbued in him was the desire to excel," said Las. "I've always been very hard on myself, and I think Karch is hard on himself, too. I pushed Karch as a kid; but I don't think I did it in any cruel way. I was insistent."[3] Although Karch's mother sometimes thought her husband went too far, everyone who knew the family then says Karch always came back for more.

After Las's internship ended, the family moved back to Michigan and Las started practicing medicine, hoping one day to return to Santa Barbara. He joined the Ann Arbor YMCA indoor volleyball team and for the next few years played on weekends in competitive club volleyball tournaments all over the Midwest, and Karch tagged along.

In 1971, the Kiraly family moved back to California, this time to the San Jose area, although they made a number of summer trips to Santa Barbara, where Karch's partents hoped they could eventually move permanently. When in Santa Barbara, Las and Karch would play at East Beach, their favorite spot. "The first time I ever played on a [beach] court, I was nine years old and I played against my dad,"[4] Karch recalled. "He picked the best player on the beach willing to play with me and paired him with me. His name was Bill Conway, and he was the unofficial 'mayor of East Beach,' a great player."[5]

In addition to playing, as Karch grew older he became a student of the game. He subscribed to volleyball publications and read anything he could get his hands on about the sport. In one story, Karch was surprised to learn that Larry Rundle, perhaps the greatest American volleyball player up to that point, competed in his first tournament at age eleven. Youth volleyball in the 1960s and 1970s was extremely limited, and Karch had always believed he would have to wait years to play in a tournament against adults, but the article about Rundle gave young Karch an idea.

"Why not go out and play in tournaments now?" Karch asked his dad, thinking it would be fun to match Rundle's feat.[6] Las agreed, so they drove to Corona Del Mar in Orange County to give it a try, and like Rundle, Karch played in his first tournament at age eleven, partnering with his father. "He was my first teammate and my first partner for the next four or five years of competition in volleyball," Karch said.[7]

Karch and others who played on the beach did so for the pure love of the game. "There was no money in volleyball," Karch said, reminiscing about his early years. "There was Olympic indoor volleyball, but there was no beach volleyball in the Olympics yet, so there was really no extrinsic reward to play for. Everybody who was playing in those weekend tournaments—and in those days people couldn't get enough of volleyball, it was all-day Saturday and all-day Sunday; we would go to Playa del Rey and there would be 128 or more teams—everyone was in it to just get better and to try and win the next game."

Because youth volleyball or club volleyball didn't yet exist, Karch never played against kids his age; he only played against adults, which he credits with furthering his development. "No grown man wants to lose to a kid," Karch said. "Their friends are going to heckle them for a year, so they didn't hold back. And when you see adults playing, you see how it should be done. I got more chances to see and read the game."[8]

Opposing teams looked across the net and saw Las teamed up with a scrawny teenager and often pinpointed Karch as the weak link. To gain a tactical advantage, teams deliberately served to Karch, forcing him to pass to his father, who would then have to set to Karch. Barely able to jump higher than the net, Karch couldn't yet spike the ball downward. The opposition much preferred that to Las's spike. Instead of discouraging Karch, however, the tactic only motivated him to get better.

What Las wanted most was for Karch to always give his best effort and compete with intensity and focus. Las was tough on all his volleyball partners, even if that partner was his son. If Karch missed a spike, Las would call out, "Come on, you've got to put that thing away," or Las would say, "Rise and think!" Or if Karch wasn't being vocal enough, he'd say, "Call it. Call it. Talk to me!"[9] Other times he would exclaim with a thick Hungarian accent, "Jump and hit that ball Karch!"

Las could be loud and vocal on the court, but that was one of his father's traits that Karch didn't emulate. Karch let his performance on the court do the talking for him, leading by example.

Soon Karch's actions spoke louder than Las's shouting. The father–son pair had, up to that point, avoided "open" tournaments, which tended to attract the most dominant players, but while still in high school, the Santa Barbara Open was coming up and Karch was approached by another player to be his partner and compete in the tournament. Karch had only ever partnered with his dad. Conflicted, he asked his father what he should do.

"Karch, you're getting way too good for me," Las said. "You need to move on. If you were to stay with me, I would hold back your development."[10] Karch entered the tournament and although his team was unseeded, they played well enough to go up against Jim Menges and Greg Lee, the best team in beach volleyball at that time.

Karch credits the beach as being crucial to his development as a player. By his own admission, even in his prime, he said, "I'm not the best in the world at hitting the volleyball or blocking or serving, but I can help the team in a lot of different areas. That's my virtue. I have a strong all-around game. And a lot of that I learned playing on the beach here in California. Because you're forced, with only two men out there, to learn an all-around game."[11]

In 1973, Las moved the Kiraly family back to Santa Barbara. It was a dream come true. Karch enrolled at Santa Barbara High School as a freshman. The volleyball action at East Beach in Santa Barbara was as intense as ever, and Karch soon became a regular. Word began to spread up and down the beaches of California about a young player with a funny name who had serious game.

Around this time, Karch noticed another teenager playing at East Beach who also appeared to have gotten bit by the beach volleyball bug, John Hanley. Hanley was dragged to the courts by his older sister, Kathy, who was a great player in her own right, but soon he was going down to the beach to team up with Karch. "John Hanley and I were obsessed with this sport," Karch said. "We tried to figure out every way we could to get good at it, both on the beach and indoors."[12]

The sand courts at East Beach were always "open," but the few indoor courts around Santa Barbara had limited open gym times. Hanley found a creative solution, bending a coat hanger to jimmy locked doors and slip into local gymnasiums. "We were not there to vandalize or do damage. We were there to just play volleyball," Karch said. Soon it was "open" gym just about any time, at least for Hanley and Karch, at Santa Barbara City College, the Boys and Girls Club, and Santa Barbara High School, where they would turn on the lights, set up the nets, and play for hours. If they were discovered, the first question was usually, "What are you doing here?" They would play innocent and answer, "Oh, we just thought it was open gym."[13]

When Karch started to attend Santa Barbara High School, he joined the volleyball team coached by Rick Olmstead, a regular at East Beach, where he often partnered with Las Kiraly. A great player in his own right, Olmstead became another role model and mentor for Karch.

Olmstead had seen a lot of athletes in his day, but he found Karch, even as a high school freshman, to be "the most intense, focused and motivated athlete I've ever coached," and he believed Karch's father had a lot to do with it.[14]

Karch loved playing for Olmstead. "His intensity was phenomenal," said Karch. "He had a hunger to see us do as well as we could possibly do, but probably most of all he instilled in us a crazy work ethic. He made demands of us and we fulfilled those demands and we learned we were more capable then we thought."[15]

Olmstead set out to build a team around Karch and Hanley. Their team-mates were mostly new to the sport, and the team struggled at first, but under

Olmstead's guidance and with Karch leading by example with his commitment and dedication, the team quickly improved.

In the summer of 1975, Karch followed the U.S. National Team's quest to qualify for the 1976 Olympics, scouring every magazine and newspaper he could find for stories. When he learned the National Team was scheduled to play a qualifying match against Cuba in Los Angeles that summer, he had to be there. The American team that summer was coached by Carl McGown and featured Chris Marlowe, Paul Sunderland, and Doug Beal, who was injured and couldn't play. Las and Karch watched from the stands as the United States got absolutely crushed, losing to Cuba in three straight games.

Even though the U.S. team failed to qualify for the 1976 Olympics, the following summer fifteen-year-old Karch spent two weeks glued to the television watching ABC's coverage of the Montreal Games. He endured endless programming of track and field, swimming, gymnastics, and other more popular sports, all in the hope that ABC would broadcast something, anything on men's volleyball. "I timed my bathroom breaks to commercials in order to minimize the risk of missing a fleeting glimpse of volleyball," he said.[16] In the days before the Internet and YouTube, there was no other way for a young fan of the game to watch the best in the world.

"I wanted to see Poland. I wanted to see the Soviet Union. I wanted to see these people I'd only seen in pictures. These high-flying Cubans and the great Polish players, [Tomasz] Wójtowicz and [Edward] Skorek." Karch waited patiently. "Basically, nothing ever came on."[17]

Finally, toward the end of ABC's 1976 Olympic coverage, the network broadcast a few fleeting minutes of the epic five-game gold medal match between Poland and the Soviet Union—the same match that Aldis Berzins drove from camp to attend. Karch liked what he saw but was disappointed in the limited coverage. He desperately wanted to see how the game was played at the highest level.

"That's when it hit me," Karch said. "The only way that volleyball is going to get on [television] is if the U.S. is good enough (a) to qualify, because the U.S. wasn't even competing in that Olympics, and (b) is a contender in the medal rounds, or has a chance to be in the medal rounds."[18]

Karch began to dream big about an American volleyball team competing at an Olympics someday and even winning a medal. "That's when I made a goal for myself, to help the U.S. team be good enough to qualify for the Olympics and good enough to medal."[19] It was an ambitious objective, but Karch never let go of it.

In the summer of 1977, between his junior and senior years, Karch had a big opportunity to make progress toward his goal when he was invited to a try out for one of the first-ever U.S. junior national teams at Loyola Marymount, a two-hour drive down the coast from Santa Barbara. That summer he also worked a construction job with a friend whose father was a contractor. He arrived at the job site every morning at 7 a.m., worked in the summer heat until 2 p.m., and then set down his shovel and drove ninety miles south to Loyola Marymount. He then practiced hard with the junior national team for two hours, got back in his car, and drove home to Santa Barbara, only to do it all over again the next day.

He *loved* it.

At sixteen years old, Karch was one of the youngest athletes at the tryout and still developing as a player. When it came time to select the team, there was one last spot and the coaches agonized over the decision but eventually gave it to Karch. "They went with potential, not how good I was then, but how good I could be," said Karch.[20]

That summer Karch mostly rode the bench for the junior national team. Since he wasn't getting a lot of time on the court, the coaches gave him a job to stay busy—collecting stats. Sitting on the bench with a clipboard and pencil in hand gave Karch a front-row view of the future of U.S. volleyball and a chance to study the game.

The team was packed full of young talent, made up of a group of teenagers who loved the sport and who had logged thousands of hours playing volleyball on the beaches of Southern California. One of those players was Steve Salmons, a 6'4" middle blocker who played for UCLA. Salmons hated to lose, and Karch admired that.

Like Chris Marlowe, Salmons was from Pacific Palisades and had attended the same high school as Marlowe, although their time there didn't overlap. He grew up two blocks from the ocean, and when he wasn't surfing he was playing volleyball on the beach. At Palisades High School, he focused mainly on basketball but was close to many of the volleyball players. In his junior year the volleyball team reached out for his help, so he joined the team on a whim. Salmons discovered he not only liked the indoor game, but he was also pretty good. His senior season he began to take the game more seriously and led Pacific Palisades to the L.A. city championship.

Another player Karch met on the junior national team was Dusty Dvorak, an all-star setter from Laguna Beach High School. Karch was also a setter and learned from watching Dvorak and competing with him during practice. Dvorak had great hands and the ability to place the ball exactly where a hitter wanted it. Salmons's Pacific Palisades high school team defeated Dvorak's Laguna High School team for the California Interscholastic Federation (CIF) championship. Eventually, Salmons went on to play for UCLA while Dvorak went to USC.

Joining Karch, Salmons, and Dvorak on the junior national team in 1977 were two more players who would become teammates with Dvorak at USC, Tim Hovland and Pat Powers. Hovland, an outside hitter, was a phenomenal athlete with a full-ride scholarship to USC to play football and volleyball and in 1977 had been named Southern California prep athlete of the year. He had quick hands, could jump, and had a hammer for an arm. Powers was a tall and lanky outside hitter with a massive vertical leap and a devastatingly effective arm. When he was on, he could intimidate another team with his vertical reach and physical presence. Both players benefited from Dvorak's excellent judgment on where to set the ball and the precision and skill to place it there. As teammates at USC, the three young men collectively made each a better player. Dvorak made Hovland and Powers better hitters, and they, in turn, made Dvorak a better setter.

One other player on the 1977 junior national team stood out. His official name was Charles St. John Smith, but as a child, everyone called him St. John. The pronunciation of St. John, particularly in British and Commenwealth contries is "Sinjin," and over time that's how he came to be known, and eventually wrote his name the way it is often said. "Sinjin" Smith was a teenage phenom who had been playing two-man beach volleyball tournaments since he was fifteen. He played for UCLA in college and won the Manhattan Beach Open in 1979, two years after Marlowe's back-to-back victories.

Karch, the emerging prodigy who would one day dominate the sport and become widely recognized as the best player of the twentieth century, was in the perfect environment. Surrounded by an absurdly talented U.S. junior national team that included Salmons, Dvorak, Hovland, Powers, and Smith, he soaked it all in, growing exponentially as a player in a short period of time.

What all these great players had in common was the beach. "I had played ten years of beach volleyball before I even played indoor," said Dvorak. "I was part of that generation that had a beach foundation. I believe that is what made us successful; the ability of beach players to adjust and adapt and make a play."[21]

The U.S. junior national team went to Hawaii that summer and won the Pacific Rim Tournament, securing a spot in the first-ever World Junior Championships, hosted by Brazil. The team stayed at the Sheraton in Rio de Janeiro across from the famous Ipanema beach. This was the first exposure to the international game for Karch and his teammates—playing competitive indoor volleyball against teams from all over the world and then, when given free time, heading out to Ipanema to play beach volleyball with the locals. The young U.S. team didn't dominate the tournament, but they were competitive and had fun together as they gained experience and confidence playing the best junior teams in the world, including those from the Soviet Union, Brazil, Japan, and China. Together, they shared a collective sense of excitement about the future.

Karch came back from Brazil riding high from his experience on the junior national team. That fall, Olmstead, Karch's high school coach, could see a change in the young player. During Karch's senior year at Santa Barbara High School, volleyball became a nearly unstoppable force. He carried the team all the way to the sectional state championship for Southern California.

Despite his success on the beach and at Santa Barbara High School, few college programs recruited Karch. "Either they weren't interested in me or they somehow figured out I had interest in UCLA and backed off," said Karch. "I really only talked with Al Scates at UCLA and Ernie Hix at USC."[22]

Karch intended to pursue a medical degree, like his father, so he wanted to go to a school that offered both a good education and a strong volleyball program. "Both of those schools offered that," said Karch. UCLA was the more successful program at the time, and the winning tradition established by Scates was a draw, but there were other considerations as well.

Coming out of high school, Karch was both a setter and a hitter, and he intended to play setter in college. "USC had one of the all-time great setters at the time in Dusty Dvorak," said Karch. "And they were running a one-setter offense, and Ernie expressed interest in continuing to run the offense."[23]

Scates, on the other hand, ran a two-setter offense, where two setters are on the court at all times, each taking on the role of either setter or hitter depending on the rotation. One of the starting setters for UCLA, Dave Olbright, had just graduated and there was an open spot. "Al Scates didn't promise it to me, but certainly, he said, you have a chance to contend for the spot." And the other setter position was filled by Sinjin Smith. The thought of pairing up with Sinjin appealed to Karch. "If I could win that spot," Karch said, "I could set a two-setter offense and run it with one of the all-time great players in Sinjin.

"It just seemed like a better opportunity," said Karch, and he enrolled at UCLA. Scates wasted no time in getting his team on the court. "There were no limitations to training. The first day of school was the first day of practice. We practiced five days per week," said Karch.

Karch loved playing for Scates, who in volleyball circles is referred to as "the other Wizard of Westwood." While John Wooden, the more well-known head basketball coach at UCLA from 1948 to 1975, won ten national championships, Scates won nineteen in men's volleyball during his storied career. "Al is a charismatic, magnetic personality and a superb coach."[24]

The year before Karch's freshman season at UCLA, the Bruins had lost to Pepperdine in the championship game. Senior Sinjin Smith and junior Steve Salmons were determined to avenge that loss. Together with Karch, they brought the Bruins back to the 1979 NCAA National Championship game, where they faced USC.

The Trojans, led by veterans Dvorak, Powers, and Hovland, jumped out to an early lead, winning the first game. Then Dvorak, while going for a block, landed awkwardly on Sinjin's foot, breaking his ankle. For USC, it was like losing their quarterback. With Dvorak out of the lineup, that was the end for USC. The Bruins rolled to the national championship, capping off the first-ever undefeated season in NCAA men's volleyball history, finishing 31–0. Although Sinjin had a great year and Karch was improving rapidly, Salmons was named the NCAA Player of the Year.

In Karch's sophomore season, the Bruins once again faced their cross-town rivals for the NCAA championship. In addition to Dvorak, Powers, and Hovland, USC had added a young middle hitter and blocker with a lot of passion and intensity from Newport Beach, Steve Timmons. With his strawberry blond hair, everyone called him "Red," and he sparked the USC offense. This time Dvorak remained healthy, but Salmons was out with a back injury all season. Nevertheless, USC was unstoppable, winning the championship as Dvorak was named the Most Outstanding Player of the tournament.

After the game, the UCLA players found out where the Trojan victory party was being held, and they showed up to pay their respects and throw back a few beers. The UCLA–USC rivalry was intense, but it never drifted into bitterness, as so many of the players were teammates on the junior national team and had grown up playing against each other at beach tournaments.

Scates encouraged his players at UCLA to play beach volleyball during the summer. "Al loved it," Kiraly recalled, "because now they are playing all summer long. Guys were touching a ball, and playing two different versions of the game, and giving their bodies a break, in the summertime, on the softer sand."[25] In the summer of 1979, Karch teamed up with Sinjin to play beach tournaments. They made a formidable pair. "We won every tournament we played that year," said Karch, including the prestigious Manhattan Open, to officially be crowned "Kings of the Beach."

While Karch and his teammates on the junior national team were cavorting on the Southern California beaches, Doug Beal and the National Team were still stuck in Dayton, swatting away gnats in the summer and shivering through the winters. Yet Beal was well aware of the young crop of players from USC, UCLA, and Pepperdine during this period.

"The chance to coach someone like that doesn't happen very often," Beal later said of Karch. "He makes plays nobody else in the world could make, yet he's never happy with his performance."[26]

With the 1980 Olympics approaching, Beal, unsatisfied with the performance of his team in Dayton, began to dream of the National Team he could put together if he could somehow convince Karch, Dvorak, Powers, Smith, and Hovland to move to Dayton. But he knew that if he added so many skilled yet inexperienced players to his roster at the same time, the team would really need leadership on the court, a setter who played selflessly and was dedicated to the good of the team, to help everyone improve and work together.

There was no one currently on the team, especially at the setter position, to fill that role, yet each time Doug Beal looked in the mirror, he thought he knew who that could be.

It was time for Doug Beal to return to the court himself.

· 6 ·

San Diego

lthough most Americans were barely aware of the sport, in volleyball circles there was a growing controversy, talk that the "Dayton" team wasn't even the best team in the country, that they couldn't beat the best collegiate teams from California. Players on the West Coast weren't familiar with many of the players training with Beal in Dayton and barely even acknowledged the existence of the National Team. Marc Waldie, Rich Duwelius, and Aldis Berzins were relatively unknown in California and, as far as the West Coast players were concerned, were just names on a page. People wondered, *Just who are these guys, anyway?* Although Beal knew of the young talented players at USC and UCLA, and had a great deal of respect for their accomplishments, he was certain his National Team players, who had devoted years to training in Dayton, were far better as a team.

That, however, didn't dispel all the talk. It also didn't help with recruitment efforts for the National Team. In 1978, both to help prepare his team, and—perhaps—to dispel the rumors, Beal invited USC, a team that included Dvorak, Powers, and Hovland, to Dayton to play the National Team. The question of just how talented this new crop of players was and just how good the National Team that Beal had been developing in Dayton was would be answered, not in a debate swirling through the world of volleyball, but on the court.

"The players on [USC] thought they'd come in and romp us," said Beal. "We won every match.

"This was telling for me as well as the detractors," said Beal. "It showed readily what kind of effect a year-round training can have on even less talented players. Our program, for all its faults, was working."[1]

For the National Team, the victory over USC was a vindication that all their training in Dayton and the years of playing against the best players in the world were paying off. Yet even though they were defeated, the match provided Dvorak, Powers, and Hovland a chance to showcase their talents for Beal and simultaneously show them just how much the national program could help them improve as players. For Beal and the National Team, the game was a "win-win."

Sure, they had proven they could beat the best collegiate team, but that hadn't qualified them for the 1980 Olympics. They had already failed to qualify at the 1978 World Championships in Italy, but two more opportunities remained. They could qualify at the Zone Championships, hosted by the Dominican Republic, where they would face Cuba, Canada, and other countries from the NORCECA region. And if they failed at the Zones, there would be one final opportunity in Bulgaria, but they were hoping to punch their ticket early and avoid playing in Bulgaria altogether.

After the disappointing showing at the World Championships in 1978, Beal felt the team needed more veteran leadership on the court, especially at the setter position, before making their next attempt to qualify at the Zones. "Although we had capable older players on our team, no one assumed a leadership role," said Beal, "either from a lack of ability or a lack of acceptance."

As he looked up and down his roster, he didn't see where that leadership would come from. "I was looking for any player who could come into the starting lineup and make a positive change in the team," said Beal. Although he was past his prime as a player, Beal began to think he could do more good on the court than he could from the sideline. "I hadn't totally adjusted to coaching," said Beal, looking back at this pivotal decision. "My mentality was still directed at playing."[2]

He turned to McGown and Neville for advice, and they both told him the same thing: "Don't do it."[3]

Neville made it even more clear for Beal: "You either play or you coach, you don't do both."[4]

Beal knew this, but he was frustrated by the criticism the program was facing, especially after the nineteenth-place finish at the World Championships, and he was motivated to help the team in any way he could. The goal of qualifying for the Olympics was so close, and so alluring, he was willing to try just about anything. He made the decision to lace up his shoes again and join the team as a player-coach. "I believed that the most important change I could make to turn the team into a winning Olympic prospect was to resign and return to playing."[5]

Beal saw it as a temporary move. He didn't want to officially resign as coach, which would have triggered a search to find his replacement. "We certainly couldn't advertise the position or go through a long, protracted search for the new coach," Beal said. There wasn't time for that. Beal informed the USVBA about his plans, and although they initially resisted, they reluctantly agreed. Now Beal had to find an interim coach, and there was only one man he wanted.

Beal reached out to his old friend and mentor, Jim Coleman, the coach of the 1968 Olympic team. Beal came from the Coleman coaching tree, and Coleman had been a technical advisor to Beal since he took over in Dayton. "If a new coach came in and changed the whole program, my desire for maintaining continuity would have been dissipated," explained Beal. "I felt that Coleman was the only person who knew our program and could take over the team."[6]

It was a package deal; if Coleman agreed to step in, Beal would return to the court. Coleman, who was living in Chicago at the time, agreed and temporarily moved to Dayton. Coaching duties transitioned from Beal to Coleman, and Beal made a smooth transfer from coach to player.

"Unfortunately, nothing else worked out quite as well as the transfer," said Beal.

In preparation for the Zone Championships, the team traveled to Miami for final training, so the players could acclimate to the tropical weather and be closer to the Dominican Republic. Optimism was running high.

Looking back on it, Beal credits the optimism to "more the eternal optimism of the American athlete than any realism, given our team and the ability of the Cubans."[7]

The Americans were promptly blown out by Cuba. "We were completely disorganized, and not only did we lose to the Cubans but we lost to a team from the Dominican Republic."[8]

A sportswriter covering the team, who had been highly critical of the program even before the Zones, got on the bus with the team after the game and berated the players over the loss, expressing disbelief that the United States could lose to a team [the Dominican Republic] that had been together only about a month. It wasn't true—their opponents had been together longer than that—but it was demeaning and humiliating nonetheless.

"Nobody said anything back to him," said Beal. "We were too hurt ourselves."

It was a low point for Beal and the program. "We were probably a worse team in the Zone Championships in 1979 than we had been at the World Championships in 1978," said Beal.

These were tough words for someone who switched from coach to player with the expressed goal of making the team better.

Beal, Coleman, and the team from Dayton were getting desperate.

They were down to one last chance to qualify, at the tournament in Sofia, Bulgaria, in January 1980. Beal and Coleman recognized that Waldie and Sunderland, the two best players on the team, needed more talented players around them if they wanted to win. And they knew where to find those players. They just weren't sure how to convince them to move to Dayton. They came up with a new approach. Rather than wait until players graduated from college, they approached players who were still playing in college and invited them to train with the National Team in Dayton for a semester. Beal reached out to Dvorak, Powers, Hovland, Salmons, and Karch, as well as recent grad Sinjin, to "beef up the team," as Beal called it.

The plan was for these players to play in the Pan American Games that summer and then temporarily enroll at Wright State, a college in Dayton, and live in the dorms for the fall semester to train for the qualifier in Bulgaria. Karch was the only player to decline, although not because he was dismissive of the National Team. The problem was Dayton. He planned to enroll in medical school after graduation and needed to take specific classes at UCLA to complete his prerequisites. The others, however, agreed to move to Dayton in a last-ditch attempt to qualify for the Olympics.

At the Pan American Games in Puerto Rico that summer, Steve Salmons, the NCAA Player of the Year, and the leader and teammate of Karch's on the UCLA team that went 31–0, injured his back. The organizers were trying to make the game move quicker for TV.

"They weren't allowing the floors to be wiped," recalls Salmons. "It was 100 degrees, humid, and there were puddles forming on the floor. I came down wrong, slipped, and hurt my back. By the end of the tournament, I couldn't feel my legs." The United States finished a disappointing fifth out of eight teams, behind Cuba, Brazil, Canada, and Mexico. After the tournament, Salmons traveled back to California to get treatment on his back, while the rest of the team traveled to Dayton to continue training for the Olympic qualifier in Bulgaria.

When the group of college players from California first arrived in Dayton in the fall of 1979, a cultural rift between the two player factions was obvious. The California players stuck together, had strong opinions about training and tactics, and weren't shy about expressing themselves. "The guys who had been with the program in Dayton desperately wanted to win," said Beal. "They knew the new players had outstanding talents and would help, but on the other hand, they had a tough time accepting them since none of them had invested in our program."[9]

Beal had been working with his Dayton players for three years and had developed his own philosophy and approach. The young collegiate players from California added an uncomfortable new dynamic to the squad, and Beal and Coleman struggled to maintain a cohesive team culture.

The U.S. Men's National Team that competed at the 1979 Pan American Games in San Juan, Puerto Rico. Standing, left to right: Gary Moy (team manager), Jim Coleman (head coach), Dave Olbright, Sinjin Smith, Mike McLean, Rich Duwelius, Aldis Berzins, Doug Beal, Kerry Klostermann (assistant coach). Seated, left to right: Tim Hovland, Steve Salmons, Paul Sunderland, Marc Waldie, Joe Battalia, Pat Powers. SOURCE: DOUG BEAL ARCHIVES

"The new guys from California began making derogatory statements about the effectiveness of the Dayton program, some of the players and even some of the coaches," said Beal. He expected the younger, less experienced players to listen and learn from the veteran players and coaches who had been developing a system in Dayton. Hovland, Dvorak, Sinjin, and Powers didn't extend the same deference to coaches that Beal and his generation showed to their coaches as they came up as players. "As a group," Beal recalled, "they seemed to have enormous egos, were lazy, and generally resisted coaching."[10]

The rift between the Dayton players and the California players was quickly becoming a chasm.

Another source of frustration for Beal was his aging body. He was thirty-two years old and hadn't played at the international level in four years. Physically, his body couldn't take the stress, and he spent more and more time out of the starting lineup, nursing injuries. When he did get on the court, the

California players weren't impressed. "Beal was more of a player-coach," recalls Hovland. "And when he was playing, it wasn't pretty."[11]

The logic behind creating the national training center in Dayton was to develop a group of players under a single system and coaching philosophy for three years. Consistency and stability were crucial if the program was to succeed, yet now, just months before a major Olympic qualifying tournament, by adding new players and returning to the court in an attempt to qualify for the Olympics, Beal risked it all for one more shot at the Olympics. It was a Hail Mary, and it almost worked.

Things started off well in Bulgaria in January 1980, as the team made it all the way to the final four, but that's where their Olympic dream ended. In their final two matches, when the team began to struggle, they simply didn't have the resilience and confidence to stay composed and turn things around, falling to Bulgaria and South Korea and failing to qualify. Although the team demonstrated a new level of athleticism and skill in the tournament, providing a hint of the kind of team they could one day be, they simply didn't have enough time to play together and gel as a team.

The split coaching structure had also proven awkward. Coleman had a terrific volleyball mind but wasn't always the strongest coach. "Jim wasn't always on top of things during the game," said Waldie, "but he always had a smile,"[12] something the players rarely saw from Beal.

While Coleman was ostensibly the head coach, a lot of players still looked to Beal for guidance, and that led to confusion. "Beal was coaching but Coleman was also coaching," said Hovland.[13] Salmons recalls Beal was more of an "assistant player coach."[14]

For some of the Dayton players, despite Coleman's shortcomings, having him as head coach had been a welcome change. Coleman's style wasn't as strict and authoritarian as Beal's. "Jim provided a fresh outlook," said Waldie. It was "a weight lifted off our shoulders," and for the first time in a long time, he enjoyed playing volleyball. "We got competitive again," he said.[15] And if Beal made a mistake on or off the court, it was magnified. For one match, Beal was finally healthy, but the players were surprised when he sat on the sidelines the entire game, until they discovered he had forgotten his athletic shoes. If one of the players had forgotten their shoes when Beal was head coach, they never would have heard the end of it.

Becoming a player-coach hadn't provided the solution Beal had hoped it would. "I simply wasn't as good a player as I thought, and didn't make nearly the impact on the team that I hoped for," said Beal, later referring to his decision to return to the court as "one of the stupidest decisions in my life."[16]

For the players who had spent the last three years in Dayton, the failure to qualify for the Olympics was heartbreaking. They and their families had sacrificed almost everything to train and prepare for the Olympics, only to have those dreams crushed. Ultimately, after the Soviet invasion of Afghanistan, the United States boycotted the Games, and "some of the sting was taken out," said Beal.[17] The boycott was even tougher for the U.S. women's team because they had qualified and had a shot at a medal.

Yet there was a silver lining for Beal and the national program. "I realized then we had the makings of a special team," said Beal. "I was more determined than ever to mold a championship team." But this time there would be no doubt about his role. "I decided, what I really wanted to do was coach the team again, and I realized any real chance of success would have to come from a venue outside of Dayton."[18]

After the team failed to qualify, Sinjin and the college players moved back to California and the USVBA took a step back to assess the state of the National Team. Although it was obvious the team and the program had improved in Dayton, it still fell short of its goal, and part of the reason was Dayton itself.

"It simply was the wrong place to train a volleyball team in the United States. It is essentially a Southern California sport," said Beal at the time.

The problem was obvious: the best players in the country were from California, and they were reluctant to move to Dayton, and if they did move, very few stayed. "We had players leave us who simply could not handle the cold and snow," said Beal. "These were guys who went surfing in their spare time, not cross-country skiing." USA Volleyball got the message and made the decision to look for a new home.

If the players wouldn't come to the national training center, the center would come to them.

USA Volleyball identified several locations in Southern California, and San Diego stood out from the other candidate cities because of its ideal climate, strong economy, and the enthusiasm of the business community to embrace the team. In late 1980 the national training center for men's volleyball relocated to San Diego.

The USVBA also took a hard look at Doug Beal. Was he the right man to lead the program for another four years? Under Beal's leadership in Dayton, the program showed improvement, but his ill-fated attempt to step down to become a player, and the team's failure to qualify for the 1980 Olympics, raised doubts.

Beal wanted the head coaching job, but he also wanted the top candidates in the country to apply to give the program the best opportunity for success. With Los Angeles hosting the Olympics in 1984, the United States would receive an automatic bid. The coach for the next quadrennial would be leading U.S. men's volleyball to its first Olympics since 1968, and the Americans would be the home team. This was a once-in-a-generation opportunity to grow the sport in the United States.

Beal contacted his good friend Bill Neville, who after finishing his term as the coach for the Canadian National Team, was coaching women's volleyball at Montana State. Beal encouraged Nevillle to join him in applying for the U.S. National Team head-coaching position.

The two of them flew into Colorado Springs for a full day of interviews. In their hotel the night before their interviews, they sat up late talking about their shared approach to coaching and discussed how much fun it could be to coach together. The two men came to a decision: whoever was selected as head coach would hire the other as an assistant. Their friendship and trust had only grown stronger over the years, and they felt confident that, no matter who was named head coach, they would be much more effective as a coaching duo than either would solo.

USA Volleyball decided to stick with Beal, and he immediately hired Neville as his assistant coach. "Hiring Bill Neville was the single best decision I made in the years leading up to the [1984] Olympics," said Beal. "He has so much integrity." Beal called Neville "the conscience of our program," adding, "He has saved me from making bad decisions so many times."[19]

Neville had one of the most creative volleyball minds in the country, but his greatest strength as a coach was his ability to build strong relationships with his players. Beal maintained an emotional distance from his players. He knew he would eventually have to make the final decision about who was on the team and who wasn't and didn't want emotion to taint that decision. In Dayton, Beal didn't have someone like Neville on his staff, someone the players could relate to, and the lack of a close relationship with his players eventually became a problem for Beal. He needed someone to fill that role, and Neville was the perfect man for the job.

"Neville softened Bill's frayed edges," said Waldie. "He came to embody the spirit of the team."[20] While Beal was an intellectual student of the game, Neville was a player's coach. Neville designed most of the drills and then he would push the players hard, but always with positive encouragement. "Let's go boys, let's do it again. Harder this time!"[21] Neville would cheer them on, always in the spirit of motivation and inspiration.

"We enjoyed working hard for Nev," said Waldie. "Nev was a real motivator. He was fun to have around. He was a character, and he had all these weird sayings."[22] One of his favorite sayings was "spiral vortex," as in, "Boys, we have to avoid the spiral vortex," what Neville called the terrifying phenomena when poor play and mistakes cascade into further poor play and more mistakes until a team completely goes down the drain.

The second assistant coach Beal hired was Tony Crabb, although he didn't join the staff until later. A former National Team player from Hawaii, where he played at the Outrigger Club, the birthplace of beach volleyball, Crabb moved with his wife and two young sons from Hawaii to San Diego to join Beal's staff. His experience as a former National Team member gave him credibility with the players, and he was particularly skilled at scouting and statistics. When Beal sent him to scout a future opponent, he was confident that his team would be "a step ahead." Crabb also pushed the team to embrace the use of videotape to analyze players and gain insights. Beal describes Crabb as being "responsible for many of the technical improvements of our team." Crabb was also a counterbalance to Beal and Neville, who shared a common coaching philosophy they learned from Coleman and McGown. He wasn't afraid to "challenge the traditional ways of playing," said Beal. "He makes us constantly reevaluate our training."[23]

The three coaches had a great deal of respect for each other. There wasn't, at that time, a long history in the sport of coaches working together. As a profession, coaching volleyball was just emerging. One of Beal's strengths was putting a staff together, assigning roles, and giving them the responsibility and the authority to excel at what they're good at. All three coaches got along great, as did their families.

With the staff in place, the coaches turned their attention to the roster. A core group of veterans who played for Beal in Dayton followed the team to San Diego, including the three former Ohio State players, Duwelius, Waldie, and Berzins. So did Sunderland, who had moved back to Malibu after the team lost in Bulgaria. When he discovered the National Team training center had moved to San Diego, he quit his job selling insurance, moved with his wife to San Diego, and rejoined the team to take one more shot at an Olympics. The plan was to supplement the Dayton veterans with the talented young players coming out of USC, UCLA, Pepperdine, and other top programs.

To that end, Beal and Neville attended the 1981 Open National Championships for club teams in Arlington, Texas, sponsored by the USVBA. The Open, eligible to any talented group of players from any community across America, included many of the best players in the country, including college players, former college players, beach players, and lifelong volleyball "gym rats."

Most of the stars from USC, UCLA, and Pepperdine played with their club teams at the Open Championships that year, providing a great opportunity for Beal and Neville to assess talent, meet with players individually, and invite the most promising candidates to try out for the National Team. In fact, there was so much talent on display that Beal and Neville had a hard time keeping the number of players selected for tryouts to a reasonable number. This was a situation they had never faced in Dayton. The move to San Diego was already paying off.

Among the players with California collegiate backgrounds joining the team that summer were Craig Buck and Mike Blanchard, two former Pepperdine players. Buck at 6'8" was one of the first dominant "big men" of the sport and perhaps the most feared net attacker in the game. Blanchard, a hard-hitting former All-American, led Pepperdine to the national championship in 1978. Blanchard played at Pepperdine with setter Rod Wilde and Buck, and he had been voted the most outstanding player when Pepperdine defeated UCLA for their first national championship under their legendary coach Marv Dunphy. Four former USC players, Dvorak, Powers, Hovland, and Timmons, also joined the National Team that summer, as did the two former UCLA stars, Sinjin and Karch. Unfortunately, UCLA teammate Steve Salmons was still out with his back injury, and his future on the National Team was uncertain.

In San Diego the team practiced at the gym in the Federal Building at Balboa Park, a 1,200-acre historic urban cultural park that is also home to the San Diego Zoo. Although the Federal Building was better than the team's facilities in Dayton, it was still substandard in many ways, lacking both heat and air-conditioning. They also shared the gym with badminton teams, and the gym featured green walls so badminton players could see the shuttlecock. The team improved the lighting and added a training room, but the building was in such bad shape the players hardly ever showered there and usually arrived already dressed for practice.

The specter of the 1984 Los Angeles Olympics loomed large for everyone. The opportunity not just to play in an Olympics but to be able to do so in front of family and friends was a huge motivator. Competition was intense, with as many as twenty-four players practicing with the team, all trying to earn one of the coveted twelve spots on the final Olympic roster.

By the summer of 1981, the new San Diego–based National Team, ever so slowly, began to take shape. Team veterans and newcomers got to know one another as players while Beal, Neville, and Crabb worked hard to bring these two groups together to play as a cohesive unit.

One thing the coaching staff knew the team needed was time on the court playing together, so they upped the number of games scheduled. "We set a minimum of 50 international matches a year for our players," said Beal, "so they would be ready to compete in major tournaments. We needed to put several thousand hours a year into the gym, not a couple hundred hours."[24]

Beal aimed to improve every facet of the program. "We needed a year-round weight and physical training program, and a sports medicine program to evaluate what kind of performance the players can maintain," he said.

"The operation we were most concerned about, though, was our jobs program," said Beal. The staff put considerable effort into the Olympic Jobs Program, which was critical to supporting the players. "We asked [employers] for half-day work, a significant amount of time off for our competitions, and livable salaries."[25] It took persistence, but eventually every player who needed a job got one, mostly at banks and savings and loan associations.

"The San Diego situation was light years ahead of Dayton," said Sunderland.[26]

The players who moved with the program from Dayton were familiar with Beal's style and rules, but to some of the more free-spirited California players, Beal's discipline and structure came as a shock.

One rule in particular caused a lot of problems and generated blowback from the California players.

No beach volleyball.

· 7 ·

Beat Cuba!

"*We* are ranked nineteenth in the world," Beal told his players in 1981, referring to their disappointing finish at the last World Championships. "We have so much work to do to get better at indoor volleyball, spending time playing beach volleyball is not going get us to where we wanted to go."[1]

"We didn't take very well to that," recalls Karch. "We resisted it." Karch, Sinjin, and Hovland, in particular, were experiencing success at weekend tournaments on the beach, and they were having a lot of fun too.

Beal scheduled practice from 8 a.m. to noon, Monday through Friday, and gave the players the weekends off. Since the weekends were their time, the players felt they should have the freedom to play in tournaments.

"We felt he was caging us in," said Karch.[2]

"I was livid," said Dvorak. "I felt like we worked hard for five days, and if we wanted to play on the beach in the weekend, we could do it."[3]

To the players, summer beach tournaments were a chance to show off their skills and compete—they looked forward to them all year—but to Beal it was an unnecessary distraction that ran counter to the team's goal of being competitive at indoor volleyball at the 1984 Olympics. Beal's policy was the exact opposite to that of some collegiate coaches, like UCLA's Al Scates, who encouraged his athletes to play on the beach.

Beal walked the team through his reasoning. "I am demanding a complete commitment to this program," Beal told his team. "You can't be with the program part-time and go play a summer of beach volleyball and expect to come back."[4] Summer was devoted to international tournaments, and the demanding travel schedule didn't leave much time for beach volleyball anyway, but Beal's reasoning went deeper than that. After a full week of practice, Beal wanted his team to spend free weekends resting.

Competing in a beach tournament usually began with a long drive of sometimes four or five hours up the coast on Friday evening, then daylong matches Saturday and Sunday, fully exposed to the heat and sun, followed by a long drive back. Then there was the partying culture surrounding the tournaments. "The beach volleyball environment lends itself to all kinds of excesses that seem to go hand in hand with sports, like liquor and drugs," said Beal.[5]

"Doug saw a party environment," recalls Dvorak. "But I didn't do drugs and alcohol, I loved volleyball and I viewed it as a great game to play. Indoor I was pigeonholed as a setter. I didn't get to hit or pass or serve much. I was 'handcuffed' by indoor. In two-man [beach volleyball], I get to receive and hit."[6] Although Dvorak didn't drink, most of the players did, at least to some degree, and often the excesses of the beach culture were evident to Beal.

"Monday morning, they would show up exhausted," said Beal. "They weren't ready to practice at the level I needed them to be."[7]

There was one more reason Beal didn't want his athletes competing in beach tournaments in those days. "On the beach, there were no coaches," he said. "The players coached themselves."[8] Beach players got used to being in control of everything on the court, how they blocked and how they positioned themselves. Everything was up to them, and they didn't have to take direction from coaches, and that made the transition Monday morning, back to the indoor game where they were learning to work in a system, that much tougher.

Karch was disappointed with Beal's decision, but he respected it. He had set a goal at fifteen years old to do everything he could to help the National Team become competitive at an Olympics, even if that meant sacrificing beach volleyball for a few years. "Not everything the coaches ask will be liked by everybody," Karch said at the time. "I want to play on this team, so I do what I have to do."[9]

Hovland and Sinjin weren't as willing to give up the beach and make the same commitment to the team as Karch. They also took Beal's edict against beach volleyball personally, a shot aimed directly at them. Hovland remembers Beal saying, "I don't like beach volleyball and I don't like beach volleyball players."[10]

It didn't help that in an interview Beal denigrated what he called the "California attitude," saying bluntly at the time that many of those who played in California, and particularly on the beach, were "prima donnas." That hit a nerve with the California players and, to many in volleyball circles, confirmed the perception that Beal was biased against them.

He tried to walk it back and said, "What I meant was that the psychology of the beach creates prima donnas," but it was too late.[11] The damage was done.

Given the pushback from players, Beal tried to find a balance, allowing the players to participate in beach tournaments at certain times, but even that grew problematic and created tension.

"I allowed some participation in our first year, then cut off beach volley-ball altogether," said Beal. "After repeated abuse of my rules on the subject, the beach game was verboten."[12]

There was another distraction luring players away from the year-round dedicated training program in San Diego: professional volleyball in Italy. Since Kilgour paved the way by playing in Italy for money, the contracts and oppor-tunities had only expanded.

Even when the team was in Dayton, players like Sunderland were getting offers. After playing exceptionally well at the 1978 World Championships in Italy, Sunderland received a $100,000 offer from a team in Rome. "For a twenty-five-year-old kid making nothing in Dayton, Ohio, this was big money," said Sunderland.

He met with Beal and told him, "I'm frustrated. The team isn't doing well. I'm married. How about you give me this winter to play in Europe?"[13]

"You can go, but you can never come back," said Beal. The response was harsh, and it was in part because he wanted to keep the team together in a "year-round" training regimen, but it also reflected the risk that Sunderland would no longer be considered an "amateur" and therefore would be ineligible for the Olympics. There was a process by which former professional players could have their amateur status returned, but the rules were opaque and there were no guarantees. Sunderland elected to stay.

When National Team members in San Diego began to receive offers to play in Europe, Beal extended his rule to exclude playing overseas as well.

"You can't go to play in Italy or some of the other professional leagues and expect to come back," said Beal. "You are either with us or you're not."[14]

Beal's hard line would eventually force Hovland and Sinjin to make a choice, but at least for the summer of 1981 they were committed to the team.

Beal's personality didn't help, and his desire to keep his emotional distance too often came across as cold and unfriendly. One player told a local newspaper anonymously that Beal was "the most negative person I've ever met in my life."[15] Yet that same player was quick to admit that Beal's methods were effec-tive, saying, "He's doing a lot of good things for us, but if he had a different personality . . ."

In the same article, Beal admitted, "I'm not too easygoing. I believe that practice is important. Every time you walk into the gym you should try to do your best. I also believe that hard work pays dividends. The team that is best prepared and works the hardest will come out on top."[16]

Complaints were not uncommon. "You never smile," the players would say to Beal.[17]

"Smiling never won an athletic event," he would counter.

"Let up, Beal, we've practiced enough," the players would plead.

"We'll run it until we get it right," responded Beal. "Don't tell me you're going to get it right during the game, show me you can do it now, right here in practice."

"Beal, you never want to have fun."

"I'm not here to be your friend," Beal said. It was more important for Beal that the players develop friendships among themselves, care for each other, and play hard for their teammates. And given the divisions and factions on the squad, that wasn't happening and had become more of a concern for Beal and Neville.[18]

At times the press, others in the volleyball community, and even players' parents questioned Beal's methods and his manner. Some parents even launched a campaign to have Beal removed and replaced by Al Scates, but ultimately Beal and the USVBA remained steadfast. But until the team showed progress in international competition, his critics would remain vocal. Sooner rather than later, the team would have to show improvement on the court against quality competition.

The team soon settled into a daily routine as Beal worked the players harder than they often wanted to be worked. On most days, the four-hour morning practice was followed by jump or physical training, conditioning, and weight training before going to their jobs, the opposite of the situation in Dayton, where the team had practiced in the evening and players often showed up worn out from a long day of manual labor.

In August 1981 the U.S. team played an exhibition match against the Japanese, a return match after a recent tour of Japan where they had been swept, losing all five matches. The United States hadn't beaten Japan in any match since 1968.

The game took place at Peterson Gymnasium on the San Diego State campus, the same gym Chris Marlowe and the Aztecs packed during their national championship run in 1973. Beal was hoping to rekindle some of that same energy, and he wasn't disappointed as the stadium was sold out. There was a lot of anticipation before the match, and the crowds showed up to cheer on the home team, but the gym fell quiet as the team promptly lost the first two games. It looked like the team was on its way toward another disappointing loss.

Yet, in the third game, the Americans endured a long, hard-fought battle and eked out a 15–13 win. In the fourth game, something happened. A collective transformation overtook the team on the court and the offense started to flow. The Americans got into a rhythm, and for the first time anyone could remember, the Japanese were on their heels. Waldie and Buck began dominating the net, blocking spike angles and frustrating the Japanese hitters. If a Japanese ball did make it across the net, often a vicious, curving shot that appeared unreturnable, Karch and Berzins, working in tandem, routinely dug it out.

On the National Team in Dayton, Berzins hadn't even been a starter. Playing on the second team meant he'd been bombarded with serves again and again, and over time he became more agile and learned to react more quickly, able to meet the serve and "pass" it to the setter. Now, after years of practice and repetition handling the best serves on the National Team, Berzins was rapidly becoming one of the best passers on the team. Beal took notice. Paired with Karch, the duo was giving the Japanese fits.

The crowd could feel it. They started chanting "USA, USA" and stomping their feet on the wooden benches. Suddenly, the Japanese were talking between points and flashing concerned looks at one another. The Americans won the fourth game 15–9 and the fifth game 15–7 to take the match. For Sunderland, the longest-serving member on the team, it was a milestone. He had played twenty-five matches against the Japanese going back to 1975, and this was the first time he had been on the winning side.[19]

It felt like the start of something, yet Beal couldn't help but wonder if it was just an aberration.

He didn't have to wait long to find out. In November the team competed in the Canada Cup, a regional tournament that included the two best teams in the Western Hemisphere, Brazil and the Americans' nemesis, Cuba. Karch and Timmons returned to college that fall and weren't available, but Hovland and Smith stepped up as leaders on the court.

The United States faced Cuba early in the tournament. In the past, Cuba, a physically imposing team with big players who jumped well and were strong at the net, had always dominated, playing with swagger and confidence when they went up against the United States. Under Castro, the United States was held up as the great evil of the earth, making these games even more significant to the Cuban team.

The Americans still lost 3–2, but this defeat felt different. The games were close and the volleys extended. The Cubans had to play their best to win, and they needed all five games to put the Americans away.

Never before had an American team pushed Cuba to raise their game in order to win. By the end of the match, Cuba no longer felt invincible, and the Americans were no longer intimidated. It was obvious to Beal and the players that the transformation that had started with the victory over Japan in August was no mirage. This new team, with young players who grew up playing the game on the beach, was playing volleyball at a level beyond any team before them. They didn't beat the Cubans that day, but now they knew they could.

Next up, the Americans faced Brazil. Armed with newfound confidence and maybe a little swagger themselves, they promptly won the match in three straight games, gaining confidence with each game.

In the tournament final, the United States again faced Cuba. After their pregame warm-ups, Beal called his players over to the bench and asked them to huddle up. As Beal and Neville gave the team their last-minute instructions, they noticed someone was missing. Beal looked around and said, "Where's PP?"[20]

He was referring to former USC star Pat Powers, a member of the starting lineup and the team's "opposite" hitter. With only a few minutes before the most important game of the year, a key member of the team was nowhere to be found.

Neville scanned the gym and at the far end of the court spotted a very tall young man, in full warm-up and uniform, waiting in line at the concession stand.

Neville told Beal, "I don't think he'll be available; you better make a substitution. I'll go take care of this."[21]

Neville strolled to the concession stand and cut in line right behind Powers. Holding his anger in check, he tapped Powers on the shoulder and initiated a friendly conversation.

"What are you going to get here?" Neville calmly inquired of Powers.

"Oh, I'm going to get a Coke and a hotdog," Powers responded.

"I think you could also get a big tub of popcorn too."

"Oh no," said the player. "I don't want to be that full when I'm playing."

"You know, Pat, I don't think you have to worry about that."

"Why do you say that?"

Neville gestured to the team. "See over there. That's *your team*. And they're huddling right now, right before they go on the court for the Canada Cup Final. Now, you *were* in the starting lineup." Neville's voice became a little sharper. "And you *would* be going out on the court with them, but you're *here*," Neville said. "So I think you can get a big thing of popcorn too, if you want."

"Oh shit," Powers replied, shaking his head with disappointment. Neville turned and walked away. Pat Powers stayed in line. He was hungry.[22]

The other players on the National Team were extremely disappointed in Powers. Even as the team was still divided, a new sense of purpose was taking hold. And part of the reason was Karch. Even though Karch, still in school, wasn't at this tournament, his presence on the team had already shifted the mentality and focus of many of the players. His level of play and will to win set a new standard for everyone. They now expected more from themselves and, just as significantly, more from each other.

"Karch set the bar," said Dave Saunders, his teammate from UCLA who joined the National Team in 1982. "Even though most of us figured we couldn't get to the bar he set, we all tried to get there. Some people folded. They couldn't handle it, but others rose to the occasion."[23]

"I was sitting on the bench, trying to break in as a starter on the National Team for years," said Aldis Berzins, the former Ohio State star. "Then this UCLA beach god [Karch] walks onto the court and he's still in college and he's a starter."[24] It was tough for some of the veterans to take a back seat to such a young player, but begrudgingly, they realized why.

"Karch made us different," said Berzins. "He made everyone around him better. At the level we play, everyone can jump, everyone can hit, but what made Karch special was his mental game, his grit. He didn't sandbag, ever. Not in practice and not in a game. He would always compete and try to win, at anything he did."[25]

On one side, the team had Karch, who treated every drill in practice like it was the gold medal match, and on the other extreme there was Powers, who was older than Karch and had all the talent in the world but lacked the focus and maturity. A mental gaffe like what Powers pulled could no longer be tolerated. The coaches would soon deal with Powers, but first they had to face Cuba without one of their starters.

Despite not having Powers in the starting lineup, the United States got off to a good start. After three games, the Americans led 2–1. Now Cuba knew the Americans could win too.

Then Beal threw a changeup. Instead of sticking with the lineup he had used in the first three games, for the fourth game Beal went with a smaller lineup, inserting Berzins and Smith.

"The small lineup seemed to be a workable alternative to the usual big-guys-only look," said Beal. "Part of developing a team is figuring out who can play, where, and which combinations work best."[26]

Although Berzins and Smith were a little shorter, they were quicker and more agile, giving the Americans a shot of energy at the precise time the Cubans were beginning to become fatigued.

One play in particular demonstrated the team's progress and development. Cuba had traditionally overwhelmed the United States with its jumping ability and ball speed. Over the course of a match, they had always ground down the Americans, causing them to lose hope even before losing the contest. In the fourth game, the Cubans had a wide-open kill and delivered a devastating spike that appeared, to everyone in the arena, to be unreturnable. The Cubans celebrated the point before the ball even hit the ground, but somehow Waldie got his hands under it.

But he didn't just dig the ball out, he managed to direct a perfect pass to Dvorak. The stunned Cubans realized their mistake and scrambled to organize for a block, but it was too late. Dvorak made a perfect set to Hovland, who soared high above the net and brought down the hammer, rocketing the ball to an empty space on the Cuban side.

Only a few months before, the Americans wouldn't have made such a play, defeated even before the ball crossed to their side. Not anymore; this time the players hadn't given up on the play. They showed resilience, and Beal began to realize that how the players worked together on the court was more important than always having the biggest and strongest players.

The team was building confidence and trust in the coaching staff, starting to believe in the system that they had put in place, and it showed on the court.

The goal set by the team back in 1974, when McGown was coach and Beal was a player and they all called out "Beat Cuba!," had finally been achieved. After years of being dominated by their regional rival, the Americans ended up on top. The victory was the first international tournament title for U.S. men's volleyball in the history of the sport. Suddenly, just beating Cuba seemed too modest a goal.

Hovland, the most gifted athlete on the team and the best player in the country, was named the tournament MVP.

Although no one, not even Hovland, knew it, or even suspected it at the time, it was the last match Hovland would ever play for the National Team.

• 8 •

Eastie vs. Westie

$\mathcal{T}$he only setback during the Canada Cup was the loss of Powers to a hot dog and a Coke. Clearly, his head wasn't in the game. Beal and Neville soon suspended him but told Powers, "We want to look at you again in a year."

"We saw something that made us think, with training and maturity he would add significantly to his skills," said Beal.

Powers thought they were nuts. He knew how good he was and how good he could be. To his credit, he didn't leave San Diego but remained in the area and continued to train and work out. Beal and Neville appreciated that. "He listens. He tries. He works at making changes to improve his skills," said Beal.[1]

Powers's hole in the roster was quickly filled by Steve Salmons, now fully recovered from his back injury. He returned to volleyball in 1981, reuniting with Karch at UCLA to win another national championship. Beal also added another player from UCLA, Dave Saunders, who, like Marlowe and Salmons, hailed from Pacific Palisades and had been a star at Palisades High School.

As the calendar turned to 1982, Beal had big plans for the team. He scheduled sixty matches against international competition, the most ever. The first set of matches was scheduled for early March against Canada, yet as the team gathered to prepare, Hovland and Sinjin were absent.

With Beal's permission, Sinjin was in New York for a two-week modeling gig. When he needed an additional two weeks, Beal grudgingly agreed, but he insisted that Sinjin return immediately afterward to prepare for Canada. When Sinjin went silent and did not return, the coaching staff assumed he had moved on. Then, during the domestic tour against Canada, Beal got a phone call from Sinjin asking how things were going.

"Great," said Beal, "now that you're no longer on the team."[2]

Sinjin was stunned. The money and opportunities in beach volleyball were becoming lucrative and had led to the chance to work as a model. He wanted to pursue both careers and still play with the National Team, but Beal was adamant. "You're either with us or you're not."[3]

Sinjin was dismissed from the team, which freed him up to pursue a professional career in beach volleyball, where he became one of the first big stars of the tour and went on to have a hall-of-fame career.

Hovland proved to be a greater challenge.

"They were both exceptional players, though Hovland was especially good," said Beal. "On the court he usually delivered on his promises, and he wasn't much trouble at practice or during games. Unreliability was his problem. He was often late or absent. And he commonly showed up for practice in less than perfect condition."[4]

Yet Hovland was so talented, and so valuable to the team, that Beal felt pressure to find a way to make it work. The coach caved, with disastrous results. There seemed to be one set of rules for Hovland and another for everyone else, causing tension among the players.

"I made special concessions that were controversial to say the least," said Beal. "None of it worked."

Neville, the "conscience of the team," urged Beal to cut Hovland loose. "You're either with us or you're not,"[5] said Neville, turning Beal's words around on him.

Hovland took the summer off to play beach tournaments, and as fall approached, he told Beal he had accepted an offer to play professionally in Italy. To Hovland's thinking, playing professionally in Europe against the best players in the world would improve his game and benefit the U.S. team. "You get better by testing yourself, by playing against guys that are as good or better than you," he said.[6]

Beal didn't see it that way. He was beginning to see the problems it caused with team harmony and felt Hovland was putting his own self-interest above the team. Beal wanted him back, but only if Hovland abided by team rules and trained with his teammates instead of playing in Europe. Hovland wanted back on the National Team, but on his own terms, with permission to play in Italy *and* in beach tournaments.

Could the United States compete against the best teams in the world without one of their best players? The press, the volleyball community, and even some of the players thought it was crazy to let Hovland go.

"No one had confidence in our ability to perform without him," said Beal.[7]

But Hovland refused to back down, and eventually the team moved on without him. "Hovland was not cut," Beal said at the time. "I prefer to say he quit the team."

With Hovland off the team, that opened the door for more playing time for Salmons.

"Hovland may have been quicker and better offensively," said Beal. "But Salmons worked harder and contributed more to the total team effort on and off the court."[8] The coaching staff began to realize the impact of having team players like Salmons in the gym every day.

"He helped raise practice intensity and the quality of competition between the first and second teams improved," said Beal. "Salmons hates to lose and it doesn't matter if he's a first stringer or a sub, he competes equally hard in both situations."[9]

In the spring of 1982, the success of the National Team based in San Diego finally started to make waves within the tight-knit volleyball community in Los Angeles. Chris Marlowe took notice. After Marlowe had turned down Beal's invitation to move to Dayton in 1977, he had set aside his dream of playing volleyball at the Olympics, but the team's move to San Diego and their inspired play seemed to be a sign calling him back. He loved everything about San Diego—the beaches, the people, the volleyball-crazed fans. He had great memories of playing for San Diego State, and he had a support network of friends in the city.

Since leaving the National Team, Marlowe had stayed in shape, playing at the beach during the day, working at a restaurant at night, and taking acting jobs as they came. He also continued to play indoors, even leading his club team to two USVBA Open National Championships.

In early 1982, Marlowe asked his girlfriend and volleyball player Jeanne Beauprey out on a date to watch the movie *Personal Best* at a theater in Westwood. The film, starring Mariel Hemingway, is about a track and field athlete who trains hard to qualify for the 1980 Olympics only to have her dream thwarted by the United States' decision to boycott the Moscow Games.

Movies were special to Marlowe, given his family's long history in Hollywood and his boyhood days of watching Gary Cooper play Lou Gehrig in *Pride of the Yankees*: "If you want to do something hard enough, you can do it."

As he watched the film, Marlowe realized his Olympic dream, while dormant, was still alive. Then, walking out of the theater, he had his own Hollywood moment, only this was no movie; it was real. He turned to Beauprey and said, "I'm going to try and get back on the National Team."[10] The next morning, he sat down and expressed his intention in a letter to Doug Beal, his former teammate on the National Team from 1974 to 1976.[11]

The letter caught Beal by surprise. He wrote back, asking why, at thirty years old, Marlowe would want to come back. Still, despite his doubts, Beal invited Marlowe down to San Diego to try out. Dvorak was by far the best setter in the country and was comfortably settled into the starter role. Perhaps

Marlowe, who was also a setter, could be Dvorak's backup, but Beal began to wonder if Marlowe might fill another void on the team—a leadership role. In Dayton, Beal had tried to fill that role himself and failed. Now, with all the young talented athletes joining the team in San Diego, that void remained, as did the question of who was going to lead them and bring them together. Beal decided to give Marlowe that chance, inviting him onto the squad in the spring of 1982. The "Big Cy" was back on the team.

Marlowe's best friend since middle school, Jeff Jacobs, lived in San Diego and offered up his couch. Marlowe gladly accepted, and although it was meant to be temporary, that couch would become his home for much of the next two years.

Marlowe's first day back on the National Team was Sunday, May 2, 1982. Crabb was running the practice, a six-on-six team drill.

Marlowe wanted to impress and put a lot of pressure on himself to perform but was a little rusty, and it showed. His frustration built up until he couldn't hold it back any more. Finally, he socked the ball straight up in the air directly toward one of the antiquated lights hanging from the ceiling.

Everyone looked up. The ball collided with the glass bulb, and it shattered, sending shards falling to the floor as the players ducked and raced to get out of the way. Once it became apparent that no one was hurt, the players surveyed the damage and had a good laugh. The only one not laughing was Crabb. He took Marlowe aside and gave him a verbal thrashing. Marlowe knew he deserved it.

Feeling down about practice and more than a little uncertain of his future on the team, Marlowe made his way back to Jacobs's apartment. His roommate greeted him with a pale look on his face. Marlowe knew immediately something was wrong. Marlowe's father had died.

The death had come suddenly, with no warning. Marlowe hadn't even told his father about his renewed Olympic dream and his effort to win a spot on the National Team.

Marlowe's parents divorced when he was a teenager, and his father moved to New York and remarried. "My father and I had a good relationship, but it was strained," recalls Marlowe. In 1976 when the team played the Russians in New York City at Madison Square Garden, his father watched him play for the National Team. It was the only time.

Over the next few months, Marlowe put his head down and went to work. Although his court play steadily improved, it was becoming apparent to Marlowe that making the final Olympic team on those merits would be difficult. As the Olympics neared, Beal and his staff would have to name twelve players to the team.

POWER PLAYERS!
U.S. VOLLEYBALL TEAM
AND FORD BRONCO II

Corporate sponsorship grew when the team moved to San Diego. The Ford Bronco II became the "Official Vehicle of the U.S. Volleyball Association." The picture was taken at Dog Beach in San Diego. From left to right: Steve Timmons, Steve Salmons, Bill Neville, Paul Sunderland with the ball, Rod Wilde, Chris Marlowe, and Rich Duwelius, slightly visible behind Marlowe. Doug Beal was driving, but the advertising agency airbrushed him out of the picture, which the players gave him a hard time about.
SOURCE: FORD MOTOR COMPANY

As a setter, Marlowe was in a particularly precarious position. Dvorak was rapidly becoming the best in the world at his position. And around the same time Marlowe joined the team, another young setter was invited to join: Rod Wilde, a twenty-six-year-old from Fort Dodge, Iowa, who was still in his prime.

Wilde came from a volleyball family; both parents were longtime players and supporters of the sport. His mother had been instrumental in establishing girls' volleyball in Iowa, and his father served for sixteen years as the director for the Cornbelt Region of USA Volleyball. While most families in the 1960s sat around the television on Saturday nights, the Wilde family would clear the living room of furniture to play pepper.

When he was ten years old, Rod Wilde's dad took him to an adult tournament in Nebraska. Although Rod was there to observe and shag balls, when the team wasn't playing well, his dad asked his teammates if he could put his son in as setter. Wilde came in and started setting his dad and the other hitters on the team. Rod Wilde more than held his own, and in the wake of the tournament, on their way back to Fort Dodge, on a long stretch of highway in Nebraska, Wilde had a premonition. "Dad, I'm going to play volleyball in the Olympics someday."[12] Where the idea came from exactly he didn't know, but the goal took hold of him, and soon became an obsession.

Wilde played his college years at Pepperdine, where he and Mike Blanchard led the team to the 1978 national championship, defeating UCLA. After college, Wilde played for the Tucson Sky in a fledgling coed professional league—the International Volleyball Association—the first coed professional league of any sport in the United States. Each team was required to have two women on the court at all times, which opened up an opportunity for many female players to showcase their talent.

Wilde won Rookie of the Year honors in 1979, but after the league ran into financial trouble and folded he went to work for a tree-trimming company in Tucson. As a former professional, his amateur status was uncertain, but he was delighted to get a call in 1982 from USVBA informing him that his amateur status had been reinstated. In May 1982 he was invited onto the National Team along with two other former IVA players, Jon Roberts and Larry Benecke.

To the California players, Iowa was a volleyball backwater, and they labeled Wilde and the other players not from California "easties." Joking and ribbing came from both sides, playing on the caricatures that the "westies," players from California, were free spirits who liked to party, while the "easties," any players from "east of the San Andreas Fault," as Neville liked to say, were more staid and conservative. The players had fun with it, but occasionally the kidding had an edge and sometimes crossed a line, even making its way into the local press. Waldie, who was from Wichita, Kansas, admitted in an article at the time that "deep down I resented some of it. Nobody likes to be made fun of for who they are and where they're from," conceding that tensions "may have affected us a little on the court."[13]

Despite the team's improvement, the regional divisions that Beal first encountered in 1970 and plagued the team in Dayton now followed the team to San Diego.

And there were even cliques within cliques, occasional friction between the players from UCLA, USC, and Pepperdine, who would often show up at practice wearing T-shirts from their respective colleges, inevitably leading to trash talk. Beal told them over and over again that "your primary identity is not as a USC player, or UCLA player or Pepperdine. You need to start thinking of yourself as a National Team player."[14] The coach eventually required the players to wear USA jerseys in practice and even banned the team from wearing college T-shirts on trips as well.

Marlowe's presence on the team helped bridge the rift among the players. Older and more mature, he, more than the other California players, could see beyond the east–west divide.

"Chris Marlowe was an incredibly well-liked guy," said Karch. "More than anyone else, he connected with every single guy on that team. He brought us together with his humor and magnetic personality."[15] Marlowe's good-natured antics and quips countered the stress of enduring Beal's strict training regime. Every day was a grind, but Marlowe kept them laughing and kept them going.

Still, Beal and Neville knew that no single player, not even Marlowe or Karch, was the answer on his own. Somehow, they had to establish a culture of trust and address the divisions that ran deep. They knew the U.S. team was made up of some of the best volleyball players in the world. Their challenge as a coaching staff was to get them to play as a team.

With Neville nudging him on, Beal decided to invite Don Murray and Chuck Johnson, the team psychologists from the McGown era, and reengaged them with the program. During the Dayton years, Beal hadn't utilized Murray and Johnson, but now, with the east–west divide causing problems and the challenge of bringing all these egos together and molding them into a team, he realized how much he needed their help. Talent had taken the team as far as it could go.

When the coaches and psychologists met in San Diego, they brainstormed, trying to come up with something, anything, that might bring the team together and bridge the growing divides. What the players needed, they decided, was some kind of "shared significant life experience." For lack of a better term, they all needed to "sit in a foxhole" together.

Just what that experience might be, they didn't yet know, but they were determined to find it.

· 9 ·

A Crazy Idea

$\mathcal{U}$pon their return, Murray and Johnson hung around the training facility at Balboa Park in San Diego for a few days, quietly observing the team and taking notes, not about volleyball skills but about people skills, the way the players interacted with each other on and off the court. They met separately with the coaches, then the players, then with both groups to begin the work that would turn them into a true team. It was still early in the Olympic quadrennial, and they were beginning the foundational work to help create a positive culture and environment that they hoped would carry the team all the way to the medal platform.

"What kind of team do you want to be?" Johnson asked the players, the same challenge he voiced to McGown's team in 1974, when Doug Beal was still a player. "What ground rules do we want to adopt for how we treat each other on and off the court?" asked Murray.[1]

The question hung in the air waiting for an answer. *How* the players answered that question would prove critical to the team's future success.

One area of concern for both the players and the coaches was how the team responded when things didn't go their way on the court. One match in particular, in the summer of 1981, was emblematic of the wider issue. It was during the disastrous tour of Japan, and the United States led 14–4 in the fifth set of the match, just a single point away from victory, but rather than finishing strong and putting the Japanese away, they started to coast. "We were so far ahead we didn't think we could lose," said Beal. "Whereas, the Japanese played at the top of their abilities, one point at a time."[2]

The coaches did their best to inspire the players on the court to remain aggressive, but there is only so much any coach can do from the sidelines. It's ultimately up to the players to maintain focus and endure the violent swings in momentum typical in a hard-fought volleyball match.

"All the Japanese had to do was keep scoring, and they did," said Beal.[3] It was a classic case of the "spiral vortex." The United States lost 16–14, a shattering defeat at the time, and one that caused everyone to point fingers.

When the players later revisited the nightmare collapse against the Japanese as emblematic of their failures as a team, the response was telling: the word that kept coming up was *resilience*.

Beal reiterated his standard for greatness: a consistent high level of achievement. His heroes, Bill Russell and the Celtics, for example, never let their guard down. They competed every minute of every game.

So when Murray asked in one particularly productive meeting, "How do we want to handle those situations in the future? What are we going to do differently next time?" the players came up with a ground rule:

"[Be] willing to accept responsibility for the play, willing to think more of us as a team instead of looking for someone to blame." Johnson scribbled the principle on a flip chart and hung it on the wall.

The team psychologists then zeroed in on behaviors. "What's a helpful behavior and what's unhelpful?" they asked the players.

One of the players spoke up, saying it's not helpful to yell at each other after a mistake or a poorly hit ball. "It's more helpful when a teammate says, 'Hey, you can dig this guy' after I make an error. It conveys the same idea but exudes confidence."

Another player spoke up. "I have noticed that when things are not going well, we as a team, lose eye contact." When things are going well, the player noted that teammates give each other high-fives and slap each other on the shoulder. "This is important because it communicates that you have got people behind you, as opposed to when everyone's looking around."

The facilitators captured these comments and asked for more. *What else?*

One behavior nearly everyone agreed was unhelpful was the "dirty look." "We need to shake it off and let the coaches do the discipline," said one player. Another teammate offered an alternative: "Confident talk after a bad play is important. Waldie and some others do this very well. Talk like 'Here we go,' or 'Let's go,' or some instruction that is positive and constructive like 'Move more to the left,' or 'I'll take the deep one.'"

Another area of improvement identified by the players was mental focus. "If our thinking errors were gone, we could beat anyone," one player suggested.

Another player offered a team aspiration: "I have heard so many times, teams like Cuba are unbeatable, but I don't see it. I'm sure the Soviets are very good, but we need to see where we need to be to get to number one."

They agreed they wanted to establish a "habit of winning," defined by the team's collective ability to "dig down and pull it out no matter what."

These were high aspirations for a team that had never medaled in a major international tournament and hadn't beaten the Soviets since 1968. As one player noted during the workshop, "No doubt, this team needs to get [mentally] stronger," an observation seconded by the team psychologists.[4]

While team performance improved, team dynamics remained fragile. The players still didn't trust one another, or the staff, completely. How then would it be possible to build the necessary camaraderie to compete for a gold medal? The Pat Power incident, the continuing drama over Hovland's status, and conflicts between factions on the team all indicated that there was significant work still to be done.

With so many problems to address, the coaches met privately with the team psychologists to discuss the next steps. They identified two key issues. First, they wanted the players to get along. They didn't have to be best friends, but they needed to heal the divisions and they needed the players to respect each other on and off the court. And second, they needed to build resilience. To compete for gold, the team would have to get tougher and learn how to remain composed and confident when challenged or facing adversity.

"It became obvious that we needed to learn to rely on each other," said Beal. "To develop cohesiveness and relationships that would lend themselves to team play. Our team had broken down too many times in stressful situations, had allowed too many big leads to get away. If that occurred in the Olympics, it would be ruinous."[5]

But how could players who didn't trust one another rely on each other? For more than a year, the psychologists and staff had kicked around the idea that perhaps a shared significant life experience outside of volleyball would bring the team together. If the players were placed in an unfamiliar yet challenging environment, they would be forced to work together to achieve a common goal. In a memo to the coaching staff, the team psychologists explained: "There are a variety of studies in education and industry that suggest strong positive outcomes in terms of the cohesion of the team can occur from this kind of experience." If structured correctly, Murray and Johnson predicted, the experience would lead the players to a new mindset, embracing an attitude that says, "If we can pull through this difficult event, we will come through any kind of pressure-filled athletic event."[6]

Now they finally decided to move forward with the idea. Neville, who had served in the military, coaching the Army volleyball team when he was just out of college, offered an idea: boot camp. Military leaders are experts at taking a random group of civilians and molding them into a cohesive unit, willing to lay down their lives for one another, and Neville thought they might be able to replicate that experience. Although boot-camp-like experiences are common today, that wasn't the case in the early 1980s. Neville reached out to military leaders at Camp Pendleton, the major Marine base just north of San Diego, to see if they were open to putting a volleyball team through some accelerated form of basic training.

The answer came back: Marine Corps boot camp is restricted to Marines. No go.

Neville was never short of ideas, so he threw out another one: Outward Bound. Neville was familiar with the organization, having been involved with outdoor experiences through the YMCA, and he considered Outward Bound the best fit because it specialized in leading groups on challenging outdoor adventures that drive both individual growth and team building.

Outward Bound—the name is a nautical term describing a ship leaving the safety of a harbor as it embarks on a journey into the open seas—began as a school founded during World War II to address the high casualty rate among younger seamen facing U-boat attacks in the Battle of the Atlantic. The British were surprised to discover that while older seamen in the lifeboats survived, many younger men, who were physically stronger, perished unnecessarily.[7] The reason? Over the course of their service experience, the older seamen had developed the inner resources and drive to overcome life-threatening challenges. They stuck together and unconditionally supported one another. What Outward Bound figured out was "people who were put in challenging, adventurous outdoor situations gained confidence, redefined their own perceptions of their personal possibilities, demonstrated compassion, and developed a spirit of camaraderie with their peers."[8] The school designed a survival program of increasing physical and mental challenges to help younger seamen gain the inner strength and resilience to survive.

What Outward Bound teaches, in essence, is resilience.

Neither Beal nor the team psychologists had heard of Outward Bound before, but they were intrigued, and Beal asked Neville to contact the organization. In the letter Neville wrote to Outward Bound to inquire about enrolling the team in a wilderness course, he complimented the current group of young players as "excellent athletes—the best crop we've ever had," yet they were, as he noted, lacking in some important life skills. "These young men have not had experiences where they had to rely on themselves and make important decisions," he wrote. "None, for example, have ever had to face a military experience and all that implies. Along with our sports psychologists, the coaching staff believes the team needs 'life experiences'—experiences which positively modify behavior, teach total confidence, and team loyalty."[9]

In the letter, Neville also described what he hoped to achieve with Outward Bound: "The coaching staff believes, to complete our total training program; to ensure the team is ready, individually and collectively, for any situation which may arise; and to fulfill our philosophical obligation of providing the maximum, positive, influential experience to the people we work with, we want to involve them in a wilderness situation which uniquely taps the human resource required in every stress situation. We want our players totally prepared when they march into the Olympic Stadium to represent the United States."

In the early 1980s the typical Outward Bound experience in the United States targeted groups of business leaders or students. The leaders of Outward Bound were intrigued by the novel prospect of taking a group of future Olympians through a wilderness experience. They offered to design a challenging course to help these athletes grow both personally and as a team, and even offered to help raise the funds to do it.

Given the long history and legacy of Outward Bound, paired with the offer of financial support, the coaching staff and team psychologists decided to move forward with their proposal, but they also established a few additional requirements. First, the coaches would be going through the experience alongside the players, and that would include at least one of the team psychologists to observe and provide advice and guidance. And second, every player had to be there; participation was mandatory.

To allow the players time to clear their schedules in advance, the coaches gathered the team and announced that they planned to take a break from training in the gym and use the time to embark on a wilderness excursion.

The players thought the idea was nuts.

"We thought they were out of their minds," recalls Sunderland, the player with the most experience on the team. "We, as a team, didn't sense we had any big issues. We didn't think, 'We are really a screwed-up group.' There were guys on the team that hung out, and guys that didn't. Some were closer than others."[10] Sunderland, and many of his teammates, didn't see that as a problem.

Since the players didn't acknowledge the depth of their dysfunction, they couldn't accept Outward Bound as a valid part of their training. They viewed it as just some crazy idea cooked up by Neville and the team psychologists, eggheads who knew practically nothing about volleyball. Player after player made the point that the way to improve at volleyball is to play more volleyball and they feared that it would take time away from more traditional training—the reps and drills that helped them hone their skills.

"Nobody wanted to go," said Beal. "We went to great lengths to satisfy all their doubts."[11]

Still, some of the players' arguments gave Beal pause. First, the risk of injury was a real fear shared by every athlete, but even more pronounced for those who knew that one misstep in the woods could result in an injury that might keep a player out of the Olympics.

"We had to provide proof of Outward Bound's safety record, assuring the players that nobody was going to die," said Beal.[12]

And finally, there was the issue of spending time away from friends and family. The team's busy international competition and travel schedule already mandated long periods of time away from wives and girlfriends. The players had limited "downtime," so they valued any opportunity to recharge, get away from one another, and reconnect with friends and family—something especially important to the married players like Dvorak, Sunderland, Waldie, and Wilde. Adding an outdoor adventure to an already overburdened schedule would cause additional stress. How could they become a better team if they were homesick and miserable?

Dvorak, the team captain, was particularly outspoken in his opposition. He wasn't upset about being sent into the mountains. In fact, he loved the mountains. His family drove to the mountains often when he was a child and he was one of the few players who knew how to ski. "I was so upset that we're in a schedule that was [already] so overwhelming, and yet we were taking time to do this," he recalled. He didn't want to spend more time away from his wife.

Marlowe, the oldest player on the team, whose relationship with Beal went back to their days on the National Team, stepped forward as a spokesperson for the players, a sign of his emerging role as a leader on the team. He put the question bluntly, distilled to a single observation: "How is hiking in the wilderness going to help us win a medal?"[13]

Beal, however, was committed to the decision, and explained that "we needed a unifying experience so players would learn to get along off court as well as on. Then, if things went badly during a game, they would pull together instead of pulling each other apart."[14]

Many of the players didn't buy that argument and hoped, if they complained enough, the coaching staff would abandon the idea. They knew Beal and Neville were mavericks, but they didn't think they were crazy enough to follow through with something of this magnitude.

But over the following weeks, Neville kept updating the players on how the Outward Bound plan was progressing, keeping them apprised of the proposed time line and possible locations. As the date of departure grew closer, the players sensed the coaches were serious, so they started offering their own alternatives.

How about a week of camping on Zuma Beach? Zuma is a beautiful and popular beach in Malibu with a surf break, outdoor showers, food stands, and a nice set of beach volleyball courts. (In later years, Zuma became a location for the television show *Baywatch*.) The players argued that Zuma would be the perfect place to get away for a couple of weeks and clear their heads.

Beal and Neville promptly rejected the notion. A week at Zuma Beach was a vacation, not a life-changing experience.

"Can't we just go on a surfing trip to Mexico?" asked another player.[15] *Nice try, guys.* They might as well have asked for a bonfire and a keg party too.

"You boys don't get it," said Neville. "The more of these things I hear, the more I know you need Outward Bound."[16]

Dvorak pitched the coaches on another alternative: sailing. San Diego was practically the sailing capital of the United States, and after marrying into a sailing family, Dvorak was familiar with the sport and its dependence on teamwork. He thought a sailing adventure through the Caribbean would be thrilling, challenging, and, perhaps most importantly for the Southern California natives, warm. He envisioned the team working together to hoist the sail and navigate from island to island, maybe spend a few days on some pristine beaches. It seemed like a slam dunk to Dvorak.

The coaches dismissed the suggestion. They wanted the team to get away from the beach, not camp on it.

After one practice, the players huddled to develop a strategy for resistance. They realized that every time they complained, Neville or Beal would turn the tables by saying, "Your whining is just more evidence for why you need this experience."[17] So the players decided to simply ignore Neville's updates. Maybe, they thought, if they all stopped complaining, the coaches would realize that the team didn't need an elaborate team-building trip. When Outward Bound was mentioned, they went silent. *Problems? What problems?*

The coaches weren't sure what to make of the silence at first. They figured it wouldn't last, but the players went several months without either mentioning the trip or uttering a word of complaint.

In the meantime, before the team embarked on a six-week tour through Asia with stops in China, South Korea, and Japan, the staff decided that one of the team psychologists would join the team for the trip to help manage stress and work with the players and coaches on team building. Murray and Johnson divided up the duties. Murray and his wife tagged along on the tour of Japan that summer, while Chuck Johnson agreed to join the coaches and players on the Outward Bound trip.

During the Japan tour, Beal, Neville, and Murray called a meeting with the still-silent players to directly address the Outward Bound trip. Neville kicked it off. "I'm so excited about our upcoming Outward Bound experience!" The players held fast and looked back at him blankly. "Since you guys are no longer complaining, Doug and I are *thrilled* that you've embraced the upcoming experience. We couldn't be happier with your change of heart." The players rolled their eyes at each other. The resistance had failed, and this miserable trip was probably inevitable. Murray walked them through the studies that showed how such experiences build cohesion and trust. Neville focused his pitch on how it would specifically help the team when they faced an especially stressful situation, like a "spiral vortex."

The U.S. Men's National Team in July 1982 during a tour of Japan. Left to right:
Bill Neville, Mike Blanchard, Jay Hanseth, Paul Sunderland, Marc Waldie, Jon Roberts,
Larry Benecke, Rich Duwelius, Alex Valow (referee traveling with the team),
Steve Salmons, Dusty Dvorak, Chris Marlowe, Karch Kiraly, Steve Timmons,
Aldis Berzins, Doug Beal, Don Murray. SOURCE: MURRAY FAMILY ARCHIVES

Steve Timmons surrounded by a group of young female fans during the team's tour of
Japan in 1982. Standing 6'5" and with bright red hair, Timmons stood out, and was
mobbed by autograph seekers everywhere he went. SOURCE: MURRAY FAMILY ARCHIVES

Finally, one of the veteran players from the Dayton years spoke up. "Let's do it," said Duwelius. "If we're going to go through it anyway, why not make the most of it?"[18]

A few other players were privately excited to go and now openly voiced their support. Berzins, who spent his summers at an outdoor camp for Latvian Americans, looked at the experience as a challenge. "I wanted to learn how to survive out there," he recalls.[19] Rod Wilde, who grew up camping in Iowa and had even camped in the snow before, publicly voiced his support, as did Dave Saunders, who had been a Boy Scout.

The team begrudgingly accepted that they would be going on Outward Bound, but they still felt strongly twenty-eight days was too long.

"The majority rebelled so vigorously about going, we backed down a bit and cut the course from 28 days to 21 days," recalls Beal. "We went to great lengths to satisfy all doubts."[20]

Meanwhile, Neville consulted with Peter O'Neil, the twenty-six-year-old senior instructor with Outward Bound assigned to design and run the course. "Most of our players have a style I call 'California cool,'" wrote Neville in a letter to O'Neil, giving him background on the team's makeup. "They may be cool, but they aren't yet as tough as we want them. We want them to make good out of bad. We want them to stop blaming each other when they lose." Neville confided that although the players were "young, supremely athletic talents," at times he found them to be obstinate and difficult to coach. "These are world-class athletes," said Neville, "with world class egos."[21]

Outward Bound recognized this as a landmark opportunity, one of the highest-profile projects it had ever sponsored. If the course went well for this Olympic team, the potential upside for Outward Bound's public relations and brand building would be tremendous. At the same time, the potential risks were equally significant, particularly if the trip caused further rifts within the team or led to injuries that adversely affected their performance.

After lengthy discussions between the coaching staff, the team psychologists, and Outward Bound, they finally agreed on a winter experience in the mountains, scheduled for January 1983, with the exact route and details yet to be determined. The combination of winter weather and mountains guaranteed that both the "westies" *and* the "easties" would be well outside of their comfort zones, the "westies" because of the climate and the "easties" because of the terrain.

The time period fit into a perfect window between the World Championships in Argentina in November 1982 and a series of important matches against Cuba scheduled for April 1983. And at twenty months before the Olympics in Los Angeles, it was not so close that it might throw off the team's preparation but not so far removed that the roster might change drastically and any benefit be wasted.

Although O'Neil was more familiar with the Rocky Mountains, that area was prone to avalanches and extreme weather, so instead he designed a course that would take the team through Southeastern Utah's less challenging and lower-elevation Abajo Mountain Range and Canyonlands National Park.

O'Neil eventually designed a course that covered more than 100 miles of remote wilderness. The group would first ascend a snow-covered peak of nearly 11,000 feet, and then move through pine forests before dropping into the labyrinthine pockets and canyons of Canyonlands National Park before arriving at their final destination, the famed Needles district of the park with its otherworldly Wingate Sandstone features. The natural beauty and ruggedness of the terrain, depending on the weather and conditions, could inspire awe or inflict misery.

O'Neil knew the players were against the trip and asked for a meeting to start a dialogue and address their concerns. He hoped to clarify the goals and objectives for the course, educate the players on the overall Outward Bound philosophy, and gain their input and perspective.

In August 1982 the team invited O'Neil to watch them play a match versus Italy at the Regis College Fieldhouse in Denver. O'Neil brought along another experienced Outward Bound instructor, Randy Udall (the son of Mo Udall, a congressman from Arizona and brother of Mark Udall, who later represented Colorado in the Senate). Although O'Neil and Udall were awed by the athleticism of the players, something else stood out—the frequent, often emotionally charged interactions of the players and coaches as the team moved from play to play.

Now the larger purpose of the course became clear to O'Neil. As he later wrote in a report to Outward Bound leadership, "The hope was that the course might have a positive effect on those elements of teamwork which only superficially enter into a backyard volleyball game, but which, at this elevated level of competition may often make the difference between victory and defeat: elements of attitude, mental fortitude, leadership, spirit and compassion, and respect for one another. The course would not increase ball speed, but it might help the team develop those inner and communal resources which come into play when the chips are down, and the momentum is going the wrong way."[22]

At a meeting with the players the next day, O'Neil ran straight into a wall of resistance as stiff as any defense on the volleyball court. As O'Neil described the trip in detail and the players learned the course would entail a 100-mile hike, much of it while wearing snowshoes and carrying seventy-pound packs, their resistance only grew.

They let O'Neil have it. The players were now determined to reduce the course even more, to only a week or two, but O'Neil pushed back. He knew from experience that the length of a course was often the biggest factor in its success or failure.

"A short course too easily allows a student to 'see beyond the experience,' to live with conflicts and frustrations and to sweep important issues under the rug, knowing 'it will all be over soon,'" O'Neil later wrote in his trip report. "A longer course compels people to deal with interpersonal strife and to make real adjustments in an environment that demands cooperation, mutual respect and trust."

In the end, O'Neil and the coaching staff held firm; the twenty-one-day course was nonnegotiable.

Several players approached the coaching staff individually about getting excused from the trip. Sunderland had what he believed to be a legitimate circumstance: his wife would be eight months pregnant with their first child while he was scheduled to be in the remote Utah wilderness. Karch, who was still in college, also asked to be excused because his class schedule at UCLA conflicted directly with Outward Bound.

The coaches worried that if they started granting individual exceptions, one player after another would opt out until the exercise would become pointless, but in response, the coaching staff did their best to address concerns and preserve the trip. For Sunderland, they arranged with Outward Bound to have a helicopter available in the event his wife went into labor. Karch's situation was more challenging. The courses he needed to take in January were not offered any other time during the year, and he needed the prerequisites to apply to medical school. The coaches kept a dialogue going with him through the fall, even reaching out to his professors, in an attempt to find a solution.

Meanwhile, the team psychologists were beginning to have concerns. During his time with the team in Japan the previous summer, Murray was alarmed by the depth and intensity of the player's resistance to a winter wilderness experience, and when he returned he conferred with Johnson. Together, the team psychologists expressed a few apprehensions to Beal about the Outward Bound course. They believed the "shared significant life experience" should be one the players embraced and not something forced on them, and they worried that the player's cynicism would taint the experience. They wrote a memo to the coaches emphasizing that the trip must not only be outside of every player's life experience and require interdependence, but also be "fun," an event "they can look back on as difficult, stressful yet enjoyable."

"Were it up to us," they concluded, a less intense experience might be sufficient. Afraid the players' recalcitrance might cause them to reject the trip entirely, they proposed an alternative, a trip of "a minimum of five days."[23]

The memo landed on Beal's desk just before the World Championships in Argentina, where they suffered the devastating loss to Bulgaria, blowing a 13–5 lead in the fifth game. The loss confirmed Beal's fears—with less than two years to go until the Olympics, the U.S. National Team was unable to break into the top ten teams in the world. The players had not yet learned how to perform in stressful situations. Despite the concerns of the team psychologists, the defeat strengthened Beal and Neville's resolve to move forward with the Outward Bound trip.

Two years before, in 1981, the coaching staff had put together a plan that mapped out the team's journey to contend for a medal in Los Angeles. "We identified moments in the timeline where we would reevaluate the plan," said Beal. "The World Championships in Argentina were one of those moments. After the disappointing finish, we realized we were not on the right path."[24]

And maybe, he thought, the team still needed Hovland? Beal decided to meet with Hovland and invite him to rejoin the team—they missed his talent—but only if he agreed to join them on the Outward Bound trip.

"If he would have agreed to that, I think everyone associated with the team would have welcomed him back gladly."[25]

Hovland turned Beal down.

"I wanted to play on the national team," said Hovland, "but I also wanted to make some money and play."[26]

Hovland was willing to return, but only on his terms, and that didn't work for Beal.

"Our program came first," said Beal.[27] They'd all go forward together, without Hovland.

On December 23, 1982, just two weeks before the team was set to embark on Outward Bound, the coaching staff received a letter from Peter O'Neil. He had recently returned from a three-month mountain-climbing expedition through India and Nepal. He confessed that, during the expedition, there were many times when "our upcoming Outward Bound course in the Canyonlands of Utah came to mind."

In the letter he wrote:

> I realized that, in many respects, the experiences I was having on our expedition to the other side of the world were similar to the experiences I hope my staff and I can facilitate for you in January.
>
> It is somehow anachronistic in this age of high-speed travel to plod behind a string of porters, or in our case in the Canyonlands in January, to labor under heavy backpacks on snowshoes. Yet, by seemingly transporting ourselves backward in time to a place where the struggle for life takes on a less affected form, we can learn a great deal about ourselves as individuals and our ways of relating to others.
>
> My journal is full of tirades against unwilling and argumentative porters. Our journey [to India and Nepal] too often became a daily struggle just to keep moving, rather than a romantic mode of travel—so dependent as we

were on the whims of other human beings—yet in re-reading my journal these are the parts that I dwell on with quiet longing, for one tends to complain of discomfort and relish hardship: the more difficult the journey, the greater the satisfaction of having completed it.

And, lest you think it was all hard work, which it wasn't, I had fun. There were moments of sheer joy, moments of shared laughter within our group . . . a great deal of happiness in places and situations where I would never have expected it.

I am looking forward to seeing you all on the evening of January 7th in Grand Junction.

Over Christmas and New Year's, the coaching staff had time to contemplate the letter, which framed their upcoming course as almost a spiritual journey and reinforced their commitment to the experience. As they prepared to leave the safe harbor of San Diego to venture out into the open seas of adventure, questions lingered like echoes in a deep canyon. Would the players relish the discomfort and hardship, or would the experience devolve into three weeks of complaining and bitterness? Would they learn more about themselves and how they related to others, or would it push them further apart and increase the pressure and internal competition to secure one of the coveted twelve spots on the Olympic roster?

After a year's absence, the coaches invited Pat Powers back on the team, hoping his time away had given him the space to mature. He was just too talented to keep off the roster, and the coaches figured Outward Bound would be an excellent activity to help him bond with his teammates.

In the early morning of Friday, January 7, 1983, players and coaches assembled at the airport to board a flight to Grand Junction, the jumping-off point for their Outward Bound adventure, and the atmosphere was thick with apprehension and tension—no one knew what to expect. As the players looked around, they noticed someone was missing. *Where's Karch?*

Beal gathered the players and addressed the team:

"Karch will not be joining the team on Outward Bound."[28]

• *10* •

Into the Wild

"*W*hat the hell is this?" Wilde thought to himself, and he wasn't the only one.[1]

The coaches had been clear that this was a mandatory trip and there would be no exceptions, and now there was.

To the players, Karch's absence seemed terribly unfair. Why should they submit to this ordeal while Karch is allowed to stay and attend school in sunny Southern California?

Although they listened to Beal's explanation, some of the players attributed Karch's absence to favoritism. If there was one player who was guaranteed to be on the team at the Olympics, it was Karch. With the possible exception of Dvorak, no other players could be so confident that Beal would give them a chance if they bailed on Outward Bound. Even so, as they grumbled to each other about the injustice, they managed their irritation and boarded the plane.

The players were not aware of the delicate negotiations that had played out over the previous weeks between the coaching staff and Karch, the only member of the team still in college, as they tried to find a way for him to both earn his pre-med degree and participate in the trip. Karch had already taken a leave of absence from UCLA in the fall of 1982 so he could practice with the team full-time and participate in the World Championships, but it had come at a cost. As a premed major, he had missed several prerequisite courses, and his only opportunity to make up those courses was the winter semester, which conflicted with the trip. If he joined his teammates with Outward Bound, he would have to wait another year to take those courses and then likely take a leave from the team later, when they were gearing up for the Olympics.

The decision to allow Karch to opt out of the trip was both difficult and perilous in terms of team harmony. A major premise of the Outward Bound philosophy was predicated on *everyone* participating. If Karch didn't, how would he then reassimilate onto the team when the players returned? No one could predict how it would all play out, if Karch's absence would destroy the trip before it even started, but the decision was made, and there was no turning back. Beal thought the right thing to do was excuse Karch and hope they'd find a way to deal with the consequences.

In reality, Karch was in a unique position, and everyone knew it. He was so much better than the others—on his way to becoming a transcendent figure in the sport—and he was such a good teammate and positive force that in a sense he had earned his pass from Outward Bound. It didn't hurt that his dedication to the National Team, while tackling something as all-consuming and challenging as medical school, was so ambitious and honorable. Karch's teammates knew he wouldn't be partying up on the beach while they were freezing their asses off in Utah. He was, perhaps, the only player for whom the trip may not have really been needed and whose absence the others would accept, however grudgingly.

It was too late for the players to do anything about it anyway. They were already at the airport preparing to board the plane, embarking on a journey that would take them into unfamiliar terrain and conditions. With little to no previous wilderness experience, the rugged beauty of the Abajo Mountains and the sandstone labyrinth of Canyonlands were certain to offer a novel challenge. It was a sharp departure from their familiar volleyball world in pretty much every way imaginable.

It was a leap of faith.

The team flew to Denver that morning and transferred to a second flight to Grand Junction, Colorado. At Grand Junction a bus met them at the airport and took them to the Holiday Inn, where they were met by O'Neil and Udall. In a team meeting that evening, O'Neil reinforced the reality that enduring the harsh winter conditions would require a team effort. Whether you are the best player on the team, or just barely holding on to your spot, out here, O'Neil reminded them all, it didn't matter. What mattered was getting from point A to point B every day, staying warm, preparing and eating enough food, and learning new skills. In this environment, the players had to care for both themselves and their teammates.

Although the team had been briefed before, O'Neil and Udall conducted a final briefing on the five sections of the course and what to expect during each phase. The trip was divided into four sections: (1) the Alpine Experience through the Abajo Mountains from January 7 to 15; (2) Resupply and Rock Climbing at Beef Basin, January 16 to 18; (3) Solo in Butler Wash from January 19 to 21; and (4) Finals in the Needles District, January 22 to 27.

As O'Neil spoke, he was struck again by the size and athleticism of the players. Outward Bound had outfitted the trip with massive quantities of food, but the thought occurred to him that he may need more. The last thing he needed was for this group to run out of food on the trail, in freezing temperatures, and turn on him, the other guides, or each other. Following the meeting, he went out to purchase more food.

That night at the Holiday Inn in Grand Junction, Aldis Berzins stepped out on the balcony to get a feel for the environment and to test his body's reaction. As the wind whipped through his jacket, he was overwhelmed by the cold. After a high of forty degrees earlier that day, the temperature was plummeting toward the low teens, while wind gusts made it feel even colder. "I'm going to be out in this cold for three weeks?" he thought to himself. "No way." This would be no walk on the beach, that was certain. Yet he was eager to learn how to survive in such harsh elements.

Early the next morning, the players boarded a bus for the three-hour trip to Monticello, Utah, where Outward Bound maintained a year-round base camp. After a brief stop to pick up equipment and rations, the bus drove the team west out of Monticello toward the snow-covered Abajo Mountains. Then, abruptly, the highway reached a point where it was not plowed and the bus rolled to a stop, the way blocked by thirty-seven inches of snow. The snowpack in the Abajo Mountains was 151 percent of normal that winter.[2]

Eddie Young and Jimbo Buickerood, two Outward Bound instructors who would be joining the group, were waiting in ambush. As the players got off the bus, Young and Buickerood welcomed the players Outward Bound–style—pelting them with snowballs. It set the tone that, yes, it was a serious trip, but there would be some fun along the way too.

As the players shuffled off the bus, dodging snowballs and returning a few in Young and Buickerood's direction, local snowmobilers moving through the area did a double take, struck by the size and height of the men.

One of the first things the guides asked the players to do was empty their pockets and personal packs. The players had been told what to bring and what not to. Rolls of toilet paper fell to the frozen ground. It was not on the list. "Whatever you pack in, you have to pack out, and you definitely don't want to pack that out," said the instructors.[3]

"What are we going to use?" the players asked.

"Snow," the instructors responded.

The look on their faces said it all.

"But what if there isn't any snow?" the players asked with a hint of desperation.

"Sagebrush,"[4] said Udall with a playful smile on his face. Only he wasn't kidding. California seemed very far away.

The players were issued everything else needed to survive the extreme cold, including down parkas, packs, snowshoes, tents, extralarge sleeping bags

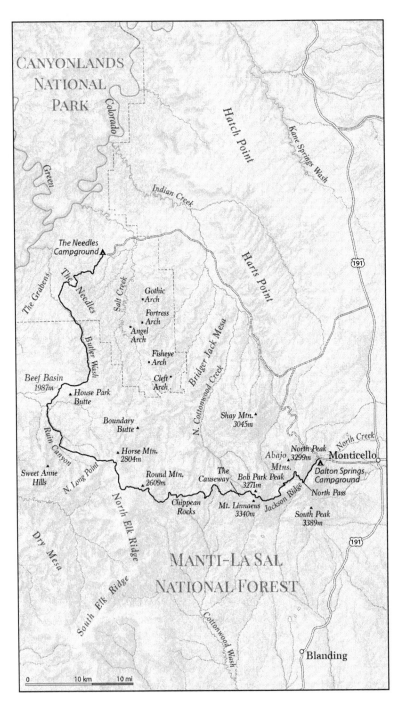

Route of the Outward Bound Course, January 7–27, 1983. CREATED BY
BEEHIVE MAPPING

with liners, Sorel boots, and all the food they would need for the next eight days. As the athletes "traded their sweat pants for wind pants, and their Nikes for snowshoes," recalled Udall, they referred to themselves as a "rare group of creatures."[5] The name stuck, and befitting the wilderness environment, they began referring to themselves as "creatures," as did the instructors.

Joining the group, too, was photojournalist Bruce McAllister, commissioned by the Olympic magazine, *Stars in Motion*, to document the alpine phase of the trip. The instructors then divided the party into two subgroups. O'Neil and Young would lead Doug Beal, Chuck Johnson, Aldis Berzins, Craig Buck, Rich Duwelius, Chris Marlowe, Pat Powers, Jon Roberts, Steve Salmons, and Steve Timmons. The players wanted a name for their subgroup, so playing off Udall's comment about a "rare group of creatures," they adopted the name *Creatures*.

Udall and Buickerood were the instructors for the other patrol which included Bill Neville, Tony Crabb, Larry Benecke, Mike Blanchard, Dusty Dvorak, Dave Saunders, Paul Sunderland, Marc Waldie, and Rod Wilde. The *Creatures* immediately labeled their counterparts the *Clerks*. It was all part of the witty banter and ribbing that often flew around whenever the players got together. According to the *Creatures*, the *Clerks* were just a bunch of nerdy, stuffy, academic-types. While the *Clerks* considered the *Creatures*, "all the guys that needed some mental work,"[6] recalled Waldie.

The division of the group into two smaller patrols, while on the surface appearing counter to the goal of bringing the team closer together, was based on research and years of Outward Bound experience. In a larger group some members can afford to "check out" on tasks such as route finding, navigating, and even basic duties like setting up camp and cooking. Groups of ten were the sweet spot, large enough that there are dynamics and dissimilarities to work out, but small enough that everyone has to pitch in and stay involved.

Equipment and food were divided between the patrols and packed into backpacks, "estimated 70 pounds at the beginning of the day, re-estimated 170 pounds at the end of the day," Neville quipped.

A snowmobile path led fortuitously uphill from the staging area, and the two patrols trudged their way up the track westward, toward the Abajos. At 8,200 feet, the air contained much less oxygen than in San Diego. With each step, their bodies struggled to adjust to the high altitude and cold environment. Their Sorel snow boots, which had not yet been broken in, were nothing like the comfortable and light athletic shoes they were accustomed to.

Eventually, the snowmobile trail played out and everyone strapped on snowshoes. The heavy, cumbersome snowshoes of the early 1980s were nothing like the light, flexible high-tech snowshoes of today. They were awkward for many of the players, especially the taller players like Buck. O'Neil was astonished at just how ineffective the snowshoes proved to be for someone who stood 6'9" and weighed over two hundred pounds. Even with the added surface area of the snowshoe, the larger players were regularly postholing two feet into the powder.

Moving through a forest of scrub oak mixed with aspen, the patrols remained in visual contact at times, but at other times they would make slightly different route choices and temporarily disappear from view. Yet both the *Creatures* and the *Clerks* moved steadily toward a common goal, a high point in the Abajos known as Bob's Peak. The urban buzz they had grown accustomed to in San Diego was replaced with an eerie silence. A landscape of snow, mountains, and trees surrounded the team in every direction. How were they supposed to find their way? The instructors patiently began teaching the players and coaches how to navigate through this new environment using a map and compass.

The group covered three miles that first afternoon, all uphill, then stopped to learn how to set up camp before the winter darkness. Each player was assigned a different task, including digging out a level area for camp, setting up tents, preparing a fire, and cooking meals. As they struggled to complete their duties with frozen fingers, the reality of the situation was sinking in, and this was only day one. Players and staff, already exhausted, retreated early to their tents. Tomorrow, they'd been warned, would be tougher. Saunders laid in his sleeping bag, shivering, as he listened to his teammates snoring. *How were they able to fall asleep in this cold?* he thought to himself.

"The second day dawned bitter cold and very windy," wrote the instructors in their trip report. Awoken shortly after dawn, the players broke camp, packed their gear, and headed out on the trail, up North Creek Canyon in the shadow of Abajo Peak, at 11,368 feet, the highest point in the Abajo Mountains. Their destination was a snow-covered saddle between Abajo Peak and Horsehead Peak called North Creek Pass, at an elevation of 10,300 feet.

"As we contoured across North Pass on steep, icy snowfields," wrote Udall, "we begin to glimpse the first signs of selfishness, as those breaking trail didn't move fast enough to satisfy those coming behind." It was, the instructors knew, a typical response among students at the beginning of a winter course. They were already seeing a reluctance "to expend the time and energy necessary to take care of oneself, and an even greater reluctance to help others."[7] With each step, the necessity for the trip became more and more obvious.

As the group slowly made their way, the instructors began harping on a theme they would return to many times over the next three weeks: "For the team to win a medal in '84, each one of them had to create a bond, an attachment, to everyone else. To excel the team needed to become unified rather than polarized. Only by surpassing this sense of separateness can the team jell [sic], play as one and compete in harmony."

Peter O'Neil, with skis attached to his backpack, leading the way above the tree line in the Abajo Mountains. Following him in the baseball cap is Jon Roberts. Note the line of players in the background making their way up the pass. SOURCE: BRUCE MCALLISTER

Yet even as they spoke those words, they already knew that "this point was easy to make, more difficult to digest, and even harder for the team to embody as a whole."

At least they weren't totally miserable. If they weren't exactly having fun, they were beginning to find some of what they were undergoing funny. On that second day, Craig Buck, the tallest player on the team, tripped and fell into a tree well. He survived intact, but his snowshoes didn't. The players joked that Buck's snowshoes suffered "a compound fracture." The instructors patched the broken snowshoe with parachute cord boiled in water and parts made out of saplings. One of the guides, Eddie Young, swapped his more functional snow-shoes with Buck, so the group was able to proceed on.

By this time, Steve Salmons's unique packing style had become a running joke among his teammates. Salmons had ignored O'Neil's advice on how to properly organize his backpack and hung random items on the outside of his pack—snow shovel, pans, rope, extra boots, and other miscellaneous objects. "He looked like a vintage nineteenth-century tinker, plying the Smokey Mountains, going from homestead to homestead peddling his wares," recalled Neville.[8] With each step, the items swayed back and forth, clinking and clanking as he made his way along the trail.

One member of the group kept falling behind: Chuck Johnson. Over forty, out of shape, and living the life of a sedentary professor in Chico, California, Johnson was the least prepared of anyone for the physical exertion required to stay with the athletes and instructors. Yet when someone in a patrol lagged behind, the group couldn't just abandon them. Salmons recognized the problem and offered to relieve Johnson of a heavy block of cheese and other weighty items from his pack. Johnson almost cried with gratitude when he handed the cheese over to Salmons. Then, whenever Johnson fell back, Marlowe would wait for him and help him catch up. The instructors and coaches took notice. It was one of the first signs that these guys were looking to care for one another, a crucial lesson Outward Bound strives to teach.

That night, Saunders shivered in his tent again, unable to stay warm.

"I just can't seem to get warm at night," Saunders confessed to his tent mate, Mike Blanchard.[9]

"I pull the draw string hoodie around my face and I'm fine," replied Blanchard.

Saunders searched his bag for a draw string, and when he couldn't find it, he realized he'd been sleeping with two liners while Blanchard had been sleeping with two sleeping bags. Once they got it sorted out, Saunders slept like a baby.

On the third day, the patrols rose early again, in anticipation of the most arduous task yet, traversing Jackson Ridge and ascending Bob's Peak. Moving up a steep section of trail, Marlowe found himself in line behind Beal and Salmons.

"We were traversing a narrow pathway on the side of the mountain," recalls Marlowe. "And on one side, there was a good slant going down."[10]

The players and coaches were drained, just trying to put one snowshoe in front of the other, when suddenly Beal's snowshoe caught a root buried just below the surface of the snow and he lost his balance. His body turned and his pack leaned downhill. Beal teetered for a few seconds, waving his hands in a desperate attempt to maintain his balance, but lost the battle. He fell and the weight of his pack increased his momentum as he barreled down the hill, end over end.

Marlowe watched it all unfold, shouting, "There goes coach!"[11] Luckily for Beal, his fall eventually slowed and he came to rest in a snowdrift. The players in the group gathered on the trail and looked intently down at the coach for a sign of movement. After a few tense seconds, they detected movement in the snow as Beal began untangling himself from his gear. As Beal stood up to signal to the players he was okay, snow fully covered the lenses of his glasses and Marlowe pointed out that he bore a striking resemblance to Mr. Magoo. "Well coach, you wanted to come on this trip," said Marlowe. "Now you've done it."[12]

Relieved that Beal was okay, they also took a little pleasure in seeing that their coach was having as rough a time as they were. But to the astonishment of the instructors, the players didn't rush down the hill to help Beal. In fact, they didn't wait for their coach at all, and instead just turned and proceeded on, figuring he could help himself. O'Neil and Young hurried down the snowfield to help Beal gather his things and get back on the trail.

The weather got worse as the day progressed. The wind came up, and the players felt their packs digging into their shoulders as their fingers and toes turned numb from the cold. Despite their athleticism, they couldn't seem to master the skill of balancing a sixty-plus-pound pack while postholing the powder in snowshoes—sand was a lot easier to negotiate—and they lagged behind schedule. The plan was to climb up and over Bob's Peak and camp on the other side, sheltered from the weather. Instead, their strength sapped by a series of false summits, as the last rays of daylight flickered, they were forced to camp below the summit at just under 11,000 feet, fully exposed to the raging weather.

"It was not an easy time for the team," wrote O'Neil. Although he and Udall designed "the Abajo crossing to provide an extraordinary challenge that would physically and mentally tax even the most fit of athletes, [we] did not predict just how much of a challenge it would be for them."

McAllister, the freelance photojournalist, later recalled, writing in *Stars in Motion*, "that night the players found the freeze-chill factor a tough handicap as we ploughed our way from false summit to false summit in lowering temperatures. It was almost like one of those [volleyball] matches in which the other team has you down two games, is about to put you away in the third, and you come back fighting with new energy."[13]

One of the players noted dryly, "This sure isn't cheeseburgers in paradise, is it?" The coaches and guides could only grunt in agreement. That was the point of the exercise. The Jimmy Buffet song caught on with the players, becoming the informal theme song of the trip.

"I like mine with lettuce and tomatoes," one player would sing. "Heinz 57 and French fried potato," the next player would chime in, as they logged mile after mile.

Big kosher pickle and a cold draft beer,
Good God Almighty which way do I steer . . .

The patrols arose early the next morning to a bluebird sky and summited Bob's Peak, where they were surrounded by a vast expanse of wilderness—mountains, forests, and canyons in every direction, as far as the eye could see. "We were standing in one state with clear views of peaks in three other states," wrote Udall.

O'Neil recognized that the players were experiencing "a kind of trauma" typical of Outward Bound expeditions. "It happens when expectations of adventure collide with the harsh realities of the logistics of adventure." But O'Neil observed that the volleyball team didn't follow the normal pattern. "Usually, the Alpine or immersion phase of a wilderness course is a good time for issues and feelings to emerge on the trail or in discussions in camp. The players were, it is true, exhausted at the end of each day, but the instructors found their groups unnaturally reticent to talk about the problems of the day, much less issues concerning the team."[14]

O'Neil expected the grueling nature of the alpine phase to bring important team issues to the surface, but that wasn't happening. Although the team was making progress on the trail, the players were so exhausted at the end of each day they had little energy or enthusiasm to discuss team issues or even share their personal experiences with their teammates. While sitting around the fire at night the instructors would bring up events during the day that obviously caused frustration or surfaced tension in the group in an attempt to get the players to open up and address issues.

"It's over," said the players in response to the instructor's prompts. "Let's not make a big deal about it."[15]

Up to this point, the instructors had been doing all the navigating, map reading, and route finding. Along the way, the guides had attempted to teach the players how to use the compass and orient themselves on a map, but few of the players paid attention.

On this morning, to the players' surprise, the instructors handed the map and compass over to the players themselves. Now that everyone had been schooled in the basics of survival, the instructors began easing themselves out of leadership roles. For the next day, it would be up to the players and coaches to navigate their way through a section of the Abajo Mountains named the "Causeway," a high, sometimes narrow stretch of flat ground with canyons breaking off on the left and right. The plan was to follow the Causeway to their next destination, Chippean Rocks, a group of rock outcroppings nestled high on a ridge, where they would camp for a day and rock climb, but first they had to get there. It was also now up to the players to select their campsites and even do their own cooking. Like it or not, they would either have to work together or risk getting lost and going hungry.

Above the tree line, the players could rely on distinctive features and landmarks to stay on course, but once they descended into the aspen forest, their navigation skills were put to the test. Suddenly *everyone* was interested in map reading and route selection. The instructors made it even more challenging by further dividing the groups into smaller teams of two or three players. This not only gave the players more opportunity to practice their navigation skills, it also prevented anyone from opting out of the responsibility.

Peter O'Neil, left, Aldis Berzins, middle, and Doug Beal, right, huddle over a map while discussing their proposed route. The Outward Bound instructors gradually handed over responsibility for navigation and route finding to the players.
SOURCE: BRUCE MCALLISTER

Neville was paired with Paul Sunderland. As the duo made their way into the Causeway, compass and map in hand, Sunderland was grumpy. The novelty had worn off. Sunderland, like many of the players, was out of his comfort zone, and he was beyond hiding his annoyance. He was tired and tempers were short.

Neville had more outdoor experience but was not in the same physical condition as the player, and his shorter legs had trouble keeping up with Sunderland's long strides. Even Neville, the eternal optimist, was becoming frustrated. Finally, Sunderland could no longer hide his irritation and began bitching to Neville. "I have an expectant wife at home—what am I doing out here? I could be attacked by a mountain lion. You know, Neville, not only is this a waste of time but it could jeopardize my one chance at the Olympics."[16]

Listening to Sunderland, Neville could feel the fatigue and pessimism building up, and he found himself silently agreeing with Sunderland's growing anger. At one especially desolate point, the two ascended a ridge and found themselves facing two valleys: one to the left and another to the right They knew one path led to the evening destination where they would rendezvous with their teammates, but which one? As they consulted their map and contemplated their route, Sunderland kept blaming Neville for their predicament.

Finally, Sunderland had enough, deciding he was sick of the "stupid" snowshoes and began to remove them. "Don't do it, Sundy," Neville pleaded. "There is a reason why we are supposed to wear these." Sunderland didn't listen, and as soon as he took off the snowshoes he sank to midthigh, unable to move.

Frustration and fatigue boiled over for both of them. Neville had been trying for days to "sell" the players on what a great experience this could be, but he was out of patience. "Now you've done it," he yelled. "Look at you. I told you not to take off your snowshoes."[17] The two men started yelling back and forth at each other.

Despite their differences, it quickly became apparent that they needed to work together to extract Sunderland from the snow and get him back on snowshoes, but they continued to snipe at each other. Neville took out his snow shovel and began digging. While offering Sunderland his hand Neville dropped the snow shovel and it landed face up on the slope. The two men then watched as it slowly began sliding down the ridge toward the valley on the right, gaining speed as it went, accelerating past rocks and trees, then disappearing from view.

This was a real problem. The snow shovel is a crucial piece of survival equipment. After extracting Sunderland from his predicament, they consulted their topo maps at length and concluded the left valley led toward the rendezvous point. The shovel had, of course, cascaded into the valley to their right.

Neville imagined echoes of mocking laughter emanating from the shovel. He gave serious thought to simply flipping the bird in the direction of the shovel and heading down the left valley. Better judgment took over as he realized the whole group relied on that shovel. He grudgingly removed his pack, trudged down the valley, and after considerable effort found the shovel. As he slogged back up to the top of the ridge, Sunderland, now back on his snowshoes, rested, and with his pack on his back, greeted him with an amused look, and asked, "Are you finally ready to go?"[18]

Neville wasn't amused. It was close to dark when the two men staggered into camp near Chippean Rocks. The rest of their troop had already set up camp and established a campfire, forming a tight circle around the flames to stay as warm as possible.

No one looked up when the two arrived or slid to the side and welcomed them to the fire. Without saying a word, Sunderland went up to his tent and Neville to his, where their tent mates accused them of intentionally going slow so they wouldn't have to help set up the tents. Both men were too exhausted to argue.

Neville dropped his pack in his tent, returned to the campfire, found a place to warm up, and plopped down. Sunderland arrived a few minutes later, walked up behind Neville, stopped, and put his hand on Neville's shoulder. Neville tightened up, preparing for an exchange of blows.

Sunderland smiled and said, in a relaxed tone, "It was great out there today, wasn't it Nev?"

"Yes," Neville said, a little startled. Then he felt himself relax and surprised to find himself agreeing. "Yes, it was."[19]

It had been an exhausting and uncomfortable day, and although they had spent much of it blaming each other, they eventually overcame the obstacles Mother Nature threw at them, and ultimately, it was the help they provided each other that made the difference.

It was, perhaps, a small turning point for Sunderland, although to this day he remains one of the players who still views the Outward Bound experience with some skepticism. But the moment was not lost on Neville. He detected in Sunderland a subtle change, suggesting maybe, just maybe, his attitude toward the trip had shifted in a positive direction. And for Neville, it was a lesson he would never forget.

Neville and Sunderland's experience that day was not unique. Several other groups also found themselves miles off course, adding hours to an already strenuous day, the kind of experience that usually provokes discussion around the campfire. That night, the instructors invited the players to share their experiences and feelings stemming from the navigation errors and additional miles. Although Sunderland and Neville had made peace, the others didn't want to talk about it. The attitude was still, "It's over now, let's not make a big deal about it."

As elite athletes, years of training had conditioned them to push through pain and break through obstacles, not confront them by sharing words and feelings. After five days, any frustrations that the players harbored remained bottled up. Most were just pushing through, just as O'Neil had predicted, hoping to get it all over with.

The next morning the instructors gave the players and coaches a lesson on rock climbing. "It was intriguing to see how the players adapted to this sport so different than their own," wrote Udall. "Some of them were immediate experts, but it was fascinating to note others whose image of themselves as athletes didn't survive the transition from flat ground to sandstone slabs."[20] The climbing experience at Chippean Rocks was merely an introduction—getting the players accustomed to roping up and belaying. They planned on doing more once the patrols met up again at the resupply point.

Jon Roberts rock climbing at Chippean Rocks. While one player climbed, tied into a rope, another player belayed from above. The players often didn't know who was belaying them. SOURCE: BRUCE MCALLISTER

That evening, while camping below Chippean Rocks, the instructors took stock of how far the patrols still needed to travel in order to reach the resupply point in time.

"We were told we were making good time," recalled Beal. "Then we found out, to stay on schedule, we had to travel 25 miles in two days."[21]

If they were going to make it to the resupply site at Beef Basin by the end of day eight, they had to push even harder. The instructors developed a plan to make up time, and they presented it to the groups. The plan entailed a fifteen-mile hike on day seven and a ten-mile hike on day eight. To the players it sounded more like a "march" or, as Marlowe started referring to it, a "forced march."[22]

The idea of a march caught on and, with some irony, the players named it after their missing teammate. It became the "March without Karch."

"The 'March without Karch' began at dawn,'" wrote Udall. "The instructors were curious to see how the team would bear up under the stress of our 15-mile day.

"The answer was, until the very, very end, splendidly," he added.[23]

The *Clerks* got an early start that morning, putting a couple of miles between them and the *Creatures*. At one point, the *Clerks* had the courtesy of leaving their late-sleeping rivals an encouraging note. The *Creatures* came upon the note in what Beal describes as "a windswept and desolate meadow."[24] It began:

Dear Creatures,

Space Shuttle should arrive momentarily. Wait here. If, for some reason, you should not be quickly and conveniently transported to the destination of your choice, ring bell . . .

At least they still had a sense of humor. They were going to need it to survive the day.

Fifteen miles was an ambitious goal, and on snowshoes, borderline insane. The stress of the day caused the team to push through its own resistance. Going faster meant that they had to work together, which meant they had to cooperate with players from other cliques or with a player with whom they were competing for the same position. For the first time, they began to see the divisions that caused Beal and Neville to come up with this scheme in the first place.

Although the players were still not talking or sharing much around the campfire at night, the instructors noticed, during one-on-one sessions on the trail that day, players finally began slowly opening up about the pressure and stress they often felt with respect to their relative position on the team. They were beginning to admit that a pecking order had emerged, based on playing time and each individual's contribution to the team. They felt intense peer pressure and the need to compete to maintain or improve one's relative position. Some players who found themselves on the lower end of the pecking order felt disrespected, but here, in the wilderness, they were all the same.

The instructors noticed that those complaining the most about Karch and his absence were the players whose place on the team was the most secure, and their commitment to the team the least significant. "For our purposes, this was a useful controversy," wrote Udall. "Because it revealed that a player's commitment was only as marginal as he could afford it to be. In other words, those players who could afford, on the basis of their talent, to bitch and moan did. And those less talented bit their tongues."

Timmons was one of those players on the margin, still trying to break in. He hadn't traveled with the team to Argentina for the World Championships. He viewed Outward Bound as more of a test of his will. "How much more can I take?" he asked himself on the trail. "How much more can I go through?"[25]

Others weren't afraid to make their opinions known.

"There was more complaining on that trip than any other endeavor I've been involved with," recalls Marlowe.[26]

Another name that came up that day was "Hovland."

"What particularly irritates some of those who have been on the team for almost two years, is that there are others right now pulling down the big bucks, who they fear might, because they are good enough, still be on the final Olympic team, to be selected a year from now," wrote Udall.[27]

Just as O'Neil had predicted, by the seventh day in the wilderness, the real issues began to surface.

One snowshoe in front of another, humming "Cheeseburgers in Paradise," deliriously making up new verses and rhymes, the players found a rhythm. *Just keep moving. Don't stop.*

Mile after mile of meadows and aspen thicket. It was a battle against daylight to reach their destination.

Berzins, the player who stepped onto the balcony at the Holiday Inn in Grand Junction wondering how he was going to survive in the frigid air, realized that the cold was no longer a problem. "They taught us how to stay warm," recalls Berzins. "It was tough at first, but your body gets used to it."[28]

Toward the end of the day, Johnson lagged behind as usual, and Marlowe stayed with him to keep him company and make sure he kept moving. Yet this time "the others waited for them to catch up so they wouldn't get lost," said Beal. "Finally we were cooperating."[29]

"With one mile to go, and fifteen minutes until dark, the instructors announced, truthfully that, 'It's all downhill from here,'" wrote Udall. "Knowing how to ski (but not on snowshoes), the players began plunging headfirst into the bottomless powder. What's worse, they weren't wearing mittens. Soon the Lord's name, repeatedly taken in vain, ascended to the heavens.

"Folks were grumpy, bitching at one another," continued Udall. "The milk of human kindness was in short supply. Empathy was in fast retreat." Suddenly, just as the team thought they had the day won, the mountains were mounting a comeback. It was the dreaded "spiral vortex" playing out in the snow at 8,000 feet above sea level

Wrote Udall, "This is a classic pattern in a talented but not particularly close or cohesive team: when they lose the winning momentum, they rarely retrieve it. Players turn negative, railing and ragging on one another even as the next volley begins."

Physically, the players were exhausted, and mentally their emotions were raw and frayed—the very conditions the Outward Bound instructors hoped to recreate. Now the question was, how would the players react, out here in the wilderness, utterly alone and dependent on one another?

Slowly and deliberately, they went about setting up camp, doing what needed to be done. The instructors sensed the players were in a frail state and stepped in to cook dinner.

"That night, sitting around a fire, we drove the point home," wrote Udall.

"The times at which it is most difficult to win and most important to cooperate," Udall told the players, "are when you're not winning! The moments when everyone is tired, things are going badly, the match is slipping away—those are the moments our teamwork customarily collapses, and we go our selfish ways."

The memory of the Bulgarian loss at the World Championships was still fresh in everyone's mind. As they reflected on their actions and attitudes, they began to admit a harsh truth: if they wanted to become an elite team, the team culture had to change.

It was not a "snap your finger change, but the start of a change," said Beal, referring to the shift he observed in the players' attitude following the fifteen-mile day.

The next morning the march continued.

As the first light of dawn filled the campsite, the players gathered their items and broke camp. "Only twelve miles to our resupply in Beef Basin," the instructors cheerfully reminded the players, with a cup of coffee in their hand and a smile on their face.

More proficient now in map reading and route finding, the team charted a route down Ruin Canyon that led directly to an open flat area, where local ranchers put their cattle out to graze in summer, called Beef Basin.

Steve Timmons in foreground followed by Chuck Johnson and Chris Marlowe (in Dodgers hat), descending a steep slope, lightly covered in snow, during the alpine phase of the trip. Outward Bound employee Chip Mehring is in the background with skis attached to his backpack. Chip was assisting photo journalist Bruce McAllister. The players were happy to be off of their snowshoes and hiking in boots, although you can still see snowshoes strapped to their backpacks, which weighed sixty to seventy pounds.
PHOTO CREDIT: BRUCE MCALLISTER

Compared to the previous day, it was a breeze. Descending Ruin Canyon, with each step the elevation lowered and the snow dissipated until it gathered only in patches and then, in a moment of elation, the players traded their snowshoes for hiking boots.

Arriving at the resupply with daylight to spare and in high spirits, the players set up camp and relaxed.

In the previous eight days, they had traversed the Abajo Mountains, snow-shoeing and hiking over fifty miles and climbing to almost 11,000 feet.

"As a staff we were now up to speed—we understood the team and its pivotal issues in a way that we hadn't a week earlier," wrote Udall.

The alpine phase of the course had tested the team. The hardship and how the players reacted revealed the team's weaknesses while also pointing to a path forward.

"It took most of eight days before players and coaches began to share feelings with the staff," wrote O'Neil, just as he had predicted.

Now the conditions were ripe to make progress on team cohesion and trust, to forge the bonds that would make the team mentally tough.

Little did they know they were about to face the biggest test of the entire expedition.

• 11 •

Breaking Point

$\mathcal{D}$usty Dvorak wanted out.

It's not that he was having any more trouble than the others on the hike; he just still didn't see the need for it.

"We spent eight months of the year together, sleeping in airports, twelve-hour bus rides. We were in each other's faces constantly," recalled Dvorak. "We learned to get along. There are some guys you like and some you don't. Any group is like that.

"Maybe what we need is time away from each other," Dvorak had told the coaches before the course began. His position had not changed.[1]

When the four-by-four resupply truck loaded with provisions arrived at Beef Basin, it carried more than much anticipated food and rations; it also provided potential passage back to civilization, and Dvorak was set on taking advantage of it.

But first, the team was rocked by tragic news. While they had been traversing the Abajo Mountains, completely isolated from the outside world, Tony Crabb's nephew was involved in a tragic accident in Hawaii and his family needed Crabb to return. Crabb's wife, working in collaboration with Outward Bound, had tried to arrange for a helicopter to lift him out, but landing in the remote location under the threat of high winds was a safety concern.

Beal and the others understood Crabb's situation and gave permission for him to leave with the supply truck. McAllister, the photojournalist, was finished with his assignment and already scheduled to catch a ride back. Now Dvorak let the coaches know he planned to join them.

The stakes were high for Beal, for Dvorak, and even for the other players. "Dvorak had been one of those most vehemently opposed to the course from the beginning and had continually verbalized his displeasure throughout the first eight days," wrote O'Neil later.[2] And now the team's number-one setter was threatening to walk out—well, really "ride out"—one week into a three-week team-building experience, leaving his teammates either to finish the course without him or, perhaps, also choose to quit.

Beal and Neville conferred with Johnson and eventually included O'Neil and Udall in the discussions as well. *How are we going to respond?*

Dvorak's demands confirmed the fears of the team psychologists and now threatened to derail the entire experience. "Most people who go on Outward Bound want to go on it," said Marlowe, looking back at the experience. "We didn't want to be there."[3]

O'Neil wasn't surprised by Dvorak's desire to leave. "People are generally both attracted and repelled by experiences they suspect will bring about change," he wrote. "Most Outward Bound students undergo a similar struggle, between the desire to go and the desire to find an excuse not to, in the months and days preceding their course." In this instance, the trip had already started, and Dvorak wasn't the only player who, if given the opportunity, would prefer to go home.

O'Neil admitted that, once the course begins, the decision to buy into the course "takes time and patience." These were fine words for instructors and psychologists, but back at Beef Basin, as far as Dvorak was concerned, he had wasted enough time already.

Beal, Neville, and Johnson didn't have the authority to force Dvorak to stay. They simply explained to him—again—the commitment they expected from players if they wanted to be a member of the U.S. National Team. Beal had lived through the more freewheeling days for the National Team, in the early 1970s, when players came and went, their level of commitment changing from month to month or even tournament by tournament. That hadn't worked.

Beal told Dvorak, "Here's the deal. You can leave, but when you get out of here, just keep on going. Don't think you'll be coming back to this team."[4]

"I love volleyball, but I'm not married to it,"[5] Dvorak recalled thinking when Beal gave him the ultimatum, adding, "I wasn't just a volleyball player. I asked myself, 'Was this really worth it?' We were playing Russian roulette a little bit."

Never one to back down easily, Dvorak also realized, "Doug [Beal] held the golden ticket. And that golden ticket was to play in the Olympics." The coach was serious, and Dvorak had already seen what happened with Sinjin and Hovland.

He briefly thought about going back to the beach, but winning the Santa Cruz Cuervo Open for $500 and a steak dinner didn't have the same appeal as the Olympics. "I was so red, white, and blue," he said. "I wanted to represent the U.S.A."

Although he figured if he did leave there was a good chance Beal would eventually invite him back on the team–there was no other setter who could step into his shoes–he also realized, "I would have to abandon my teammates, and that would have made it very hard to come back. My relationship with the players would have been irreparable.

"Luckily, I gave in," said Dvorak. "I cared about the team. I cared about the team's success and the team's goals. I told myself, 'I have to man up and get through it,'" adding, "but I wish it could have been resolved in a different way."[6]

The team had walked up to the edge of the canyon and stared into the abyss, only to take a few steps back. Now it was time to put the episode behind them and move forward.

Dvorak's relationship with Beal was broken, and Neville was the only person who could repair it, if it wasn't already too far beyond that point. The assistant coach had the innate ability to study the motivations and idiosyncrasies of players and then find a way to relate to them at their level.

"Neville is a great guy and an exceptional human being," said Saunders. "He learned the personalities of the players. He filtered the different levers to pull for different people. He was a people person. I learned a lot from him." Over the final two weeks of Outward Bound, the team needed Neville to play that role more than ever.

The next morning the Outward Bound truck drove away bearing Crabb and McAllister while the team continued its journey. The sky cleared and the sun came out, revealing the stark beauty of the desert canyons. The high alpine traverse of the Abajo Mountains had been more strenuous and physically demanding than even O'Neil had anticipated and the group needed to rest, so they took advantage of the time to put the climbing skills the players had learned at Chippean Rocks to work.

Repelling and belaying require both coordination and trust—the players were literally putting their lives in each other's hands. Although "ropes courses" are a common practice today for corporate retreats as a method to build trust, this was way ahead of its time. The instructors covered basic climbing skills: tying knots, setting anchors, and belaying their partners using the specialized climbing equipment. Then they had the players pair up and work together.

"During the rock climbing activities one player would belay another. Because of a feeling of animosity and mistrust players avoided Dvorak's rope," recalled Neville.[7]

Someone had to step up.

"When my turn came, I volunteered and climbed, basically in Dusty's control," said Neville. He knew Dvorak, standing high on a ledge above, held the other end of the rope, but he couldn't see him. Neville tied his harness to the rope and gave the signal to Dvorak, informing him that he was starting to make his way up the route. Neville didn't have the extended reach of the players, and he struggled up the sandstone cliff.

"Halfway up Dusty peered over the edge with an evil grin and said, 'Hi Nev. How you doing?' Too focused to respond I finally clamored [up and] over the edge right in front of Dvorak," recalled Neville.

The two men were alone, standing on the ledge above the vertical face. "Thanks," said Neville as he began taking off his gear.

Dvorak gave him a serious look and asked, "Why did you volunteer to climb on my rope knowing my feelings about this trip and you?"

"Because you are a competitor and hate to lose or fail," replied Neville. "There is no way you would let anything go wrong. I believed that would override any hostile feelings you may have."[8]

"Thanks," responded Dvorak.

Another player who had a breakthrough while climbing was Craig Buck.

"Buck really struggled with pushing through physical, demanding activities," said Beal. "Weight training, testing, and that sort of thing. He wasn't the most resilient and toughest athlete. We as coaches expected more from him, and his teammates did too."[9]

Then they saw him on the rocks. "Surprisingly, Buck was one of the better climbers, even though his 6'8" frame didn't lend itself to such agility,"[10] said Beal.

High above the ground, Buck moved with grace and ease, his long limbs fearlessly reaching out to scale routes and overcome obstacles no one else could. Displaying confidence and grit beyond that of the others caused his teammates to view him in a new light.

Suddenly, "Guys wanted to climb with Buck," said Beal. "They saw him in a different way. He had this respect and status."[11]

Another player who grew in stature on the trip was second-teamer Aldis Berzins. "Aldie was good with a map and compass," recalled Saunders. "Guys wanted him on their team so they wouldn't get lost."[12]

"I always had trailblazers," recalled Berzins. "Guys like Pat Powers would be in front of me, and I would be in back telling them to move left or right."

Wilde also changed how others thought of him. When it's twenty degrees, snowing, and daylight is fading, it helps to have someone who knows how to set up camp and is willing to cook. Wilde, an "eastie" and an outsider from Iowa, was unexpectedly in demand.

Engendering respect for each other beyond the volleyball court was one way Outward Bound could help the team become closer, but in the end its value was dependent on players taking that perception back to the volleyball court.

As the resupply portion of the course came to a close, the guides gathered the players and coaches together for the next phase, the solo segment. Each member of the group would hike into Canyonlands National Park and spend two days alone, isolated from the group, and be utterly responsible for their own well-being and safety. If an individual slacked off, he, not his teammates, would pay the price. Yet the logic behind the exercise went beyond that.

The larger goal in sending each man out alone was to force him to confront himself, and through an exercise in journaling, reflect on his experience so far. Hopefully they would confront some hard truths about themselves, their role on the team, and their interaction with others.

"It tends to be one of the most powerful elements of the course," O'Neil wrote in his report. "It is a chance to rest, write, think, sleep, prioritize and contemplate, and it is a challenge because it pits one against one's thoughts until they have all run out and the students must finally learn what kind of company they make."

The physical and mental demands of the program were such that many of the players welcomed the relatively slower pace of the solo. To help each player contemplate their dedication and contribution to the team, the players were prompted with questions designed to provoke introspection:

"Athletic ability aside, what would make you a better volleyball player?"

"Winning and losing aside, why do you play the game?"

Armed with their backpack, a journal, and a pen, each man set off on his own path, to spend time alone with his thoughts. Snow fell silently as they walked into the wilderness of Canyonlands National Park. Utterly alone, they charted a solo path through some of the most stunning and otherworldly terrain in the United States, moving over the "slickrock" Cedar Mesa Sandstone formations, and gazing up at Wingate Sandstone cliffs.

"For people who generally lived in bustling Southern California with nonstop sounds of transportation, construction, conversation, music, and countless ambient distractions, the wilderness silence was deafening," recalled Neville.

As they opened their journals, each player confronted questions that, despite their importance, they had never really contemplated before, at least at their deepest level.

Why do I play volleyball?

Is it to satisfy a parent? Am I perhaps chasing someone else's dream?

Is it to gain social status on the beach?

Is it just a way to get girls or money?

Is it a way to test myself and push to become better?

Is it a way to escape from something else? An outlet for larger frustrations or perhaps a way to avoid confronting other issues in my life?

"As night came on, it was cold but no wind. Peaceful," remembers Neville. "And then wafting on the silence came the sound of the lonely strains of a harmonica. Mike Blanchard. Out there somewhere he was playing. It was perfect." In such a setting, it was almost impossible for players to avoid pondering their answers.

When they all reunited after two days on their own, the instructors debriefed the team as a group. Each person was invited to reflect on what he took away from the solo excursion.

The experience proved to be profound. Many of the players opened up and shared with teammates, for the first time, their feelings about volleyball and what it meant to them. Several players were enthusiastically positive about the solo outing, others were neutral, but no one had an overtly negative response. The guides took that as progress.

While the solo experience was about introspection, the finals section of the course would be all about the team. Players were divided into three patrols of five players, and a fourth made up of Beal, Neville, and Johnson. The player groupings were carefully selected to "deliberately pair people who had prior conflicts or showed little respect for each other on or off the court,"[13] wrote O'Neil. This meant combining starters with players from the second team, "easties" with "westies," and players who just didn't get along with one another.

For the next four days, these patrols traveled independently, without instructors, charting their own course through the wilderness toward the same end point: the Needles District. The intricate canyons made map reading difficult. With the exception of Berzins, the players were still developing their orienteering skills. "Almost all the groups suffered map reading errors," wrote Udall, leading to periods of backtracking and confusion, which was precisely the point.[14] To achieve their goal, the disparate groups would have to work together—or fail.

The guides handed out assignments for each patrol. These included carefully designed routes each group was expected to follow—itineraries intended to require cooperation and teamwork.

One of the navigation teams consisted of Dvorak, Buck, Marlowe, Blanchard, and Duwelius.

"There was friction between Dusty and Buck," recalled Marlowe. "I thought they put me in that group to be the referee. It was a particularly taxing hike. We hiked two to three miles into a gorge, and we were supposed to traverse this thin opening, across the gorge—thread the needle into this pass overlooking a 1,000-foot drop."[15]

Udall and O'Neil shadowed the group, not in constant visual contact, but close enough to see how they handled any obstacles along the way.

As the group consulted their maps, they realized that a few miles back they had taken a wrong turn. "If we go right [at the fork], we will have to traverse the gorge," recalled Marlowe. "If we go to the left, we go down a wash, on a much easier descent, but both paths ended up in the same spot."

They had gone left, which took them down the easier route, but which also avoided crossing the canyon, which was the point of the exercise. The problem was they were already halfway down the easier route when they realized their mistake.

"We had a team discussion," said Marlowe. Their choice was to backtrack several miles, uphill to the fork, and complete the route that was assigned to them, or continue down the relatively easy path they were on.

"Do you want to go back?" Marlowe asked the troop.[16]

"Fuck no, I don't want to go back," was the consensus.

Standard protocol, discussed in advance, was for the group to build a cairn to alert the guides shadowing the patrol that the group had deviated from the assigned route. The team didn't bother. They happily continued down the easy route to the rendezvous point and waited for the Outward Bound instructors.

An hour later O'Neil and Udall arrived and confronted the group. The guides knew the patrol avoided the more challenging route, and they assumed it was deliberate.

"We nominated Blanchard to tell the guides what happened," said Marlowe, because he had the most credibility with the instructors.

Blanchard explained to O'Neil and Udall exactly what happened. "We went halfway down. We realized we made a mistake. We stopped and had a team discussion. We got everyone's input. We talked through our options and decided the best course of action was to continue the path we were on," he said with a smile.

And then he added, for emphasis: "We made a team decision, just like you guys wanted us to do."

Udall and O'Neil didn't buy it. They assumed the group deliberately skirted the assignment to take the easy way down, but it was too late in the day to do anything about it, so the group set up camp.

The next morning the instructors approached the group and asked if they wanted to go back and do it right. To the instructor's dismay, the group refused. It was the players' way to rebel against the instructors and carve out a sliver of independence and autonomy, but at the end of the day, the exercise nevertheless had a positive impact. Dvorak and Buck were now getting along better, and Marlowe, who for better or worse had kept the group together, emerged as a leader even though he wasn't even on the first team. Ever so slowly, some of the cliques were starting to break down.

One of the finals patrols on Outward Bound finds shelter, and a rare moment of rest, under a sandstone alcove in Canyonlands National Park. Left to right, Jon Roberts, Steve Timmons, Paul Sunderland, Aldis Berzins in beanie hat, and Larry Benecke, resting against his backpack. PHOTO CREDIT: RANDY UDALL

Another finals patrol was made up of Dave Saunders, Rod Wilde, Pat Powers, and Marc Waldie. On the morning of their second day, they took aim at a distant ridge and decided to push over it and set up camp before nightfall. The ambitious decision made for a long day. At 3 p.m., after traveling close to fifteen miles, Powers reached his limit and physical and mental exhaustion set in. "I'm tired. I can't go any more, guys."

Waldie spoke up. As a member of the National Team since 1977, many of those years as a starter, his words carried some authority. "Come on Pat. We all agreed to get over the ridge before setting up camp."[17]

Powers was having none of it. "This is like the fifth game, and I've hit every ball. I can't play anymore. I'm done," he told his teammates.

"Well, we're going over the ridge," said Waldie. "Good luck." The group marched on, leaving him behind.

Waldie, Saunders, and Wilde proceeded down the trail without Powers and made it over the ridge late in the afternoon.

All that time, however, Waldie kept thinking about Powers and everything they had learned on Outward Bound. When they got to the campsite, Waldie spoke up again. "You guys set up camp. I'll go back and get Powers." The others in the group agreed; you don't leave a teammate behind, and success meant each of them achieving the goal.

Saunders and Wilde prepared the campsite and meal while Waldie started back down the trail. Within a few miles he encountered Powers, clearly fatigued, trudging up the trail lugging his pack and struggling, but, significantly, having made the decision to rejoin his teammates. Waldie took Powers's pack, and they traveled the remaining distance in tandem, arriving in camp just before dark. The group was together again.

Meanwhile, Beal, Neville, and Johnson formed their own coaches team. On the last day, fatigued and ready for it to be all over, they found themselves in a situation similar to what Marlowe's group had encountered.

Their route called for them to climb a slickrock trail so steep that at one place a ladder had been secured to assist hikers up and over the rocks. Carrying heavy packs, the climb over the steep sandstone was intimidating.

"We could see where we had to get to but there was an easier way to get there," said Beal. A fire road conveniently skirted the obstacle then rejoined the trail.

"What do you want to do?" asked Beal.[18]

"Let's just take the fire road back," said Johnson. "It's easier." Then, after a silence. "The players don't need to know."[19]

Beal agreed.

Neville looked at his partners, shaking his head. Beal and Johnson could see Neville was dead set against any shortcuts.

"Look," Beal explained, "we are old. We aren't players. We don't need to tell the players that we took the easier route."[20]

"We didn't come out here to take the easier route," Neville snapped. "That's not the point of this exercise."

"Nevs," Johnson pleaded, "the road goes around this rock right to the place. This is going to be the easiest route to where you want to go."

"We don't want to take the easy route," Neville shot back.[21]

Johnson threw his arms up in the air. "What am I doing here?"

"Chuck, this was basically your idea!" Neville replied.[22]

For Neville, "the conscience of the team," the disagreement cut to the heart of why they were all on Outward Bound in the first place.

"We're not going to shortchange this trip," said Neville. "How can we look the players in the eye if we don't go through with it? We're going to take the road less traveled." Then he turned and started climbing.

Beal and Johnson rolled their eyes and followed him. Then, when they got to the top, they realized that getting down was even more challenging. Johnson had to slide down the last forty feet on his pack.

"I could have been killed!" he complained wryly. "I'm going to kill you, Neville, for taking me on 'the road less traveled.'"[23]

The three men then made their way to the group campground in the Needles District to await the arrival of the other teams, tired but their consciences clear.

On January 26, the last full day of the course, the guides organized a daylong "Orienteering Marathon." The team was divided into pairs, each charged with using their newly acquired map and compass skills to navigate a tactical course and in less than three hours locate thirteen different "marks" across a fifteen-square-mile area of desert canyonland. The event was meant to be fun, but it also was an opportunity for the players to integrate all that they had learned from their experience so far into a competitive situation. Would they act as individuals and cut corners to win at all cost, or would they work together as partners and stick together?

Neville was paired with Jon Roberts. Two hours into the competition, Roberts's knee started bothering him and he decided to return to base, five miles away. Although he was within shouting distance of Neville, he neglected to let him know. When Neville couldn't find Roberts, he grew worried and spent hours in search of his partner, before finding Roberts's tracks leading back toward camp, where Neville discovered Roberts had been safely convalescing for over an hour. The instructors used Neville's predicament as an example—a little communication can go a long way to eliminate problems and undue anxiety.

Rod Wilde was paired with Larry Benecke. With two marks remaining to be found, the pair realized that if they split up—Wilde collecting one mark and Benecke the other—they could win. The problem was, by design, each group was issued only one compass and one map to foster teamwork and collaboration. As they set off separately, each toward their respective marks, Benecke had the map; Wilde didn't, and without the benefit of a map, the canyonlands can be unforgiving. Even experienced hikers often become disoriented in the maze-like formations.

Berzins, the master of maps, and Saunders were the first to return and win the Orienteering Marathon, the only group to gather all the marks and return to base camp on time. Unlike the others, they had worked together and not taken any shortcuts.

Slowly, the other groups staggered back. When Benecke wandered into camp alone, he was immediately asked, "Where's your partner?"[24] Benecke had no idea.

Hours passed and Wilde was still missing. Had he fallen and been injured, or was he hopelessly lost? The folly of going their separate ways and trying to shortcut their way to victory was obvious to everyone. Crews went out searching and were relieved to find Wilde on a dirt path headed back to camp, but more than three hours late. He explained that he had taken a wrong turn and followed a trail into a canyon where he got turned around. His feet were sore and beat up, but he was happy to be at base camp. He and Benecke endured a barrage of ribbing from their teammates, but the point had not been lost.

For their victory, Berzins and Saunders were awarded a case of beer. Rather than keep it for themselves, they promptly shared it with their teammates, scoring another small victory for team dynamics and cohesion.

That evening, they all celebrated the end of their journey together in high spirits, enjoying a dinner of steaks, salad, and potatoes. Throughout the meal and into the night, they shared a few laughs and reflected on the experience. The players were both relieved it was finally over and eager to get back to San Diego.

O'Neil and Udall led the final campfire, encouraging players to share what they learned about themselves and the team. "Much of the time we had been mediators between the team's vigorous, common, shared desire to win, and all its players' various, more selfish yearnings," Udall wrote. "We were trying to meld the two."

The ultimate message the instructors hammered home that last evening was clear: "'There will be no individual *win*' we insisted. 'You will either win as a team or not at all,'" wrote Udall.

Marlowe stood up to address the team. He was by far the most gifted storyteller, and he revisited some of the group's more memorable moments: The windswept traverse of North Creek Pass, where they broke trail for each other in waist-deep snow, Beal's tumble, Buck's surprising rock climbing prowess at the Chippean Rocks, the "March without Karch," the "Space Creatures" note, their solo experiences in Canyonlands, the five-man patrols, and the "Orienteering Marathon." In the end, he summed up the trip with an surprising admission, saying, "I didn't want to come, but now that I've been through it, I can see why we did it, and I'm glad we did it."[25]

These words, coming from Marlowe, had a big impact on the other players. Before Outward Bound, he had been one of the more vocal critics, but now, having completed the journey, it suddenly made sense, and his words helped the other players make sense of it too.

The trip became a touchstone for the group as much as any volleyball match or overseas trip. "Outward Bound was an amazing experience," said Saunders. "Something we all laughed and joked and teased about in the months and years that followed."[26]

"The really cool thing, when Marlowe would tell an Outward Bound story, Karch would be laughing," said Berzins. "Even though he never went. He laughed with us.

"It didn't end the cliques completely," continued Berzins, "but it always gave us something common to talk about. No matter where we were, the stories would come out and we would laugh about our experience together."[27]

They boarded the bus for the ride back to Grand Junction and civilization. The players, now sporting thick beards, collapsed in their seats with both a sense of relief and a feeling of accomplishment. Before Outward Bound, many of the players believed that the team would improve only if they, as individuals improved their volleyball skills, or by running drills and practicing game situations. Although they knew the team needed to be mentally stronger, they hadn't believed Outward Bound could provide the solution. Yet, somewhere in the Abajos and the Canyonlands, somewhere in the snow and the cold and the silence of the wilderness, they discovered that becoming a team required something else. Their "shared significant life experience" had transcended individual goals and caused each of them to focus on the team-oriented mission. They began to admit—grudgingly perhaps, and not everyone to the same degree—that each individual, as difficult as it was, had to put his ego aside, accept his role, and play for the good of the team. If they were going to win in 1984, they would win as a team. And even if they lost, they would also do so as a team, sharing the responsibility.

When the players returned to San Diego and daily practice at Balboa Park, Neville noticed a change.

"The guys kept showing up with their heavy beards, and they carried themselves with a certain toughness. There was a pride there in what they accomplished," said Neville.

"And many didn't shave their beards for months."[28]

The American System

$\mathcal{W}$hen the players returned to San Diego, they were interviewed by a local magazine reporter about the effect Outward Bound had on the team.

"It's not something I would choose to repeat," said Sunderland. "Hopefully it was good for the team because it sure was a pain in the ass."

"I didn't want to go," said Marlowe, "but I tried to make other players see there might be some value in it. I'm older, maybe I understand [Beal's] reasons for doing things a little better than some of the younger players."

One of the players who enjoyed it more than most was Berzins, saying that the Abajo Mountains expedition was "not enjoyable, but rewarding. I like camping. I go on my own sometimes—and I thought it might be a neat thing at first. Then when I got there—Jesus! The first eight days were like a death march. . . . But after the third or fourth day you learned how to stay warm, how to keep your boots from freezing; the simplest things were the hardest."

The writer of the article talked to all the players and summed it up this way: "In retrospect, nearly every coach and player on the team says the same thing about the wilderness outing: it was hard, it was interesting, and it is virtually impossible to evaluate its effect on the team."

"It's not like we came out of the mountains and we were different human beings," observed Sunderland. "It may have helped," he added.[1]

The team settled back into its routine of daily training, and the level of intensity and competitiveness of the practices quickly returned. As everyone got back in the gym, playing volleyball again, the coaches noticed a subtle shift. Although tension between certain players still occasionally surfaced, Beal and the coaching staff believed the sheer effort required to complete the course caused every team member to respect and acknowledge the value and contribution of their teammates. Outward Bound wasn't easy, few of the players wanted to be there, and it wasn't always fun, but every player who started the course completed it, and that demanded respect for shared perseverance.

"There was a sense of accomplishment when it was all over," said Neville. "And deep down they knew that they had helped each other along the way."[2]

Every morning before practice, Beal would address the team. He started using this forum to reinforce the idea of trust and respect. "You don't have to be best friends with everyone on the team. You have to have respect for the role and character that each player brings to the team," Beal told his players.[3]

One benefit that came from the added trust among everyone connected with the team was that it gave the coaching staff increased license to experiment. Neville's mind was always churning, and he regularly came up with new drills, strategies, or plays. He even kept a small notebook on his nightstand to capture his moments of inspiration.

At the World Championships in Argentina, the team had struggled to effectively block the physically larger and stronger Bulgarian and Soviet teams. Afterward Neville started thinking, "How do we get better at blocking?"[4] Blocking is not a skill most players are excited to practice. Just as basketball players are generally not as excited about rebounding as they are about shooting, volleyball players don't get pumped up about blocking in the same way they do about hitting. Neville wanted to create a blocking drill that would be more fun and engaging.

One night he shot up out of bed, reached for his notebook, and started writing. He couldn't wait to get to practice that next morning and implement his moment of inspiration.

"Boys, I got this idea," Neville said when everyone gathered at practice the next day. "Here's what we're going to do. The attacking team, you are no longer limited to three touches; now you have seven touches. And the defending team, you have to read the situation and prepare your blocking schemes to counter the offense. Got it?"

He had changed the rules. In competition, teams get three "touches" to get the ball over the net. For this drill, Neville gave the attacking team seven, which allowed the setter to fake, send the ball back and forth, and, in theory, cause the defending team to try to anticipate the unexpected, continually read the situation and be prepared to block. Neville hoped that if they became proficient at blocking in the seven-touch scenario, they might find the three-touch game situation easy.

It was unorthodox, no doubt, but the players trusted Neville and gave it a shot.

Neville let the two teams go at it as he observed from the sideline. The ball got passed around by the offense while the defense waited for the attack, which didn't come until the seventh touch. The offensive team enjoyed the freedom of seven touches, but it didn't teach the defensive team how to block any better. In fact, it actually gave them fewer opportunities to practice blocking and didn't really teach them anything new. Despite the extreme effort it required, the drill was a pathetic failure.

Halfway through the drill Neville walked onto the court and called it off. "Stop! Please just stop!"

"What idiot came up with this drill?" he asked.

The players laughed and shook their heads, but there was no resentment toward their coach for wasting their time, because they trusted that Neville shared the team's overall goal of improving. "Whatever Neville drew up, we were always ready to try," Karch recalled. Neville would tell the players, "If a drill or activity doesn't work with you, it probably won't work anywhere." The coaches sensed an opportunity to build on the bonds that were forged on the Outward Bound trip.

"I'm sure there were times when they hated Doug and I," said Neville. "I know they did, but they trusted us. They trusted that we had their best interest in mind, and we would try all kinds of stuff to help the team get better."[5]

One topic of debate and discussion that kept coming up among the coaching staff was the question of what kind of "system" or approach to the game the American team should adopt.

Over the past few decades, volleyball coaches all over the world had been playing "follow the leader," adopting the style of play of whichever team was successful at the time. In the 1960s, Japan had been the dominant volleyball team, deploying a strategy that was uniquely Japanese and played to the strengths of that culture. Yasutaka Matsudaira, the coach of Japan's gold-medal-winning 1972 team, designed an offense that used precise ball control and quickness to defeat teams with more height and power. The Japanese coaches made no effort to conceal their philosophy or training techniques. They even made beautifully produced films that explained their approach and strategy, which other teams studied religiously. But importing the Japanese system into America wasn't going to be easy.

"When you look at Japan, the players all do everything the same way," said Neville. "But our team, everyone had their own approach and there were different techniques."

The Japanese system was also predicated on the players' individual deference and behavior. "The players would bow to their coaches," said Neville. "Dvorak wasn't going to bow to Beal."[6] He knew it wouldn't work.

Later, when the Soviet style of play became dominant in the 1970s and early 1980s, it became popular to copy their philosophy and approach. After one series of matches between the Americans and the Soviets in the 1970s, McGown and Beal met with the Soviet coach to pick his brain.

"Yuri Chesnekov, the Soviet coach, was a father figure to us," Beal wrote in his memoir. "McGown and I went to his room after the matches, and he acted like he was teaching his son how to drive. He scattered diagrams and charts all over the room for us."

Chesnekov, in his broken English, told them they were doing it all wrong. "The guy felt sorry for us," said Beal.

As the American coaches studied the Soviets, they realized the Soviet scheme was predicated on the fact that the Russians were all big, tall, and powerful. As Beal and Neville looked around the gym, they didn't see many overpowering Russian-type athletes, and neither did they see a squad of smaller, quicker players adept at the kind of precision play favored by the Japanese. They saw gifted, nimble athletes, most of whom had fallen in love with the game on the beach without the benefit of coaching. There was no consistent approach shared by all the American players; each had developed their own unique style. The Soviet system wasn't going to work either.

The answer they were looking for came from a conversation Neville had with Japanese coach Matsudaira. Asked why he freely shared the secrets of their success, Matsudaira, like a Zen master, smiled and laughed.

"Only the Japanese can play like the Japanese," he said.

His message was clear. If you tried to copy the Japanese at their game, it would be just that—a copy. So, too, with the Russian style. Matsudaira even provided an analogy to further enlighten Neville. "He compared it to making a copy on a Xerox machine," said Neville, "where the outcome degrades with each new generation."[7]

The solution was obvious. The Americans would need to discover their own style of play, one that took advantage of the diversity of backgrounds of all members of the team, because no single style of play was common among all the American players. Every college program was different, and the players had come to the game from both YMCA gyms and the beaches of California. Somehow, they needed to develop a style that allowed the mostly Southern California players to leverage their beach volleyball roots and play to their strengths but still took advantage of the discipline of players without beach backgrounds.

That, of course, was easier said than done.

In the wake of Outward Bound, the team's newfound collective willingness to experiment was, perhaps, its greatest strength, and that created the space and freedom to let an American system evolve.

"We weren't afraid to look foolish," said Beal.

The coaches discovered they could now propose almost anything and the players would mostly give it a serious effort. In fact, the team's willingness to try new ideas, no matter how crazy, became a point of pride. The door was open to try new things, and Beal was determined to step through.

The coaches started thinking about how to improve the team's passing ability. In volleyball, receiving the serve and directing the ball toward the setter is called a "pass," and the player who receives the serve is designated the "passer." A quality pass in volleyball opens all kinds of opportunities and strategies for the offense, while a poor one leaves an offense scrambling to get the ball back over the net anyway it can.

Better passing meant better setting, and better setting led to better hitting. And if the hitting improved, the team would score more points and win more matches.

Because passing is so crucial, every team member must be at least proficient. At that time, there were typically three players in the back row responsible for receiving the serve and making the pass, but some teams would position four or even five players in the service-receive area to better cover the area.

Although all the players were expected to be capable passers, and many considered themselves to be very good passers, two guys on the team were much better than the others: Karch Kiraly and Aldis Berzins. Statistically, it wasn't even close.

One morning at practice, Tony Crabb offered a suggestion: "What if only two players were positioned to receive serves?"[8]

The notion was utterly unorthodox and counterintuitive—how could two players cover the same space better than three or more?—but the staff decided to give it a try. From now on, Berzins and Karch, by themselves, would receive serve.

Only one other team in the history of international volleyball had ever designated only two players to receive serve. And even that team, the Poles in the 1970s, had never designated the same two players on every serve. The innovation was brand new, as if a major league team had two outfielders who were so fast and covered so much ground that it allowed them to play the third outfielder in the infield.

It was Neville's job, as usual, to implement the idea. At practice he gathered the team around. "Boys, we're going to try something new." The players nodded.

"We're going to place two players in position to receive serves," said Neville. "Those two players are Karch and Berzins. Everyone else needs to get the hell out of the area and give these players space to work.

"Do you see the line over there," he said, pointing to the others and gesturing toward the sideline. "Put your foot on the line and don't move until the set. If you want to be on this team, you won't be returning serve."

Dvorak, as the setter, rarely received serve, so it wasn't a big change for him, but the middle blockers, Craig Buck, Steve Timmons, and Steve Salmons, were all used to receiving serves themselves and had a much harder time adjusting.

On the first day Neville introduced the new system, Salmons struggled to stay in his place. Every fiber of his volleyball being told him he was in the wrong place, and with each serve he inched farther into the serve-receive area until he was getting in the way.

"Salmons," Neville yelled. "We're trying something new. We're not going to have you pass anymore. We're going to have you stand out of the way."

Practice would continue, and then Salmons would slowly start creeping back. Neville finally had to tell him, "Either go stand in the corner out of the way while the passers pass, or you can come over here and sit by me on the bench."[9]

That got Salmons's attention. Finally, with Buck, Timmons, and Salmons out of the way, Karch and Berzins had room to work, and it proved successful enough that they tried it again the next day, and again the day after that. It was a novel idea, and because the team trusted the coaches, they did all they could to make it work.

Soon, Salmons, Buck, and Timmons accepted their new role. Instead of viewing the situation as taking away their opportunities to pass the ball, they recognized the freedom that came from letting go of that responsibility. Now they could focus on what they did best—and enjoyed most—hitting. And because the quality of the pass improved, the offense was able to create more deception, confusing the blockers on the other team. The whole system improved.

In the traditional serve-receive formation, with four players receiving, there are three "seams" between players, but with two players receiving serve, there is only one seam. A ball served directly at a seam posed a problem: whose ball is it? Although teams worked hard on communication, inevitably, a well-hit ball into no-man's-land would sometimes freeze the two passers and the ball would hit the ground.

For Karch and Berzins, there were benefits, too. Now the players only had one seam to think about and one other person to coordinate with. The more practice they got, the better Karch and Berzins got at figuring out who was going to do what. Based on slight differences in angles and velocity, they soon knew instinctively whose ball it was. It was a huge opportunity for Berzins, a former second-teamer who now found himself on the court almost all the time. The two-man serve receive simplified the game, and it made the decision making faster and more efficient.

It was revolutionary. The effects of the two-passer system rippled through the offense in ways no one could have predicted.

"A skill that used to take up a large segment of practice now took almost no practice time for the bulk of the players," said Beal, "freeing them up to improve on other aspects of their game."[10] The concept took specialization to another level but allowed the team to capitalize on their strengths and become even stronger. The entire team improved.

Another area the coaching staff knew they needed to improve was blocking. They expected the biggest challenge at the 1984 Olympics would come from the Soviet Union, whose blocking skills were expected to be formidable. If there was any team in the world that might be able to thwart the Americans, it was the Soviets. The coaches spent hours thinking about how to design an offense to smash through the Soviets' blocking schemes.

"How can we make them smaller?" Beal asked Neville.

Neville had an idea. The towering Soviet players were most dominant when they jumped straight up. But when they jumped to the side, or had to lean hard to cover the ball, they couldn't reach the same elevation. They were, in effect, "smaller."

"You make players smaller by creating indecision," said Neville. "The blockers don't have as much time to react."[11] So the trick was to keep the Soviet blockers guessing and moving so they could never be 100 percent certain where the hitter was coming from.

The team started experimenting with an offense Neville developed during his time coaching the Canadian National Team called the "flair" offense. The name was a little tongue-in-cheek because he spelled it "flair," as in a unique talent or ability, but the idea was that the hitter would hide behind the setter and then "flare" to one side or the other to keep the defense guessing.

Beal and Neville built off that idea, developing what they called the "swing" offense. The key was utilizing Karch and Berzins, the two designated passers, to take advantage of their athleticism and hitting skills. Karch was a great hitter, so why not incorporate him into the attack?

When hitters come from the outside, everyone in the gym knows where they are going. An outside hitter can be powerful, but not always very decep-tive. The coaches wanted to get Karch and Berzins involved in the attack, but they didn't want their opponent to know where they were always going. So the hitters, instead of going outside to positions, went inside. Once Karch or Berzins passed to Dvorak, they would start the attack by going "inside out" and "swing" one way or the other to hit.

"We wanted to take advantage of their abilities," said Beal. "And since they were starting in the middle of the court, we wanted to take advantage of going either left or right. It allowed us to use their physical attributes, quickness and good ball control, and we could set up a game plan for them to hit to the weaker blockers."

It also became known as the "side-to-side" offense. "Karch and Aldis would pass from the left side and then go and hit on the right side," said Marlowe. "No one had done that before. It was a combination of Doug and Bill recognizing the skill of some to the players. Other teams couldn't stop it."[12]

Neville soon had another idea. The coaches noticed in practice the players executed at a high level because the carefully choreographed drills meant the players knew where the ball was coming from and what to expect. Yet, in the frenetic pace of matches against international opponents, amid the noise of the crowds and the intensity and pressure of ever-changing game situations, the players would sometimes become disoriented and less sure of themselves. Everything was more challenging during a match, so Neville devised a drill to simulate the chaos and confusion that often emerged at matches. He called the drill "piles."

Neville instructed one player to lay on the court while a second player laid across and on top of the first player, and a third player laid across and on top of the first two, creating a "pile" on the court. Then the coach bounced the ball hard against the floor so that it flew into the air. In the pile, the players were looking down and had no idea where the ball was or where it was going to land. At the sound of the ball striking the court, they had to react, untangle from each other, organize themselves, and play the ball before it hit the court. The player on top had to hustle to locate the ball, make a play on it, and pass it to the setter. The other two players had to quickly determine who was in position to set and who was going to hit, and then execute their plan. It forced players to take on roles outside their traditional assignments, and to communicate and coordinate their actions while dealing with uncertainty.

Neville would even deliberately place Dvorak on top of the pile, so he couldn't be the setter. "Piles" was intense, competitive, and chaotic, just like a real game situation.

"It was a good drill," said Neville, "because the players had to get good at dealing with diversity."[13]

Neville loved it, and the players hated it, but they knew it was good preparation for the uncertainty of game situations.

The Americans weren't done innovating yet. They decided to add one more layer of deception. The offense was set in motion when either Berzins or Karch received the serve and passed the ball to Dvorak. As the ball was being passed, Dvorak would call out the play, much like a quarterback calls an audible at the line of scrimmage in football, dictating where the hitters would go. That was standard procedure for elite international teams at that time, but the American players felt confined in that system. What if, during the course of the play, a hitter recognized an opportunity on the court and wanted to change the play? Basically, the hitters wanted to call their own play too. On the beach, hitters called their own play, and that's what they had grown accustomed to doing.

Would it be possible to allow both the setter and the hitter to call the play? If the Americans could work that out, it would allow for maximum freedom and creativity on the court.

The team decided to give it a try. Once Dvorak called the play, the hitters, Buck, Sunderland, Timmons, and Salmons, would then call out what option they were going to run for that play. The option might be to angle from the outside or cross the net or even hit from the back row. Dvorak might hear "back" from one player, "hut" from another, and "red" from a third. He then had to decide, depending on who had the best matchup, who to set. For the player who received the set, his job was simple: avoid the block and try to get the kill. It was complex and required good decision making, especially at the setter position, to run smoothly.

The system played directly into Dvorak's strengths.

"Dvorak was the Babe Ruth of setters," said Beal. "And he didn't let us down."[14]

Dvorak had an intuition and feel for where to set the ball, and he was adept at lightning-fast decision making. The end result was that the opposition often had no idea which hitter was going to receive the set—it wasn't given away beforehand. That forced the blockers to spread out along the net and make late decisions on where to block, guessing where to position themselves for the ideal block. The resulting confusion on the defensive side of the court often left gaping holes for Dvorak to exploit.

The combination of the "two-passer serve receive," the "swing offense," and the hitters calling audibles constituted an entirely new style of play. What Beal, Neville, and Crabb cocreated, along with the players, was the distinctly *American* system that had previously been so elusive.

It was an exponential advance in team play. Even more, it brought the team together under the same umbrella, feeding the strategic needs of players more accustomed to a patterned system while allowing the beach-bred players the freedom and creativity they craved.

"It was developed out of trial and error; evolution; 'what-if' meetings; no judgment brainstorming," said Neville, "always based on the need to beat the best teams of the world. It was an evolutionary process."[15]

When it was done right, and the players found their "flow," their collective movement exhibited beauty and grace. It was more jazz improvisation than a symphony.

"Our guys taught us who they were," said Neville.

The "American system" provided enough structure to leverage teamwork, but also enough freedom to let the creativity that defines beach volleyball emerge on the indoor court. It allowed the players' personalities and unique skills to shine, and it was, arguably, the fastest and most innovative volleyball system in the world.

"It's a system that is enabling us to beat everybody," Sunderland said enthusiastically at the time. "It's like the Los Angeles Lakers discovering the fast break."[16]

"We had the best offense in the world," said Marlowe, looking back at the accomplishment. "And we had the players to run it."[17]

Yet only through hundreds of hours of practice and the newfound collaboration in the gym could such an offense evolve. The biggest problem going forward, apart from getting more comfortable in the new system, would be to decide which twelve players were best equipped to put it into practice. Over the next eighteen months, that would be Beal's greatest challenge.

The first big test for the team—and the new system—took place in a series of matches scheduled against Cuba in April 1983. Karch was in his last quarter at UCLA, so he stayed behind, depriving the team of a key player, a real challenge to making the new system work. Marlowe was also left behind so Wilde could get some playing time.

The matches were hugely important, not just to see if they could beat the Cubans, but because it would be the first time the coaches would be able to assess the progress of team building and trust after Outward Bound and try out the evolving "swing offense" in game competition.

It was *a lot* of change all at once. "The trip to Cuba had its ups and downs," said Beal. "We used our system well, although we were still not comfortable with it."

The coaches could see the potential for the new offense but realized the team needed more time to adjust and gain confidence in their new roles. Cuba beat the United States four out of five matches.

"Some of the teamwork ideas we were supposed to learn on Outward Bound had still not taken effect," said Beal. "And there was also some grumbling about our system. It was not traditional volleyball and some of the guys did not want to experiment with new concepts.

"It takes time to learn new systems," added Beal. "So we weren't too disappointed with the reactions."[18]

Although Dvorak set most of the matches in Cuba, Wilde had played setter in the only U.S. victory, and that got the coaches' attention. In twelve months, Beal knew he would have to make a decision between Wilde and Marlowe about who would be backup setter, and the decision wasn't getting easier.

The next big set of matches came in June against Poland, gold medalists at the World Championships of 1974 and Olympics of 1976. Now Marlowe had a chance to demonstrate his value. And Karch, only hours after finishing his last final exam, flew to Europe and joined his teammates for a warm-up match in Finland, where they easily beat the Finns in four straight matches.

When the team landed in Warsaw to play the Poles, Marlowe's luggage was missing. He had no uniform, no shoes, no anything except the clothes he was wearing. Dvorak and Wilde agreed to lend Marlowe what he needed if Beal put him in the game, and sure enough, in the third match, he was tapped to go in.

He scrambled to put on Dvorak's wrong-size shoes and Wilde's uniform and stepped onto the court. On his first play of the game, Marlowe served the ball across the net to the Poles. Lech Lasko, their best hitter on the left, took the set. Lasko spiked the ball down the line, crushing the ball off Marlowe's forehead and launching the ball forty feet in the air.

Karch immediately called out, "I got it,"[19] and set the ball to Powers, who put it away. Head ringing, Marlowe thought, "Wow, here we go!" From that point on, it was Marlowe's night. Although not as talented a setter as Dvorak, and not as physically talented as Wilde, he could still get the team to play at its peak. In games like this, Marlowe felt confident that he was going to make the team.

The United States won three of its five matches against Poland, defeating one of the best teams in the world on their home soil while gaining confidence not just in each other but in the new system.

As the team prepared for their next big tournament, the NORCECA Zone Championships, the offense began to click as players settled into their roles. However, several players from the Outward Bound trip were nervous about their chances of making the team. Steve Timmons in particular was facing an uphill battle to earn a spot on the final Olympic roster.

Crabb, in fact, wanted to cut Timmons, who was still maturing on and off the court, but Neville saw something special in him. "I don't think you want to cut this guy," he told Crabb.[20] Timmons knew he had to impress the coaches if he wanted to make the team, so even before Outward Bound he made it a rule to never complain and during the course stayed positive, even during the toughest stretches.

Instead of traveling with the team to the Zone Championships, Timmons was sent with a group of college players to the World University Games in Edmonton, Canada to give him more playing time. Neville sat him down to explain the decision, saying, "Your chance to make the Olympic team is dependent on how you behave and carry yourself as a leader at the World University Games. I'm going to call your coach every day and ask how you're doing. I'll be asking about your attitude. If you have a bad attitude, you're toast."[21] Timmons decided to accept it as a challenge rather than a demotion.

Neville followed through on the phone calls and every day received the same answer from the University Games coach: "He's fabulous. He's really showing up as a leader."

For the time being, Timmons still had a shot at making the team, but he was left off the roster again in August at the pre-Olympic tournament. Sitting in the stands watching Salmons, Duwelius, and Buck play the middle blocker position—his position—he made a promise to himself.

"I realized what a precious opportunity this was,"[22] said Timmons and he resolved to do everything he could to make the team.

Just as the team was gelling that summer and the new system was beginning to work, Hovland asked to rejoin the team. The staff was divided over the request. Neville was done with Hovland and thought it was time for the team to move on without him, but Hovland's talent left Beal torn. Even some players lobbied for his return, as did their parents.

"You can screw up and be forgiven," Berzins said at the time. "But Hov screwed up over and over again. I want to win at the Olympics . . . these last few years have been a sort of filtering system, for filtering out the best volleyball players in the country and those of us who are left, we're strong. You have to earn your spot on this team."[23]

In the end, after considering several alternatives, Beal and Hovland couldn't find a way to make it work, and Beal finally closed the door for good.

Looking back on it today, Hovland, a unique player with unique talent who went on to become one of the most dominant beach players of all time and earn admission to the USA Volleyball Hall of Fame, is circumspect about the experience. "If I would have given in a little bit and Beal would have given a little bit," he said, "it would have worked out. It is what it is." The question of Hovland highlights a deep philosophical question that every great coach faces at some point: is the best team formed with the best players, or the players who play best together as a team? Beal decided the team was stronger without Hovland, and he never looked back.

"Without Hovland on the team, that opened up the gates for Kiraly and Timmons and all these guys," said Neville. "It was Johnson and Murray, too. They would give advice. Chuck [Johnson] said, 'Somewhere along the line, you'll have to cut someone significant to seal the team you have.'"[24]

At the final tournament of 1983, the Canada Cup, the United States dominated and Karch was MVP. It was obvious to everyone in the volleyball world that the fortunes of the U.S. team were headed in the right direction. The team ended the year on a high note, winning 77 percent of their matches for the year, the best performance ever for the U.S. National Team and a drastic improvement over the Dayton years, when the team struggled to win 40 percent of the time.

Sunderland summed up the feeling among the players. "If you look at a curve for the performance of the U.S. men's volleyball team in the last few years," he said, "it's like this," holding his arm and palm nearly vertical.[25]

The trend was up, but a question remained: could they continue to improve and challenge the Soviets at the Olympics? Beal and his staff knew that the answer to that question might well lie in the makeup of the final roster.

And questions remained for Marlowe, Wilde, Timmons, and Blanchard, four players from the current fourteen-man roster who were on the bubble. Only twelve could walk into the Coliseum in Los Angeles for the opening ceremonies as members of the Olympic Team.

· *13* ·

The Straw That Stirred Our Drink

𝒯he countdown to Los Angeles had begun.

As the calendar turned to 1984, everything surrounding the National Team seemed to quicken in pace. Each match took on more meaning, and the competition for playing time intensified. Players lived in fear they would suffer an injury, preventing them from competing at the Olympics, and Beal noticed that smaller injuries suddenly seemed to "heal" much faster than normal. No one wanted to give the coaches any reason to reduce playing time or keep them off the team.

The Olympic Games were highly anticipated in Southern California. The press kept the public informed as the Los Angeles Olympic Organizing Committee prepared each venue and sport for the upcoming competition. Essentially L.A.'s "hometown" team, the U.S. men's national volleyball team had never before been so celebrated, or so scrutinized, so much so that the team psychologists worried if they might crack under pressure or if the sudden attention would go to their heads. They were rock stars, and volleyball was hot.

To prepare for the competition, the team scheduled a series of friendly matches against the Cubans in February. Timmons was fighting for a spot on the team and running out of time to demonstrate his value. On the flight to Havana, Neville sat next to Timmons.

"Red, I love you. I want you to be on this team," Neville said. "But you have to convince two other coaches: Tony Crabb and Doug Beal. If there is anything you can do to solidify your spot, you have to do it now."[1]

The Americans had asked for the matches to be played in a large arena, to better prepare both teams for the Olympic atmosphere in Los Angeles. Cuba complied, scheduling the matches for the 15,000-seat Coliseo de la Ciudad Deportiva in Havana.

During the first match, Buck was having trouble with a sore ankle and Timmons replaced him. In one play early in the match, Dvorak set the ball to Timmons from the back row, a rarity in the Americans' offense. Dvorak usually focused on setting the ball to the outside hitters. Hitting from the back row is tricky, requiring near perfect coordination and timing between the setter and hitter.

Timmons played the ball perfectly from the back row, executing a devastating kill. A short time later, Dvorak did it again, and Timmons was again perfect, catching the Cubans off guard. Dvorak and Timmons were in sync, and Dvorak, realizing Timmons was lighting it up, returned to him again and again.

Marlowe watched from the bench with amazement. He immediately recognized that Timmons had upped his game. Hitting from the back row was a game changer. The Cubans couldn't stop him. Nothing could stop him. "We have to give Red a new nickname," Marlowe implored his teammates on the bench. "We should nickname him 'God.'"[2]

That night Timmons kept his roommate, Berzins, up most of the night as he replayed the match in his head, going over again and again what transpired on the court that day and what it might mean for his chances to make the team. Timmons was so jacked up he barely slept in anticipation of playing again the next night.

The following evening, Buck started as usual, but when Timmons subbed in, he once again lit up the scoreboard, proving his performance was no fluke. Now Dvorak had another solid option. He could set a high outside ball to Powers or Sunderland, do a quick set to Buck, set Karch on the "swing" attack, or set Timmons in the back row. That was a revelation. Now every player was an offensive weapon, and the opposition had no idea what to expect. The potential of the American team appeared limitless.

"Originally, our back row offense depended upon Hovland," said Beal. "When he left, we didn't have the hitters there, until Timmons."[3]

By the fourth match in Cuba, Timmons not only became a starter, he played the entire match. And he played the entire fifth and sixth matches, too. Six months earlier, he hadn't even made the travel squad, and now Beal couldn't take him off the court.

For well over a year, the competition between Marlowe and Wilde for the backup setter position had been heating up. With Dvorak getting most of the playing time with the starters, Marlowe and Wilde, just as Timmons had, needed to take advantage of every opportunity. Whenever Beal turned down the bench and called out their name, they had to be ready to go, physically and mentally, especially if they got a chance to play with the starting group.

A glossy magazine called *Countdown to Los Angeles*, produced by USA Volleyball to build interest in and support for the team, contained a blurb about

The 1984 U.S. men's volleyball team. Back row, left to right: Doug Beal, Paul Sunderland, Steve Timmons, Mike Blanchard, Rich Duwelius, Marc Waldie, Mark Miller. Middle row, left to right: Billy Taylor (trainer), Steve Salmons, Craig Buck, Pat Powers, Dusty Dvorak, Chris Marlowe, Ron Wilde, Tony Crabb. Bottom row, left to right: Mark Herschberger (trainer), Dave Saunders, Karch Kiraly, Aldis Berzins, Bill Neville. SOURCE: DOUG BEAL ARCHIVES

each player. Wilde's profile read, "Wilde has the finest pure technique of the setters and is quicker than heat lightning. He's the best on the team at setting the bad pass and has excellent range on defense." On the other hand, Marlowe's note read, "Marlowe has the unique ability to draw the best out of everyone around him. He is a leader and a strong competitor."[4]

What was notably missing was a single word about Marlowe's skills, either his setting talent or technique. He could set, but as the magazine noted, and as the staff and even the players sensed, his most valuable role was that of a leader.

"Chris was the straw that stirred our drink," says Karch.[5]

"Chris had a way of getting the players on the court to feel something," said Timmons, "to play harder, to want to win."[6]

For the last year, the coaches knew they had a very difficult decision to make between Wilde and Marlowe. Do they go with the younger more physically talented setter in Wilde or the more experienced, charismatic leader in Marlowe?

"Chris always had the chatter on the team, retelling stories," recalled Timmons. "He was a great historian of volleyball, and everything revolved around Chris. He wasn't the best athlete; he wasn't the best setter. Rod was a better athlete and a better setter, but Chris was the 'hub' of the team."[7]

As Neville recalled, "The three coaches agreed that we could only carry two setters and we had three good ones—each with unique strengths: Dusty was the best tactician, having an instinct to know who to set and when. . . . Wilde was the best athlete: quick; gymnastic; pure setting technique . . . always eager to please. He would give you the shirt off his back.

"Marlowe was the best leader," continued Neville. "He made everyone around him better.

"As coaches we bantered around what was ultimately best for our chances in the Olympics? We created 'what-if?' scenarios. If Dusty went down and was out, who would best replace him? We debated and concluded Wilde would be the best because of his extraordinary athletic tools. We had to make decisions [based] on the worst-case scenarios."[8]

Responsibility for the decision ultimately rested on Beal.

In late March 1984 Beal designated a day for personal evaluation meetings with each player. None of them knew if this was just a routine check-in meeting so the coaches could give the players feedback or whether one or more players might be cut from the squad.

Dvorak met with the coaches first, and Marlowe was supposed to come in that afternoon, the tenth player evaluated. But around 10 a.m. Beal phoned him and said, "Come down early. I'm going to meet with you now."

Marlowe suspected something was up. "Why was I getting called out of order?" he wondered.[9] Marlowe drove to the team offices and saw Beal, a somber look on his face, standing in the parking lot to meet him. He feared the worst.

Beal greeted him at his car, something he'd never done before, and the two went to the coach's office. As Marlowe entered, he saw Neville and Crabb sitting, both bearing the same heavy look. As Beal began talking, the other two coaches looked down, their eyes fixed on the ground.

Beal had told the players he had already met with that he planned to cut Marlowe. They hadn't liked it and told Beal he was making a mistake, imploring him to change his mind. Beal had tired of hearing that over and over and, dreading the meeting with Marlowe, called him in out of order, determined to get it over with.

Beal told Marlowe he was being cut from the team. He explained what a difficult decision it was and then walked Marlowe through his thought process, explaining that he had decided to keep Wilde because he was a setter who could also come in as a back row sub, dig and pass balls, and contribute that way. Beal also explained that in the event Dvorak was injured and couldn't play in the Olympics, Wilde simply gave the team a better chance to win.

It was a challenging decision for the entire coaching staff and an emotional one for Beal, whose friendship with Marlowe went back a decade, to when they had been teammates on the National Team. It was one of the most difficult things Beal ever did as a coach. "I had a ton of respect for Chris," Beal said. "The fact that he had come back. The respect he had from the other players, and his role on the team."[10]

Although Marlowe had always known he might be cut, he had never allowed himself to admit it. Usually the most talkative guy in a room, for the first time in his life he just didn't say anything, surprised but not shocked, and just listened. He knew there was no way to talk his way back on the team. Neville and Crab kept their heads down as Beal continued to explain the decision.

As the meeting came to an end, Marlowe finally spoke up. "Gentleman," he said, "I think you're making a mistake, but I'll respect your decision. I know you're trying to do what's best for the team." The whole experience was gut-wrenching and emotionally painful for everyone involved, and now it was time for it to end. No use dragging it out. They all stood and shook hands. As Beal walked him out to the lobby, he told Marlowe, "Look, stay ready. Keep in shape. If something happens, we will need you."[11]

When Marlowe sat down in his car, alone, the full weight of the news hit him. He was devastated. His Olympic dream went all the way back to the 1975 team that failed to qualify in Rome. He had gone through a great deal since then—giving acting a try, dealing with the death of his father, and trying to make a comeback as the oldest member of the team. And now—*pfft*—it was all over.

Word traveled fast, and Wilde was ecstatic when he learned the news. His Olympic dream was finally within his grasp. He thought back to his very first volleyball tournament at age ten, when on the drive home he told his dad he would one day play on the Olympic team. Now, here he was, seventeen years of hard work later, on the cusp of realizing that dream.

Neville later debriefed Wilde and was blunt, saying, "Rod, you are the only one who is happy about this. . . . They [the team] do respect you [but] they love Marlowe.

"You were chosen because of your great athletic skills and would give us the best chance to win if Dusty faltered. So, here is the deal: Don't say a word. Don't criticize, compliment, give directions, joke. Play like you can. The boys are angry—mostly at Doug and, to maybe a lesser degree, me—but they will take it out on you, so keep your mouth shut and just play."

Many of the players were shocked and disappointed that Marlowe was cut. "The whole point of Outward Bound was to create the best team dynamic, the best trust, the best connections," said Karch. "Chris Marlowe fostered that more than anyone, hands down. That's why cutting Marlowe confused us so much, it sent the direct opposite message of all we were trying to build."[12]

"When they made the choice to cut Chris, it was a mistake," said Timmons. "It is not the best player versus best player, it was the player who can help the team. And Chris was the player who could help the team."[13]

The following Monday, instead of going to practice, Marlowe went to his part-time Olympic job at the bank to tell his coworkers that he hadn't made the team. He broke down in tears, unable to get the words out.

Marlowe packed up his belongings, said goodbye to his best friend and roommate and the couch he called home for two years. He moved back to L.A. and got a job tending bar at the Malibu Chart House.

He was still "The Big Cy," one of the living legends of beach volleyball in Southern California, two-time winner of the Manhattan Open. And now, with the Olympics around the corner, and the biggest volleyball tournament in the world coming to his hometown, he was tending bar. His friends kept calling him and stopping by. Everyone wanted to know, "What happened?"

It was too painful. He wanted to go into all the details and explanations; the Outward Bound experience and the time in Poland when he rallied the team and all the stories, but the most gregarious guy in the room was once again silenced. He simply answered, "I got cut and I'm an alternate."[14] That usually ended the conversation. People understood.

After he got over the shock of being cut, he picked up the pieces of his life. Ever the optimist, he decided to stay in shape, just in case. He continued to work out every day, running and lifting. He kept his volleyball skills sharp by playing at the beach.

A good friend from San Diego, John Schroeder, was doing TV work at the time. He reached out to Marlowe to do a segment about his time on the National Team and his experience getting cut. They took half a day to do some stand-ups and interviews.

"What are you going to do now?" Schroder asked.

"Well, go back and resume my real life," answered Marlowe.

"Are you going to continue to work out?"

"Yes, I will. I feel somehow it's all going to work out."[15]

Many of Marlowe's teammates were crushed too. "Part of our 'soul' was missing," said Karch.[16] They all felt his absence. The coaching staff anticipated a letdown after cutting Marlowe and had intentionally done so just before a series of matches with Czechoslovakia so the team would have to focus on volleyball instead of their feelings.

Czechoslovakia had not qualified for the Olympics that year, but as a big, physical team, they resembled some of the teams that had. The United States won all three matches comfortably and, as Neville hoped, the matches provided Wilde a chance to prove himself on the court and to be embraced by the team.

With the roster now down to thirteen players, Beal had one more big decision to make to trim the team down to the twelve players who would walk into the Olympic opening ceremony together on July 28. He rotated all thirteen players on the court to help with his decision and give the second team playing time and confidence.

The coaches knew that the powerful Soviet team would be favored to win the gold medal. The team, coached by Viacheslav Platonov, was the reigning world champion and Olympic champion, and nothing in their recent play indicated they were ready to give up their titles.

Beal had scheduled a series of matches in early May against the Soviets to gauge his team's progress before they began final preparations for the Olympics. In many ways, the team's performance in these matches would be a test of three years of hard work and tough decisions that started with moving the national training center from Dayton to San Diego, all the way through Outward Bound.

They warmed up with a two-match stop off in Bulgaria, winning both matches handily. Beal continued to experiment and in the second match started Timmons and Buck together for the first time, providing both size and more opportunities for Timmons to score out of the back row. At their best, Timmons and Buck proved to be slightly better than Salmons and Duwelius, the other two middle blockers. The victories provided a confidence boost and sweet revenge for the devastating loss at the World Championships in Argentina two years earlier. It was obvious the team had come a long way since then. But the real test remained ahead. The Americans had not defeated the Soviets in sixteen long years, since the 1968 Olympics, when many of the players were barely in grade school.

The team traveled to Kharkov, in what is now Ukraine, for matches on May 8, 10, 12, and 13. While physically dominant, the Russians could also be predictable, almost machinelike in their tactics and strategy. Over the previous year, Tony Crabb had traveled to Europe multiple times to watch the Russians, compiling a detailed scouting report. Beal, Neville, and Crabb had already spent years studying and learning from Platonov. Now, with Crabb's insights, they put together a game plan to exploit the weaknesses of the Russian system.

When the team walked onto the court in Kharkov on May 8, 1984, something was different. They were not intimidated. For the first time they faced the Soviets with confidence. They believed they could win and they believed in each other.

The two teams were evenly matched in terms of talent, and they battled it out for the first four games. With the match tied at two games each, there was a five-minute break before the fifth and final game. When the Russians returned to the court, Platonov and his staff flashed concerned looks and the normally fiery coaches appeared distracted.

Beal could sense right away that something was wrong. Seeing the worried looks on the faces of their coaching staff, the Russians seemed to lose fire. In the final game, the full effect of the new "American system" finally began to break the Russians down. With Karch and Berzins positioned to receive serve, and Dvorak executing the swing offense and Timmons flying toward the net from the back row, everything was falling into place for the team. The Americans won the fifth and decisive game in dominating fashion, 15–6. The win shook the foundations of the volleyball world.

"The Soviets did not lose even in friendlies," said Beal. "Platonov did not like to lose at all."[17] The Americans had studied the Soviets for years. "They had taught us so much about volleyball," said Beal. "And now we were throwing it all back at them, with some new twists."[18]

Beal and the players erupted into celebration. The victory, coming in Russia's backyard, was a huge accomplishment, validating everything the team had been working toward for the past three years.

At that moment, while celebrating on the court, Beal looked around at his players. He began to believe that his team was the best in the world, and he could see that the players were beginning to believe the same thing. "We were going nuts in the locker room," recalled Karch. "We are on our way. We are close to arriving now. We just beat the number-one team in the world on their home floor."[19] But the celebration didn't last long.

Immediately after the game, Beal was pulled aside and informed that the Soviet Union had just announced a boycott of the Los Angeles Olympics, citing "chauvinistic sentiments and an anti-Soviet hysteria being whipped up in the United States."[20] The decision had everything to do with politics and nothing to do with sports. In 1980, the United States had boycotted the Moscow Olympics due to the Soviet invasion of Afghanistan—this was simply payback.

Beal surmised that the Russian coaches had likely been informed during the break, before the last set, and it was the shocking news of the boycott that had caused the distraction. After the game, Platonov approached Beal and offered his congratulations, but his face was ashen. "We are not going to Los Angeles," he told Beal, confirming what the U.S. coach had already feared.[21]

Beal wasn't yet certain whether the boycott was just a threat or a reality. He conferred with Neville and Crabb, and together they decided not to tell the team of the Soviet boycott right away and let them enjoy the victory while they gathered more facts.

The following day, May 9, was a national holiday in Russia commemorating the end of World War II in Europe, and the Russians had planned a joint appearance for both teams at a local memorial. After practice that morning, just before they left for the memorial, Beal gathered his team and informed them of the boycott that now included several other Eastern Bloc countries and Russian allies.

"We were looking forward to a bigger showdown at the Los Angeles Olympics," said Beal. "That's what we wanted. That's what our players wanted. That's what our country wanted. We wanted to beat the best team at the best tournament. Now that was impossible."[22]

It was a major letdown. As athletes, the Americans felt terrible for their Russian counterparts. They were rivals, yes, but the U.S. players respected the Russians and knew how hard they worked for the opportunity to play in an Olympics. And they felt a sense of loss for themselves too. They desperately wanted to compete and win against the best in the world in Los Angeles. Without the Soviets and other Eastern Bloc countries competing in Los Angeles, they feared it wouldn't be the same.

Still trying to absorb the news, the team joined the Russian coaches and players at an impressive World War II memorial in Kharkiv. During the ceremony, Beal could see Platonov breaking down in tears. Beal couldn't figure out if Platonov was crying over the boycott or the memory of the war. Platonov, who had become a personal friend, later told Beal that his father had been killed in the war near this memorial.

Suddenly, volleyball didn't seem as important. Beal had great respect for Platonov and Russian volleyball. In many ways his goal over the last eight years had been to create a team as dominant as the Soviets and to establish the United States as the best team in the world. Now, standing next to Platonov and taking in the gravity of the moment, he had a sense that this journey was about something bigger than volleyball.

Ideally, sport is supposed to transcend politics. Athletes are not soldiers. The tradition and purpose of the Olympics, going all the way back to the ancient Greeks, was to bring nations and city-states together, in the spirit of peace, to participate in friendly, yet spirited, competition. Beal believed strongly that athletes should not be prevented from competing for political reasons.

But it wasn't up to Beal or Platonov. Greater forces were in motion, and the Russian and American athletes were at the mercy of global politics.

Over the following days, Beal observed the Russian team as they came to grips with the boycott. Several Russian players had originally planned on retiring after their gold medal victory in Moscow in 1980 but had rededicated themselves to the team with the singular hope of competing in Los Angeles. Now, after four additional years of hard work and training, that dream was over.

Beal realized another lesson, that "a team or individual shouldn't place all their focus on one goal. Sure, the gold medal and playing in the Olympics is important, but the goal is the process, not the end result."[23]

A few days after the boycott was announced, the Russians hosted the U.S. players and coaches for a "real American barbeque," albeit with a distinctly Russian flavor. There was lamb sautéed in vodka, caviar, fresh meat, fresh fruit, and shots of vodka all around. In between rounds of drinks, the players would all take a sauna, sweat out the vodka, then come back to the party to eat and drink more. The Russians were intense on the court, but they also knew how to throw a party. As the two teams bonded, both sides were more disappointed than ever that they would be unable to compete against each other at the Olympics.

Over the years, Beal and Neville had grown close to one of the Soviet scouts, an older man who did research for the Soviet team. Neville, always thinking of "what-if" scenarios, asked Beal, "What if the U.S. had a scout that scouted our own team? What would they tell us? What is our vulnerability?"[24] Of course, they didn't have such a scout, but now wondered, since the Olympics were off the table, might they get some information from their old friend?

Beal and Neville invited the Russian scout to their room to discuss life and volleyball. Although Neville was a teetotaler, Beal and the scout shared a few obligatory shots of vodka, and then they asked their Russian friend what he thought about the new "swing offense."

"Aw," he said with a smile. "It's a spaghetti bowl. We have *no idea* where your hitters are going."[25]

Beal and Neville smiled. If the Russian couldn't figure it out, the American system was working. Even if there had been no boycott, they now believed the U.S. was likely the better team.

In the remaining matches, the Russian intensity and competitiveness so evident in the first match never materialized. The Russian players just didn't have their heart in it, and the United States dominated. Nevertheless, it was good practice and preparation for the Olympics.

One of the highlights during the first few matches in Russia was the improved play for Wilde, not only setting but also coming in to play the back row. Wilde was in a tough situation because Marlowe was so well liked, and for some of his teammates the disappointment of losing Marlowe lingered, but just as Neville had counseled, he handled himself well and delivered exceptional performances on the court. No longer sharing time with Marlowe, Wilde got more reps with the starters and played his best volleyball, appearing to justify Beal's decision.

In the last game of the last match in Russia, the match firmly in hand, Wilde subbed in to replace Dvorak. It was mop-up time. The ball was on the

Russian side of the court. Oleksandr Sorokolet, one of Russia's top outside hitters prepared to spike.[26]

Wilde was near the net. Although he normally blocked on the right side, in this instance Wilde, who often tried to do more than he needed to on the court, moved over to be a third blocker on the left side, something the team hadn't practiced. Maybe it was his way of proving to the guys he was up to the job.

He leaped in the air, arms extended, in an attempt to block Sorokolet. As Sorokolet came down, a little out of control, his foot landed under the net across the center line, a not uncommon occurrence and still within the rules, but directly under Wilde. Wilde came down awkwardly, landing on Sorokolet's foot.

Crack!

"You could hear the bones breaking from the bench," said Neville. "It sounded like something I remember hearing in the forest when I lived in Montana. In the late winter, when the snow gets too heavy on the limbs of trees, they'll snap and it creates an echo. It's an ugly kind of sound, especially when it's a guy's leg."[27]

Wilde heard the crack and went down hard on the floor but didn't feel any pain at first. Buck hunched over him on his left side and Karch did the same on his right. Still in shock, Wilde attempted to lift his leg off the floor, but his leg below the break didn't move, flopping down on the court. Wilde had suffered a double fracture in his lower leg, breaking both the tibia and fibula, the bones between the knee and ankle.

"I looked at my leg and there was a huge gap in my sock," said Wilde.

The trainer for the U.S. ran onto the court to assess the injury.

"Rod, this is bad," the trainer said.[28]

"Yes. I know. I can see it," Wilde said, still in shock. As the severity of the injury set in, Wilde's thoughts went immediately to the impact on the team. "Thank God this wasn't Dusty," he said to Karch and the other teammates around him.[29]

Wilde was crushed inside. He feared his Olympic dream might be over.

Beal and the players felt terrible for Wilde, but suddenly they needed a backup setter for the Olympics. Everyone knew the obvious choice was halfway around the world pouring margaritas and chatting up the locals at the Malibu Chart House.

Wilde's injury wasn't exactly front-page news in the United States, and in those days it wasn't easy to send a message across the globe. A telephone call from Russia to the United States was an expensive and complicated affair involving international operators, and the coaches couldn't get a call through. Later that night, Karch tried to call Marlowe to give him a heads-up and tell him to get ready. Although Karch was the youngest player and Marlowe the oldest, they were close.

Karch wasn't able to reach Marlowe either, but he was able to reach his own family and relay the message to his father. Laszlo Kiraly immediately understood the gravity of the situation. He recognized the positive impact Marlowe had on his son, and as much as he respected Wilde's volleyball skill, he hadn't agreed with Beal's decision to let Marlowe go. Las promised his son that he would reach Marlowe and let him know what had happened.

Back in Los Angeles, the team's success in Russia was featured in the *Los Angeles Times* that week. Marlowe was happy for his teammates but couldn't help feeling a sense of loss. Just as he closed the front door on his way to work the evening shift at the Malibu Chart House, he heard his phone ring. He paused for a moment, wondering if he should go back and answer it, then turned around, went back inside, and picked up the phone.

The voice on the other end of the line spoke with a thick Hungarian accent.

"Hello Cy," Laszlo greeted him.

"Hi, Las," Marlowe answered, recognizing the voice and Hungarian accent right away.

"Have you heard zee newz?" Las asked.

"Yeah, we are beating the Russians, pretty amazing," Marlowe said, sounding deflated.

"No, not zat!" Las interrupted. "Rod Wilde just broke hiz leg. And if zat Beal doesn't fuck you over again, you'll be back on zee team!"[30]

Marlowe was stunned. "At that moment I wasn't sure what it all meant," he said. He felt terrible for Wilde, but at the same time he felt a measure of guilt that Wilde's misfortune might, for Marlowe, turn out to be a good break and open a door for him to return to the team. He also couldn't help but wonder if Wilde's injury would heal in time for the Olympics.

He got as much information as he could from Las before going to work. That night, as he tended bar, he tried to process it all.

"It was a strange feeling," said Marlowe. "I was in a daze. I probably drank more cocktails than I served that night."

The next day Marlowe answered another phone call, this one from Beal.

"I want you to come back on the team," said Beal.

Marlowe already knew his answer. "I don't want to come back unless you can guarantee me a spot on the team for the Olympics. I can't go through that again," he said.

"I can't guarantee that," said Beal. "If Rod is able to come back, you might be off the team again."

Marlowe just couldn't bring himself to agree to return on those terms. It would be too emotionally painful to be cut again, and this time around it might come just weeks or days before the Olympics. Beal and Marlowe went back and forth. Finally, Beal offered a grim prognosis: "Look," he said. "He has a broken leg and it's pretty bad. Chances are he is not coming back."[31]

Marlowe thought for a moment and agreed to return. The next day he drove down to San Diego, moved back into his buddy's house, and reclaimed his spot on the couch.

A short time later, when the team reconvened in San Diego, Beal invited the players to vote for a team captain and Marlowe was voted in unanimously. The players sent Beal a message: "You cut him, now he's our captain."[32]

In Chris Marlowe the players now had a captain to unite and inspire them.

The straw was back in the drink.

· *14* ·

Pullman

*C*hris Marlowe was humbled. Although few of the players knew it, Marlowe had been named captain of the National Team once before, in 1976, for a series of domestic matches against the Russians. Too young and immature to realize the crucial role that a leader plays in a team sport, a few days later when the team hosted a players-only dinner, he blew it off, opting to go out with his girlfriend and some friends instead. The coaches stripped him of his title.

"I decided to take the captain role seriously this time," said Marlowe.[1]

He knew, better than anyone else on the team, just how rare and special was the opportunity to play in the Olympics. Although the team had come together far better than anyone had anticipated, it was now Marlowe's responsibility to make certain that remained the case. As Wilde's injury had demonstrated, team dynamics are an ever-changing process. His job was to keep the team united and playing together as one. He would soon have an opportunity to prove he was up to the task.

Doug Beal had another big decision to make. The team still had thirteen players, and one more player had to be cut. After a four-match domestic tour against China in mid-June, Beal gathered with his staff to make the final cut.

They had known for some time that the decision would come down to keeping either Marc Waldie or Mike Blanchard. Waldie had been a leader and driving force on the team when it was based in Dayton, but with the younger players like Karch, Powers, Timmons, Salmons, and Buck coming aboard in 1981, he wasn't getting as much playing time. Waldie's value to the team diminished further with the introduction of the two-passer system, the swing offense, and the move toward specialization.

"Waldie was a good all-around player. He could set, he could pass, and he had good ball-handling skills," said Beal.[2]

"In 1983 we changed how our offense worked," said Waldie. "It used to be the more well rounded, the more valuable you were to the team.

"I didn't like the two-passer system," Waldie continued, "because it led to less playing time for me." But eventually he came to realize, although his personal role was diminished, overall play of the team improved. "It took our best skills and accentuated them and took our worst skills and 'de-accentuated' them," he said.[3]

Blanchard filled a different role on the team. His job was to come off the bench and provide a spark. Neville would tell him his job was to be a "fireman."

"You have to have someone who can go put the fire out on the other team, or put the fire into your team," said Neville.[4]

Since joining the team, Blanchard had been on every international trip, never missing a tournament, and he was the consummate team player. "He followed every rule and did everything right. But he never was a starter and never earned his way onto the court," said Neville. Still, there was a role for Blanchard to serve as "the fireman," but only if the coaches trusted Blanchard would get the fire started.

That became the deciding factor. "Blanchard could go into a game, but he would wait to see how the team was playing to see how he would play," said Neville. "He'd play the way the team did, and that wasn't quite the role he should have been for us." In June, after a series of domestic matches against Argentina and China, Beal made the final cut, deciding to keep Waldie over Blanchard.

"I couldn't make a decision on whether or not I 'liked' a player," recalled Beal. "And I liked Blanchard a lot." Everyone did. So did Neville and his teammates. No one wanted to see him go, but Beal had to pare the roster to twelve athletes.

"The day he was cut was emotional and short," said Beal. When he told him, Beal got the words out quickly, and his voice broke. For Beal, personally, this was the hardest cut to make, even more difficult than cutting Marlowe.

"He [Blanchard] was such a great guy," said Beal. "And he was there for every day of training and every trip."[5]

"He felt betrayed," said Neville.[6]

Marlowe, more than any other player, knew what Blanchard was going through. He felt for him, but he also understood it was his job as captain to heal the emotional wounds and help the twelve remaining players come together as a team.

Beal kept a journal with notes for every match. On June 22, 1984, he wrote down in his notebook, in large red letters, "Olympic Roster," and underneath he scratched down twelve names and their jersey numbers:

1—Dvorak
2—Saunders
3—Salmons
4—Sunderland
5—Duwelius
6—Timmons
7—Buck
8—Waldie
10—Marlowe
12—Berzins
13—Powers
15—Kiraly

"For the next month, things settled in" recalled Marlowe. "The first team was set. The second team was too. We practiced, we practiced, we practiced."[7]

The coaches and team psychologist had one final worry before the Games began: pressure. Each day the expectations for the team grew, the stress from their families, the press, and the public increased. On the national stage, no one had ever given volleyball a second thought, but now the players were giving television and magazine interviews and being mobbed for autographs.

A few years before, just making the Olympics would have been a celebrated accomplishment. Now, with the Soviets out of the way, the United States wasn't just expected to medal but to win the gold, quite a change for a team that had never won a major international tournament.

"At that time, we felt a responsibility to volleyball," recalled Timmons. "We had to do well in the 1984 Olympics for the sport to grow. If we didn't win and justify what we were doing, it might just go away. The future of volleyball in the U.S. was at stake, and the players wouldn't have a future in volleyball."[8]

"There was a lot of pressure on the team," recalled Beal. U.S. men's volleyball hadn't been to an Olympics since 1968. There were no Olympic veterans on the team. "Every player on the team would be participating in their first Olympics, and it was my first Olympics too. We didn't really know what to expect," he said. And they would be playing in their home country.

"Playing at home can be a big advantage, but it also comes with a certain pressure," said Beal, "playing in front of family and friends."

"The team played better out of the country," added Beal, because there were fewer distractions.[9] That was a huge concern for the coaches and the team psychologists.

"The goal was for the team to peak at the Olympics," said team psychologist Don Murray, "which meant the team had to play its best volleyball in Los Angeles despite all the distractions and pressure from friends and family. We spent a lot of our time, during the run-up to the Olympics, helping players cope with the pressure and manage the stress."[10]

To counteract the pressure, Murray and Chuck Johnson wanted to make the players as comfortable as possible during the Olympic experience. To help them prepare, and to avoid major surprises, the coaching staff, along with the team psychologists, prepared a detailed Olympic "dress rehearsal." A few years before, at the 1982 World Championships in Argentina, there had been nothing but surprises. The bus trips took longer than expected, their hotel rooms weren't ready, meals were delayed, and the trainers even forgot to bring doxycycline to treat common stomach ailments, which often crop up at these events.

This time around the coaches left nothing to chance. Pulling a page from live theater, in advance of the Games they replicated the Olympic schedule, so the players could experience in advance every detail of their Olympic routine.

The coaching staff wanted this dress rehearsal to happen somewhere outside of Los Angeles, away from the daily distractions of the city and all the pre-Olympic hype. Jim Coleman, the former National Team coach, was now coaching the women's volleyball team at Washington State University in Pullman, making it an ideal setting for the Olympic dress rehearsal. Coleman helped the team arrange for housing, practice facilities, and access to an arena at the university.

In July 1984, just weeks before the Olympics, the team traveled from Los Angeles to Pullman and moved into a dormitory. The team's Olympic schedule was replicated, minute by minute, for two weeks. Each day, the players would rise at the exact time they would rise during the Olympics and experience the same daily Olympic routine. *Everything* on the schedule was replicated, including meals, travel time on buses, pregame routines, matches, practices, and off days. If two players were scheduled to be roommates during the Olympics, the same two players roomed together in Pullman.

"They wanted to take us out of town, to focus, get cohesion," said Marlowe. "And they had this great idea to go to Pullman, Washington, for a week or two to practice up there.

"It turned out to be kind of wild," Marlowe added.[11]

Like many of Beal's decisions, the players didn't like it. They understood that preparation was key to achieving their potential, yet the international travel schedule that year had been grueling, and the players were looking forward to relaxing in Los Angeles for the last few weeks before the Olympics.

"The coaches were trying to reduce stress and increase acclimation," said Karch, "It was well meaning but it increased stress because it took us away from our family and friends. And we were focused entirely on volleyball. You can't think about volleyball all the time. You need a break.

"I went stir-crazy," added Karch, and he wasn't alone.[12]

In Pullman, with their schedule scripted and controlled, there was no built-in vehicle for stress relief. At least during Outward Bound they'd ended each day physically exhausted. As important as volleyball was to each of them, they all found it difficult to focus on volleyball all day every day, with no release valve.

About the only distraction they had were public scrimmages, generally the starters versus the second team, matches designed to replicate the Olympic schedule. Intrasquad scrimmages were nothing new to the U.S. team—they had already played and practiced against each other for thousands of hours, and the first few scrimmages in Pullman were routine.

"If a team got up 2–0, we would say, put us out of our misery," said Karch, "so we can just take a shower and go read a book and stop thinking about volleyball."

One scrimmage in particular was billed as "Youth Night," and kids from Pullman and the surrounding area were invited to attend. Whether by chance or design, the team was divided that night along the latent fault lines that had more or less been invisible since Outward Bound.

One team had the three former stars from USC, Dvorak, Powers, and Timmons. They were joined by the three former Ohio State players: Berzins, Duwelius, and Waldie. On the other team were the three former UCLA stars, Karch, Salmons, and Saunders, joined by Buck and the two veterans, Marlowe and Sunderland. Crabb coached one team, while Neville coached the other, allowing Beal to observe and take notes.

The former USC/OSU team won the first two games and held a commanding 10–6 lead in the third. It appeared as if Karch and his team would soon be showering and then nodding off while reading in bed.

That's when it started, innocently enough, with Marlowe being Marlowe. He couldn't accept that his team would lose quietly, so he started doing what he did best.

"This was classic Marlowe," said Neville, who was coaching Marlowe's team that night. "Using his stage voice, he began exhorting his team: being animated, cajoling, overcelebrating when the other team made an error. And when his team executed a winning play, he was energized, running around, slapping hands, loudly claiming they were going to attack the net, and score."[13]

In a routine play, Marlowe set Karch high above the net, but when Karch went up to hit the ball he was stuffed by Powers.

By this point, Powers had tired of Marlowe's antics.

"Pat went into this excessive celebration," recalled Karch. "Yelling, he snapped a little. It wasn't directed at me, but it came out at me."[14]

Powers's primal scream followed by yelling and over-the-top high-fives triggered something in Karch.

"Inside, I reached a boiling point," said Karch. He wasn't going to take it another minute. The team huddled between points, and Karch called for a blocking pattern that would allow him to go up and block against Powers. Sure enough, the next play fell into the precise pattern Karch was hoping for. Karch went up and stuffed Powers.

"Now I went into an excessive end zone celebration," recalled Karch.

"What goes around comes around and now it's coming around," said Karch, loud enough for the other team to hear.[15]

"That just sort of set things off," recalled Marlowe.

"Now things are testy and we don't want to be put out of our misery," recalled Karch. "Now it is on."[16]

The level of intensity and emotion of both teams went through the roof.

"We are bickering back and forth and things are being said under the net," said Karch.

Trash talking in volleyball is as old as the game itself, but for intrasquad scrimmages there had always been a line. After all, at the end of the day everyone is on the same team, playing for the same goals. But on this night they let loose with the kind of no-holds-barred verbal fire power generally reserved for the likes of Cuba and the Soviet Union.

After Marlowe directed another comment at Timmons, Dvorak snapped, jumping in to defend his teammate. "Fuck you, Marlowe," he said. "You shouldn't even be here. You weren't even picked for this team."[17] The comment touched a nerve with Marlowe and he turned back to the net and fired back at Dusty, loud enough for the whole arena to hear, "Fuck off!"

"This was Marlowe's wheelhouse," recalled Neville. "Nobody could match Marlowe's mouth."[18]

"Taunting Chris was a bad idea," said Beal. "He was humorous and the expression on his face and body language. Don't inflame someone that is going to make your opponent play better."[19]

The Youth Night crowd was alternately thrilled and mortified. They were witnessing high-level volleyball, but hadn't expected to have to cover the ears of their children. The language was becoming embarrassing for the coaches.

"If the arena was full, the spectators would not have heard anything on the court," said Beal, "but there were only a thousand or so, so you could hear everything."

Gary Colberg, the referee, tried to calm the players down, but the players turned on him too.

"We took our frustrations out on him," recalled Karch. "[Later] we all signed a ball for Colberg, filling it with apologies."[20]

At one point, Timmons ran under the net and got in Marlowe's face. The two were almost nose to nose at this point. Karch, sensing that things were spiraling out of control, jumped in and tried to diffuse the situation. Timmons and Karch were best friends, as tight as two players could be. They roomed together on the road and shared an apartment in San Diego.

Karch appealed for everyone to take it down a notch. "Let's tamp this down," he said, then reached his hand out in a gesture of peace, saying, "Let's shake on it. We're all teammates here."[21] He thought for sure Timmons would help him diffuse the situation by embracing the handshake. Instead, Timmons rolled his hand over and raised his middle finger at Karch.

Karch was stunned. "Okay," he said, as he went back under the net to his team, all the time thinking, "Oh yeah, fuck you, too. It's on.

"We played the most intense match of our lives," said Karch. Pride was on the line now, and neither team was going to back down. The scrimmage became an all-out dogfight, this match suddenly meaning far more than anyone could have foreseen. Meanwhile, the crowd of mostly kids and families got an education in elite-level volleyball trash talking, complete with loud claps, intimidation stares, and finger-pointing.

The coaches prayed the two teams wouldn't come to blows. Between games and during time-outs, Crabb and Neville tried to diffuse the situation and bring the emotional intensity down.

"I always said, 'Celebrate with your back to the net,'" said Beal. "Don't put it in their face. It will only antagonize your opponent."[22] But the players were having none of it. Not even Marlowe wanted to make peace.

"It got out of control," said Beal. "It started to get personal. It was clear everyone was 'edgy.'"

Beal even considered stopping the match. "As coaches, you have to decide, how much will I allow this to go on? Will it spill over? Will players remember it? Will it create animosity and friction?" But he reluctantly decided, as painful as this match was to watch, it was better to let the players resolve it on the court.

Karch's team battled back and won the next two games. The match came down to the fifth game. On the next-to-last play, Dusty tried to dump a ball but Salmons blocked him. Then Marlowe blurted out, loud enough for both teams to hear, "That's the best fucking block of our lives!"[23] Dusty, Timmons, Powers, and their teammates were steaming.

Now it was match point. On the next play, Karch and Marlowe's team won. Game over. The teams went to shake hands.

"The teams always shook hands," Karch said, "but not this time. After the game, the other team just walked off. They didn't even shake hands."[24]

"What just happened?" thought Beal. It was only two weeks before the Olympics and he felt as if he had witnessed an earthquake rip his team apart. His mind began racing: "What does this mean? How can we recover?"[25]

Neville, however, had the opposite reaction.

"Yes, now we're ready for the Olympics! This is what I've been waiting for. Now we're ready."[26] He witnessed a team that was so competitive and so intense, they weren't going to back down from anyone—even each other. They were all in and prepared to go all out to win and leave nothing on the court but their own sweat.

"I don't know if that made us better," said Marlowe, "but it revealed the character of the team: we were competitive. We had a tremendous team spirit."[27] And Marlowe was as determined as ever to channel that competitive drive toward winning a gold medal.

"With emotions running high and Chris's team winning," recalls Neville, "he [Marlowe] immediately called for an all-team meeting—without coaches—to get everybody back on the same page again. That is leadership and what his teammates relied on."[28]

Later, when Marlowe had time to reflect on what had happened, and how he might turn the scrimmage into a positive, he remembered something Beal told the team.

"In 1982 Beal said, 'We can win a medal.' I was not so sure. We were thirteenth at the World Championships, but Beal said, 'If we can get to where I know we can be, the competitive spirit of USA will take over.' And it did. He was right."[29]

The following day was a much-needed off day. Beal and Neville huddled with Murray and Johnson. *What to do? Should we have a team meeting? Should we talk about this?*

Ultimately, the coaches and team psychologists determined what the players needed most was a day away from each other and away from volleyball. They gave the players more freedom than usual that next day, encouraging them to spend time with family, relax, or just hang out.

When the team came back together the following day, the page had turned. No one mentioned the scrimmage. The team simply put the incident behind them.

"It took some time to heal," said Karch, "but we didn't break apart. We got past it."[30]

Whatever had transpired on that court in Pullman or in the players-only meeting, the lasting takeaway they all had was if they took that kind of intensity and competitiveness and unleashed it on the court at the Olympics, they would be unstoppable.

Over the past three years, Murray and Johnson had periodically asked the players to complete a survey to help them assess the culture of the team. The idea was to identify trends over time and then use the data to help them design specific team-building interventions and exercises. So far, the trends were pointing in the right direction. The data showed that the team's culture had improved each year, and Murray and Johnson were eager to get one more assessment before the Olympics, particularly after the scrimmage. They handed out the assessment to the players in the evening and told them they'd all meet again to collect them in the morning.

Chris Marlowe spoke up. "Don't bother," he said. "I'll *personally* go around and collect the surveys for you."[31]

The next morning the psychologists asked Marlowe for the surveys. He looked up at them with a playful grin on his face. "Sorry, guys. I can't find them anywhere. I must have mistakenly thrown them out."

Marlowe knew when to protect the team, and he figured they were done with the coaches and team psychologists and all the poking and prodding. No more blood draws, no more grueling practices, no more trash-talking scrimmages, no more hikes in the wilderness, no more isolation training, and no more psychological tests.

It was time to play volleyball. The players were ready to step out on the world's biggest stage and find out just how good they were.

The remaining matches in Pullman were completed without incident. Just as Neville had predicted, the team had passed its own test. It was now worthy to go up against the best. On July 22, just six days before the opening ceremony, the team boarded a flight back to Los Angeles.

It was time.

• 15 •

Olympics

July 22, 1984: In 1974 I vowed I would play on three USA Olympic teams: 1976, 1980 and 1984. In '76 I did make the team, but we weren't quite good enough to qualify for Montreal. Down to two Olympics!

Four years later in 1980, President Carter announced the USA would boycott the Olympics in Moscow. And again, our team wasn't quite good enough to qualify for the Olympics. Down to one Olympics!

In 1982 I returned to the team with the hope of making it in 1984. One last chance. In March of '84, after playing with the USA Team for two more years, I was cut. Down to zero Olympics.

I was crushed. What had happened? I didn't know. For two months I tried to reshape my life without the Olympics. Then it happened. I heard the news that Rod Wilde had broken his leg. Call it fate, karma, bad luck for him, good for me, whatever, I was back in the Olympics.

My final conclusion? It takes four factors to reach the Olympics; 1) You need to be good enough to make the team, 2) Your team has to be good enough to qualify for the Games, 3) You have to be lucky with injuries, 4) You have to be lucky your country isn't boycotting that year.

In 1984 I was dealt four aces![1]

$\mathcal{C}$hris Marlowe's diary entry was written on the day the team flew directly from Pullman to Los Angeles for the Olympics, scheduled to begin on July 28. Upon landing, the team went straight to the airport Marriott to get ready for the big event the following morning—the long-awaited handing out of Olympic uniforms and apparel.

"Sometimes I think the athletes live for this day more than any other," said Beal.[2] Levi Straus was outfitting American athletes in 1984, and they lavished the athletes with gear, everything from a special outfit for marching in

175

the opening ceremony to sweats intended to be worn on the medal stand—if they medaled. For the first time, the players would get to see themselves wearing gear that identified them as Olympians, just like the heroes they'd grown up watching on TV.

The U.S. men's volleyball team received their gear alongside the more well-known and widely celebrated U.S. men's basketball team. Although both teams at the time consisted of "amateur" athletes, the chasm between the two groups couldn't have been wider. On one side were soon-to-be-millionaires Michael Jordan and Patrick Ewing, already household names, and Indiana coaching legend Bobby Knight. On the other side were athletes still holding part-time jobs to try and make ends meet.

The distribution of uniforms and gear only served to increase the contrast.

As the volleyball players responded to their free Levi's and sweats with high fives and whoops of celebration, the basketball team was distinctly less enthusiastic. At one point, Marlowe looked over to see Bobby Knight trying on a pair of skin-tight, leotard-like sweatpants. Knight laughed at how ridiculous he looked, and promptly discarded the clothing like day-old fish.

The scene underscored what is today an often overlooked aspect of the Olympic Games, that it is both a competition and an experience, one that, at its core, is about (or at least is intended to be about) bringing people together from all over the world as one team, Olympians. Of course, as athletes, each team and individual also wants to win for each other and their country. The challenge for the U.S. volleyball team would be to find a way to enjoy the experience of being at the Olympics, to have fun, and at the same time complete the mission they had spent the past several years working toward.

At its best, the Olympic experience itself should inspire the best performance, and to that end the coaching staff obsessed over every detail. Housing was one of the most important. While many teams elected to stay at the Olympic Village throughout the Games, Beal and company chose a hybrid approach. On most days the team would stay at the Olympic Village, located on the University of Southern California (USC) campus, where they could mingle with athletes from other nations. The Olympic Village is an integral part of the experience, but one that can also provide a great many distractions; imagine the world's largest college dormitory the first week or two of freshman semester.

However, on game nights, they wanted to keep distractions to a minimum and ensure the team would play its best. With the help of corporate sponsors and actor and team supporter Tom Selleck, they stayed at the Breakers Hotel in Long Beach, just a few minutes from the competition site.

The Olympic volleyball matches would take place at the Long Beach Arena, a forty-five-minute drive from the village at USC. The coaches were worried about the unpredictability of L.A. traffic, and by staying close to the arena after game nights the players could also spend more time after each match with the large contingent of family and friends who lived in the L.A. area.

On July 23, the team checked into the Olympic Village, but everything took longer than expected, and Beal reluctantly canceled practice for that day. The team had now gone two straight days without practice or training, and Beal was antsy and concerned.

The players, on the other hand, were more than eager to explore the Olympic Village.

"I've never seen the guys on the team so euphoric," wrote Marlowe in his diary. "Everybody was juking, slapping five and really taking it all in." "We are in the Olympics!" they kept saying to each other in amazement.

The players soaked in the whole experience, sampling the free food, free video games, free movies, and free live music. Even the haircuts were free. The opportunity was too tempting to pass up, and one after the other each got their hair styled. Steve Timmons, known as Red due to his rusty-colored hair, went in with the feathered-back California beach look that most of the players sported . . . and came out with a crew cut. The bold move quickly became the talk of the team, giving Timmons a sharper, more edgy look. Beal told him he looked "punk."

The change in appearance seemed to spark something in Timmons, who would soon start playing with more energy and zeal. Marlowe called Timmons a "reverse Samson," gaining more confidence with less hair, not more.

Of particular interest to Marlowe, still single at the time, was the Olympic Village outdoor disco, Colours. He recruited Pat Powers, Steve Salmons, and Craig Buck to accompany him to the dance floor that first evening, where they mingled with athletes from all over the world.

Security was intense throughout the Games, especially in and around the Olympic Village. Sharpshooters stationed on the rooftops served as a grim reminder of the terrorist attack against the Israeli athletes at the 1972 Games in Munich. For security reasons, the athletes were told when they left the village to avoid wearing anything that would identify them as U.S. Olympians.

Fat chance. Although some players obeyed the warning, Marlowe, Salmons, and Timmons took it as a challenge. They promptly left the village proudly dressed head to toe in their Olympic sweats, brandishing their IDs and enjoying every second of the attention they attracted on the street.

While the players were having fun, Beal was increasingly stressed about the disruptions and the time away from volleyball. On July 24 the team finally got back on the court at the Long Beach Arena for their first practice since Pullman.

When they walked into the arena, they were blown away. They had played in Long Beach Arena before, and they knew it as drab and cavernous, but the

Olympic Organizing Committee had utterly transformed the site, draping it in vibrant banners and other colorful decorative features that made them feel special.

Beal got there early to savor the moment and become familiar with the redecorated venue.

"I must have walked around and sat in one hundred different seats," said Beal. "I walked into all the locker rooms, medical rooms and offices. I wanted to see everything."[3] Just like the players, he wanted to see and experience as much of the Olympics as possible.

Then practice started. Beal was rarely happy with practices, but this one was particularly horrible. Players were tight, pushing too hard, trying not to make mistakes, and as a result making more than usual.

"The two days off showed," wrote Marlowe in his diary that day.

Although the team had reached incredible heights in 1984, culminating in their victory over the Soviets, there was one fact that could not be ignored; the United States had never won a major international competition.

Never!

Despite having invented the game, and given all the talented players to wear a U.S. jersey through the years, the Americans had yet to field a men's volleyball team that medaled at a major international tournament. Any medal, not to mention a gold medal, was far from a certainty.

On July 28, the opening ceremonies were held at the Los Angeles Coliseum. The team gathered with other athletes in the nearby Los Angeles Sports Arena for three hours, waiting for their time to enter the stadium. The experience was worth the wait. For many of the players, it was the most thrilling moment of their lives.

A global television audience of 2.5 billion watched as athletes from 140 nations paraded through the Olympic stadium, pulsating with music and dancing, a celebration on a grand scale. The opening ceremony set the tone for the Olympics. It was now evident to the players: this was going to be the biggest competition of their lives on the biggest stage in the world.

As the American Olympic delegation entered the stadium, the 92,000 spectators became even louder, erupting and roaring for the American athletes. As the crowd sang along to the Diana Ross hit "Reach Out and Touch (Somebody's Hand)," the athletes started holding hands, and then everyone in the stadium joined in. Marlowe found himself holding hands on one side with Paula Weishoff, a star on the women's national volleyball team, and a boxer from Tanzania on the other. The camaraderie between all the athletes was evident. Everyone was laughing, smiling, singing, and dancing.

Duwelius turned to Marlowe and said, "Cy, this happens once in a lifetime."[4]

Linked hand in hand with the athletes around them, they looked over and saw something they had never thought possible. Doug Beal cracked a smile. "I swear to God!" vouched Marlowe in his diary. The coaches were as overwhelmed by the experience as the players. Beal's girlfriend, Nonie McKinnon, who later became his wife, ran down on the field and took a picture of Beal and Neville with their arms around each other, each sporting a wide grin.

Former American Olympian Rafer Johnson, gold medal winner in the decathlon at the 1960 Olympics in Rome, lit the torch, the first person of African descent to light the Olympic torch at an opening ceremony. It felt like a huge symbolic step forward for the world and was one of the highlights of the Games.

Aldis Berzins recognized his parents in the stands and ran over to embrace them. The other players were soon looking around for their parents too. Marlowe recognized his mom and ran over to her and gave her a hug.

Then the Games began. The very next night, on July 29, the team faced off against Argentina in their first match. As the host nation, the United States

Bill Neville (left) and Doug Beal (right) at the opening ceremonies of the 1984 Los Angeles Olympics. This photo was taken by Nonie McKinnon, Beal's future wife.
PHOTO CREDIT: NONIE MCKINNON

selected their opening opponent. In 1984 a total of ten national volleyball teams qualified for the Olympic tournament, divided into two "pools" of five teams each. After the round-robin pool tournament, the top two teams from each pool would then advance to the medal round. Originally, the U.S. pool was to consist of Brazil, Poland, Bulgaria, and Argentina, but after Poland and Bulgaria joined the boycott, they were replaced with South Korea and Tunisia.

The players and coaches considered Brazil the most formidable team in the pool, followed closely by Argentina and Korea. The United States could have chosen to play Brazil in their first match, but Beal decided to open the tournament against Argentina because he knew they tended to get better as they advanced in a tournament. He wanted to play them early and hopefully get them out of the way.

As the host nation, the United States also had the option of picking when it played its matches and, afraid of coming out flat, avoided playing in the morning. Besides, ABC, the Olympic broadcast network, informed USA Volleyball that the team would have a much better chance of television coverage if they played later in the day. Beal understood that prime-time Olympic coverage could be a game changer for USA Volleyball, the players, and the sport itself. Whenever possible, Beal chose to play in the 8:30 p.m. time slot. That decision would pay dividends.

> July 29—Opening Match. I've played volleyball for 20 years of my life, six on the USA team. I've played in every kind of volleyball competition, been everywhere and done everything volleyball has to offer. But tonight is the night I've waited for my entire athletic life.

As captain, Marlowe led the team out of the tunnel. As soon as the fans caught site of the team, they cheered wildly and waved flags. The team broke into a run as they approached the court, and the crowd went nuts. The squad had never before experienced such an entrance. The match against Argentina before a crowd of 13,000 was the largest to ever see a volleyball game on American soil.

The starting lineup was beginning to solidify, but Beal liked to keep his options open. For this game, he started Karch and Berzins at outside hitter, working the two-man pass-receive strategy that was key to the system. Buck and Timmons started at middle blocker, and Powers lined up opposite the setter, Dvorak.

Soon after Beal turned in his starting lineup to the officials, he realized he mistakenly had placed Duwelius in the starting lineup instead of Timmons. Because each team is only allowed six substitutions for each game, he would have to pay a price to correct it.

"We had to use a substitution to make a substitution before the game to get the right team on the floor," said Beal. "The first lineup I ever turned in at an Olympics, and I screwed it up."[5]

There were a lot of nerves on and off the court.

Then, the first match of the Olympics began, and during the first few volleys, players were feeling the pressure and excitement of the moment.

"In the first set we had to sub out Timmons because he was hyperventilating," recalled Beal.[6] Back on the bench, Timmons breathed into a paper bag to calm himself down.

Beal made sure to use the entire roster against Argentina. He wanted everyone to get some Olympic experience, and if that cost the team a set, he was fine with that. He knew it would be a challenging tournament, and he wanted to get everyone involved early. Also, to receive a medal, players would need at least some time on the court, and he wanted to ensure the entire team would be on the medal stand if they were able to get that far.

"We talked a lot about starters and finishers," recalled Beal. "We considered it a plus we didn't have a stark division between starters and finishers. It was more fluid. . . . We thought it was important to keep guys excited about their role on the team, even at the Olympic Games."

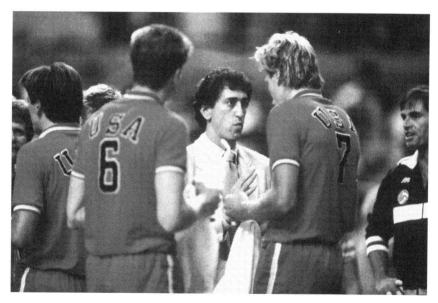

Head coach Doug Beal talking with Steve Timmons, left, and Craig Buck, right, during a break in the action at the 1984 Olympic Games in Los Angeles.
© PHOTO BY BRUCE HAZELTON

The United States won in four games. Dusty Dvorak, on what was also his twenty-sixth birthday, got his birthday wish.

In a stroke of luck, ABC broadcast the game live to a huge national audience. Gymnastics was scheduled to be televised in prime time, but the competition was running late so ABC switched to volleyball. Kirk Kilgour, the former National Team player whose injury while playing in Italy in 1976 left him a quadriplegic, had turned to broadcasting and served as the color commentator for the broadcast. His deep knowledge of volleyball helped the American audience understand the intricacies of the game and contributed to the surprise popularity of both the men's and women's teams at the Los Angeles Olympics.

For many Americans, it was the first time they had ever seen volleyball played at the highest level, and they liked what they saw. This group of young, tall, handsome, fit young men not only dominated on the court but seemed to have a lot of fun doing it. Their athleticism stunned most first-time viewers, amazed by their vertical leaps, quickness, and coordinated play. This wasn't anything like the game they knew from the backyard and junior high gym class.

"U.S. volleyball, as it kept winning, became the feature of ABC's evening coverage on match nights," said Beal.[7] It was a far cry from the scant few minutes of volleyball coverage Karch and his teammates savored while watching the 1976 Olympics.

There were only two concerns coming out of the match with Argentina: the play of Powers, and Buck's sore foot. Against Argentina, Powers struggled with his rhythm approaching the net, so Beal pulled Powers for part of the match. With Powers on the bench, Sunderland got more time with the starting rotation and played well, but not having Powers at his best was a concern. When he was on, the play and intensity of Powers lifted the entire team. The coaching staff needed to find a way to get him going.

Buck came out of the game with a sore foot and was having trouble jumping, so in the next match, on July 31 against Tunisia, Beal elected to play Salmons in his place. As a late alternate for the Games, the Tunisians were the weakest team in the pool. Beal was worried his team would look past the match. Marlowe described the pregame morning meeting for Tunisia in his diary:

> July 31—Our 10:30 meeting today went as predicted. Doug kept telling us that Tunisia is a "good ballclub . . . they did well against Korea . . . they can side-out," and "they have some big guys."
>
> Whenever Beal says things like that you know the team is a dog.

Marlowe was right. The Americans won in three straight games as Tunisia scored only eight points the entire match.

In the postgame meeting, Neville told the team, "Four miles to go." He was referring to the four remaining matches, two more in pool play and then, hopefully, two more in the medal round. Four more victories meant gold, but it was also a subtle reference to Outward Bound and the long journey this group of young men embarked on three years earlier.

The more competitive showdown that evening was the one that occurred between Beal and his team captain.

Just before the match, Beal approached Marlowe about a problem. There was some confusion about how to get water to the team during the time-outs. International volleyball competitions have strict rules about who can be on the court during time-outs. A volunteer from the Los Angeles Olympic Organizing Committee had been taking water to the team during time-outs, but now that practice was being questioned. In the event the Olympic Committee banned the volunteer from the court, Beal asked Marlowe to come off the bench with water for the team during the time-out.

When Marlowe balked at becoming the team water boy, Beal became insistent, saying, "Yes, you are. You will do it!"[8] In Beal's mind, if something needed to be done for the good of the team, they did it.

Just about anything Beal asked Marlowe to do for this team, he would, but this was one thing the proud captain wasn't going to agree to, even if he didn't play another minute during the Olympic Games. "No, no I won't do it," replied Marlowe. "I'll crawl for this team, but I won't grovel!"[9]

Fortunately, it turned out to be a nonissue as officials from the Organizing Committee allowed the volunteer to continue delivering water during time-outs. Yet after the match, Beal and Marlowe got into another shouting match over the incident, as neither man was willing to let it go.

The team witnessed it. Thirteen thousand spectators filing out of the stadium saw it. A writer for the *Long Beach Press Telegram* saw it.

The next day the *Telegram* reported, "Marlowe and Beal were seen to exchange harsh words after the match . . . a personality clash is known to exist."

The first part was true, the second part . . . not so much. Marlowe commented on the episode and the subsequent article in his diary:

> What a bunch of bullshit. If anything, I get along with Doug as well as anyone on the team, perhaps better, because I know where he's coming from.
>
> Oh well, there's an old movie adage: "I don't care what the newspaper says about me as long as they spell my name right." With the amount I'm playing, I need all the publicity I can get.

Despite the spat, Beal and Marlowe had tremendous respect for one another. If anything, the open confrontation was a sign of a healthy relationship; each man felt comfortable to communicate his true feelings. On dysfunctional teams, similar conflicts often get buried and fester, only to return when the pressure is the greatest. This team had reached a point where honesty and the truth were more important than anything else.

Beal and Marlowe put the incident behind them and focused on their next match, and the biggest to date, against South Korea on August 2. Beal continued to try different combinations with the starting lineup. Buck's ankle was still sore, so he got a shot the morning of the match and Beal kept him in the starting lineup, but Sunderland started over Powers.

The United States fell behind early in the first game and Karch raised his hands, pleading with the crowd to make some noise. The response from the American fans was intense and seemed to unnerve the Koreans as the crowd at the Long Beach Arena became a real factor. Although Korea was competitive, the U.S. team won in three straight games.

The team was getting better with each match but still had not peaked. The two-person serve receive of Berzins and Karch was working beautifully. They seemed to get to every ball, so Dvorak had multiple options when setting. The crew cut was working its magic, and Timmons was playing the best volleyball of his life. Dvorak's skill as a setter paired with Timmons's ability to hit from the back row was a lethal combination. The only lingering concern was Buck's ankle, which was still preventing him from playing to his full potential.

The next test for the team would be against Brazil on August 6. A victory would secure the team a spot in the final round.

Karch going all out to dig a ball at the 1984 Olympics. Kiraly made plays on the volleyball court that seemed beyond the limit of human ability. © PHOTO BY BRUCE HAZELTON

Then the unexpected happened. Underdog Korea beat Brazil 3–1, meaning the Americans were certain to finish in the top two of their pool. Before even taking the court against Brazil, they had already qualified for the final medal round.

Suddenly the nature of the upcoming Brazil match changed how both the United States and Brazil approached the game. To reach the medal round, Brazil absolutely had to beat the United States in pool play.

For the Americans, the stakes were different—they didn't have to win. The Americans wanted to win, and certainly would still play to win, but didn't absolutely have to, an always dangerous situation.

Beal worked the team hard the next day at practice and had the "starters" and "finishers" scrimmage each other to keep everyone sharp. Just like in Pullman, both teams were competitive, but unlike Pullman, everyone pulled in the same direction. The team was aligned and focused and together like never before.

That night Beal gave them the evening off, free to do whatever they wanted. Most players went home to visit family, but Marlowe, Karch, and Saunders went to the Chart House in Malibu for dinner.

"It seemed strange after I walked in, and it hit me," wrote Marlowe. "Two months ago I was behind the bar pouring margaritas for the locals. Now, through one twist of fate, I am captain of the USA volleyball team and leading it out on the floor in front of 13,000 screaming fans."[10]

Patrons streamed by their table, offering support and wishing them luck. After dinner they watched the U.S. women's team beat China. Jeanne Beauprey, Marlowe's friend who was at the movies with him the night he vowed to get back on the National Team, played for the United States, fulfilling her own Olympic ambition.

The night before the match with Brazil, the team huddled around the television together at the Olympic Village and watched Edwin Moses win a gold medal in the 400-meter hurdle. As the medal ceremony began, the room went silent.

"It's an eerie feeling watching Americans being awarded gold medals," wrote Marlowe. "The room gets very quiet, and our players become transfixed. Maybe that's the one thing that drives the players and coaches alike, a desire to do our best and come away with a gold medal.

"I'm sure the guys in the room were thinking the same thing" continued Marlowe. "In six days, we have a chance at that same glory."

"The only thing held out there as a reward was being an Olympic champion," recalled Timmons. "There was no contract, no guarantees, just the medal."[11]

August 6,

It seems like only yesterday. The year was 1975 and we were playing in the Pan American Games in Mexico City. The team was very different back then. Beal was not the coach but one of the starting setters. I was the other.

Paul Sunderland was our big outside hitter. Dave Saunders was 14 and in junior high school. No one had ever heard of Karch Kiraly!

. . . If we beat the Brazilians, we would get the silver medal. If we lost, we would get nothing. We were confident and playing well and in the fifth game we built up a 12–3 lead. We seemed to be on our way. . . .

We never scored another point. We all seemed to run out of gas at the same time and Brazil played great. They put in a new hitter at 12–3, a 19-year-old phenom named Bernard Rajman [*sic*]. He put every ball away. Eventually he would be All-World at 21.

Now back to reality. Rajman [*sic*] is now 27 and not the player he used to be. Beal is the coach, I am a reserve and oh yes, everyone has heard of Karch Kiraly.

Tonight, we play Brazil with a chance to give them nothing. That's right. No medal, no nothing. If I sound like I want revenge, you're right! I want to beat Brazil as badly as we can beat them.

Paul Sunderland (left) looks on as Steve Salmons, center and Karch Kiraly, right, go up for the block against Bernard Rajzman (#12) for Brazil in the pool round match. © PHOTO BY BRUCE HAZELTON

Aldis Berzins digging a ball near the back row while Steve Timmons looks on. Berzins was an integral part of the two-passer system, and he was the best passer for the United States at the 1984 Olympic Games. © PHOTO BY BRUCE HAZELTON

During the Olympics, Marlowe and Timmons had developed a pregame ritual. With millions of Americans watching the match on television, they wanted to look good for the camera. Marlowe would drop by Timmons's room to borrow a little Dippity-Do hair gel Timmons used to spike his crew cut, which was generating buzz in the volleyball world and beyond. But before the match with Brazil, Marlowe forgot. When Marlowe met up with Timmons on the van ride from the Olympic Village to the arena, he realized that Timmons had also forgotten to put Dippity-Do on his own hair. And Timmons without his Dippity-Do was like Samson without his hair.

Whether it was the lack of Dippity-Do or the fact that Brazil played with a desperation the United States didn't have or couldn't find, the team, like Timmons's hair, came out flat during the match with the Brazilians and stayed flat. Beal had changed the starting lineup by going with Sunderland and Salmons, but he realized early on it wasn't working. Powers came in off the bench and played great, but the rest of the team just wasn't clicking. Karch had only four kills the entire match, which was more like his average per set. Meanwhile, Rajzman played like a much younger version of himself and dominated. Brazil won in three straight games. Even more humiliating, the United States scored only two points in the final game, losing 15–2.

It was the first loss for the United States going back twenty-eight matches. Had the old ghosts returned? Were they falling into the same old patterns again? Was this Mexico City in 1975? Was this Argentina in 1982? Just as the team feared, Brazil didn't just win, they dominated and vaulted into the final round with confidence.

Beal tried to put it in perspective after the match to the media: "They played good ... (long pause) ... we played bad."[12]

Marlowe reflected on the match in his diary after the game:

> It will be very interesting to see how everyone reacts at practice. Can we come back to the finals? Is everybody down or up? How's the confidence level of the players? Only tomorrow's practice will tell.

· *16* ·

Can We?

*A*s a downtrodden U.S. team entered the gym the next morning for practice, they realized the cost of losing. The South Korean team was just finishing a meaningless practice, and it appeared as if the last place they wanted to be was on a volleyball court. Although Korea may well have been the second-best team in the tournament—like the United States and Brazil, they went 3–1 in pool play—they had lost more sets and been eliminated in a tiebreaker. The U.S. players knew all too well how it felt to be sent packing at a major tournament, and most wandered down to where the Koreans were practicing and offered sympathetic handshakes and pats on the back. It was going to be a long flight back to Seoul.

Once the Koreans left the gym, the team quickly regained focus. Karch told his teammates to forget about the loss to Brazil and put it behind them. "We didn't need to win to get into the medal round, so don't worry about it."[1]

"I said the same thing," said Beal, "but Karch's statement reinforced it. The guys really paid attention to him."[2]

The team turned to the task at hand, beating Canada, the Americans' opponent in the semifinals. Everyone was confident that, if they played to their ability, they would capture the real prize, the chance to play for a gold medal. They also knew they had a secret weapon: Bill Neville.

Neville had been the Canadian National Team coach for the 1976 Olympics and had developed many of Canada's players and their system of play, but he left the position in 1977 after a dispute with the Canadian Volleyball Federation.

"Every person on the team has certain teams they dislike and want to beat badly," wrote Marlowe. "Some dislike the Soviets or the Bulgarians, but no one gets up for a match like our assistant coach Bill Neville gets up for Canada.

"When we play Canada, Nev becomes a man possessed," Marlowe continued. "He gets this look on his face that looks like the one Tony Perkins had in *Psycho* every time he picked up that 10-inch knife."[3]

Neville knew everything there was to know about Canada and its players going back to 1974, and he put together a plan that he believed was bulletproof. "I like to say I've never lost a match on paper," joked Neville.[4] If the Americans executed, Canada didn't have a chance.

The morning of the semifinal match against Canada on August 8, the team was scheduled to practice at Manual Arts High School. On the way to practice, without explanation or warning, the bus was suddenly diverted to another practice site, L.A. Trade–Tech.

The U.S. team had practiced for about an hour when the Canadian National Team showed up for their practice and demanded use of the court. The Canadian coaching staff was visibly upset. According to their schedule, this was their gym, and they wanted to know what the U.S. team was doing there.

The Americans were on the court and planned to stay until they finished. The Canadian trainer then ordered his players onto the court. It was "game on."

The American players refused to be bullied off a court they believed they had every right to be on. The team that had once been split into a half dozen factions now spoke as one, chanting, "Hell no, we won't go!"[5]

"So we served balls at them until they retreated," wrote Marlowe. "At this point they were very angry and frustrated.

"We ended up leaving a short time later, but we clearly won the intimidation war," concluded Marlowe.

On the way back to the Olympic Village, questions started to fly. The players couldn't figure out how the mix-up happened. Why had the bus, they wondered, suddenly gone to Trade–Tech instead of Manuel Arts?

"The guy who took us to Trade Tech for practice was a genius," wrote Marlowe, "(or was it just an honest mistake . . . eh, Nev?)."

They never got a straight answer at the time, but the devilish grin on Neville's face said everything.

For the semifinal match later that evening, Beal decided to tweak the starting lineup again. Powers and Buck, the latter's foot feeling better, were back in the starting rotation, paired with Berzins, Karch, Timmons, and Dvorak.

"This is the starting team that has had the most success," reflected Marlowe. "So we should be very confident."[6]

The United States fielded its most formidable team, at least when everything was clicking, and that night against Canada, everything was clicking. Although Canada broke out to small leads early in each game, they were never really in the match. The United States proceeded to eliminate Canada in three

Timmons preparing to hit a well-timed set from Dvorak, as Karch Kiraly looks on, during the semifinal match versus Canada at the 1984 Olympics. SOURCE: USA VOLLEYBALL

straight games, guaranteeing, at the very least, a silver medal. A few years before, that might have been enough for the team, but not anymore.

Among the bedlam and cheering during the match, Marlowe was scanning the crowd and saw something that surprised him. In a sea of faces, he spotted a familiar one: Tim Hovland, cheering wildly for the United States. Also in the stands that night were Rod Wilde, his leg still in a cast, and Mike Blanchard. They had been invited by USA Volleyball, as guests of the team, and given rooms at the Hyatt adjacent to the arena. Still, it was bittersweet for Wilde and Blanchard as they watched the United States put Canada away and move one step closer to the ultimate goal: a gold medal. As happy as they were for their former teammates, they couldn't help wondering, "What if . . . ?" Their emotional scars were still so raw, it was hard at times for each to watch, but it meant a great deal to their former teammates to have them in the stands.

Now it was on to the gold medal match. In the other semifinal match, Brazil faced Italy, a last-minute replacement team in the tournament due to the boycott. A energized Italian team beat Brazil in the first set, but after that it was all Brazil. The Americans would have to play the Brazilians again, this time with a gold medal at stake.

The gold medal match was set for August 11 on the eve of the closing ceremony, one of the last competitions at these Games and certain to draw a huge television audience. With three days to prepare, Beal, Neville, and Crabb went over everything that went wrong in the loss to Brazil during the pool round, plotting a response. In pool play the Brazilians had utilized a jump spike serve, a relatively new skill and one that had given the U.S. team trouble.

Volleyball teams today, when facing the jump serve, use four passers.

"When the Brazilian players jump served well, it presented a major challenge for us, because we only had two passers," said Beal.[7]

In the pool play match against Brazil, the United States had elected not to try and block the serve but to focus on the return. That simply hadn't worked. This time around Beal and the coaching staff came up with something new. They briefly considered tossing the two-passer system, because if Brazil had an especially good night serving, the United States might be exposed, but instead they chose to devise a blocking strategy against the serve, cutting it off at the net. Under current rules, serves cannot be blocked, but that wasn't the case in 1984.

Over the next three days, the team studied the extensive scouting reports they were provided on each Brazilian player. They knew the Brazilians were a good team, and sometimes a great one, but they weren't unbeatable. They had recognizable patterns, weaknesses that could be exploited, and the coaches had a strategy to exploit them. The coaching staff developed a plan that would neutralize the jump serve and shut down Rajzman, who had given them so many problems before.

"We had never utilized a serve block strategy against the jump spike serve before," recalled Beal.[8] "We went over the scouting report rotation by rotation," wrote Marlowe. "With the second team impersonating Brazil," allowing the first team to get their blocking tuned to Brazil's offensive patterns.[9]

"We made one key change," said Beal, "we changed Berzins' blocking assignment. In our first match against Brazil, Aldis had no stuffs and our team only had nine."[10] With the new plan in place, the hope was that Berzins would be much more effective at the net. A few early blocks by Berzins would be a good indicator whether or not the plan was working.

Beal was rarely, if ever, content with his match plan and the preparation that went into it. Perhaps it was a reaction to his time as a player on the National Team in the 1970s when the team never seemed to be as prepared as their opponent.

"No matter how much we prepared for a match, I could think of things we'd forgotten," said Beal. "I could see problems, not so much with the players as with the match plan. I was never satisfied."[11]

The coaching staff had developed a match-day ritual at the Olympics, meeting in Beal's hotel room to finalize the game plan. The morning of the gold medal match, the three coaches met again.

In the foreground, the three U.S. men's volleyball coaches at the 1984 Olympics, from left to right: Tony Crabb, Bill Neville, and Doug Beal. Sitting behind the U.S. coaches, from left to right: Yuri Chesnokov, behind and to the left of Crabb, was a former gold medal player from the USSR in 1964 and coach of the Soviet team at the 1972 and 1976 Olympics. Between and behind Crabb and Neville is Bill Baird, an American who represented USVBA at the L.A. Games. On the right, between and behind Neville and Beal, is Yasutaka Matsudaira, Japanese men's coach from 1962 to 1972 and the gold medal winner in Munich in 1972. SOURCE: USA VOLLEYBALL

"This one lasted about three minutes," said Beal. "The reports were all over my bed. We looked at each other and laughed. There really wasn't anything more to talk about.

"We had our rotation down. We had our setting tendencies down, our passing down. Our matchups were perfect," added Beal.[12]

Beal and Neville were almost never on the same page when it came to a match plan. "I was the one who expressed apprehension," said Beal. "And Neville was the eternal optimist.

"We rarely agreed, except for the gold medal match!" he added.[13]

The game plan was solid, and everyone knew their assignment, but more than anything, the U.S. team was peaking. Everything the coaches and team psychologists had put in place to prepare the team to play its best volleyball at the Olympics seemed to be paying off. The two-man serve receive, so novel and unorthodox that they risked "looking foolish" for even trying it, and the swing offense, the "bowl of spaghetti" the Russian scout had found impenetrable, all of it was working even more effectively than Beal or Neville had ever imagined. And now the lethal threat of Timmons timing a perfect kill from the back row was paired with the virtuosity of Dvorak and the abundance of options he faced when deciding who and where to set. And added to that was the deepest roster in the game, with Sunderland, Salmons, Saunders, Waldie, Buck, and Duwelius available off the bench to fill specific roles and to provide a spark.

And leading them all was Marlowe, "the straw that stirs our drink." Every player now not only knew his role but embraced it. They weren't just players from USC and UCLA and Ohio State and a few other places thrown together, they weren't beach volleyball players and gym volleyball players, laid back Californians and stodgy Midwesterners. For the past three years, this group of individuals had been slowly coalescing.

Steady improvement had been the goal. Three years before, knowing that as host nation they would play in the Olympics, they had set out to see if they could become a team and then see how far that would take them, and now the team had a chance to compete for gold.

There had been arguments and injuries and ups and downs, days of sweat and nights filled with anxiety . . . and an awful lot of laughs too. The goal was now in sight, but the trail hadn't been easy.

For three long years, they woke up early each morning and practiced for four hours in a run-down, badly lit, and sometimes freezing cold gym in San Diego. They put their lives and careers and everything else on hold. They turned down offers to play professionally in Europe. They passed on beach tournaments and the all-night victory parties. They spent six weeks traveling through Asia in the heat of summer. For twenty-one days they snowshoed across the Abajo Mountains of Utah and hiked through Canyonlands National Park. They beat Poland in Warsaw, Bulgaria in Sofia, Cuba in Havana, and they beat the Soviet Union, the reigning World Champions and Olympic Champions, in four straight matches in the Soviet Union.

They had overcome their individual egos and their self-interested desire for individual playing time and glory. Now it was about the team. There had been bumps and twists along the way, but here they were, one match away from achieving their goal. What had once seemed so hard to achieve now seemed obvious: they would win gold together as a team, or lose as a team.

Each player prepared in his own way for what was about to come. The afternoon of the gold medal match, Marlowe reflected in his diary:

August 11—Can We?
It all comes down to this! Only one more mile to go! Our backs are up against the wall! This is it, make no mistake! Had enough?

It is 3pm now. Tonight is the culmination of every volleyball player's dream and many players careers (including mine). When we talk about big games, this is the BIG GAME.

It's the type of thing that can make or break your life in one way or another.

The interaction between the players today is very interesting. Lots of smiles, knowing looks and excitement in everyone's eyes. There's the air that this is the greatest event on earth and we're in it.

I know one thing—we will not be satisfied with the silver medal. We've worked for gold, we want the gold, and I think we're going to get it!

To beat Brazil, each player knew one thing: they had to play as a team. If volleyball truly is the ultimate team sport—and many of the players believed it was—then to win the ultimate prize would demand a team performance like no other. If the team fell behind, there would be no finger-pointing, no blame, no "spiral vortex" . . . only absolute support and trust in each other

Beal, Neville, and Crabb got to the arena early, before the team arrived. A disheartened Canadian team had lost the bronze medal match to Italy earlier in the day, and the arena had cleared out. It was completely empty of spectators.

Beal and Neville sat in the empty stands to take it all in. They thought back to their early days together on the National Team, Beal as a player, Neville as a coach. They thought about the years of separation, with Beal building the U.S. program in Dayton and Neville coaching the Canadian team. They recalled all the U.S. teams of the past that failed to qualify for the Olympics, and the accompanying heartbreak and dejection. They reflected on the move to San Diego in 1981 and setting the audacious goal to medal in 1984. They reminisced about Outward Bound, with Beal cartwheeling down the snowy mountain and Neville chasing a runaway snow shovel into a remote valley, the entire experience washing over them . . . the cold . . . the hunger . . . the exhaustion . . . the conversations around the fire after a long day . . . the realization that your survival depends on your "brother." And how something had clicked, and the team had broken through its selfish tendencies to become a team, and then, through trial and error, coaches trusting players and players trusting coaches, they had, together, discovered the "American system."

Then Beal took some time to be alone and reflect.

"I wandered around the arena and sat in different spots in the stands," said Beal. "Some low, some high.

"I was thinking about how amazing it was to play for the gold medal in the city most of the players were from," continued Beal. "In front of a home crowd. Having a team that might be the best in the world."[14]

Beal thought about how he and the coaching staff would process the game, win or lose. "Did we feel confident with the decisions we made and the challenges we took on?

"I was thinking about what a long journey it had been. And I was feeling good about everything we had already accomplished." Whatever happened tonight, well, that was gravy.

"I took a fair amount of time being really grateful for the experience," recalled Beal. "The four years leading up to 1984 and sharing that experience with Bill and Crabb."

There was no more game planning, no more practice, no more surveys, and no more talk of team building. There was really nothing left to do but play the game, to learn if the team would stand together on the Olympic podium with gold medals around their necks.

When the team arrived at the arena, Neville joined them on the court to take them through their warm-ups. Beal stayed in the locker room. He wanted to be alone. He kept pacing from the locker room and looking through the tunnel to the arena where he could see people slowly filling the seats. He saw so many familiar faces, so many people who in ways large and small had in some way contributed. Yasutaka Matsudaira, the great Japanese coach whose team won gold at Munich in 1972, sat just behind the U.S. bench as part of the Olympic jury. Then Yuri Chesnokov, the coach of the Soviet team that won silver at Montreal in 1976, took his place near Matsudaira. Beal had learned so much from these men through the years, and to the American coach they represented the history of the entire sport. They had been his mentors, his teachers, and now they were here to see how their student would perform at the biggest stage.

"During the day I was trying to come up with a 'final few pump-up words' that Lombardi would have been proud of," said Neville. "But I was coming up blank."[15]

As Neville took the team through warm-ups, Marlowe asked the coach if he could read something to the team before the match. Neville agreed. The players completed their warm-ups and came together one last time for the pregame meeting.

In the locker room there was an inverted canopy bubble from a World War II B-17 gun turret, and placed in the shell, which formed a bowl, were M&M's. "Nobody was in the mood for eats," recalled Neville, "except Pat Powers, who stood by the bowl and gobbled the candy."[16] Well, at least he wasn't in line at the concessions stand.

"We were crowded into the room," recalled Neville. "The players were decked out in the Gold Medal match-required warm-up suits provided by Levi. The players had fresh haircuts and groomed for the show."

"The locker-room was very quiet and very confident," recalled Marlowe.[17]

Neville let the team know that Marlowe was going to say a few words.

"Chris pulled out his dog-eared, coffee-stained, dirt-stained, Outward Bound journal," said Neville. "I remember it being in complete contrast to the perfectly groomed group of players."[18]

During the three-day solo portion of Outward Bound, each player was asked to keep a journal, to reflect on the experience, but also, to consider the greater journey—the journey of the team as it prepared for the Olympics—and the role each person played toward helping the team succeed. That was the experience Chris Marlowe chose to tap into and share with his teammates before the most significant match of their careers

"As he started to read the memories came back," said Neville. "I looked around at the players' faces. It appeared they were thinking back as well."[19]

It was all there—the bitter cold, the heavy packs and the seemingly endless hike, over 100 miles across windswept, snow-covered passes and sandstone slickrock canyons. But he also brought back memories of the cooking of meals together, the camaraderie and smiles around the campfire, the awe-inspiring views that lifted their hearts, and the sense of accomplishment when it was all done.

Although Marlowe lost the journal many years ago, the words he read that evening had, in a sense, prophesied this very moment.

"Marlowe's reading was very personal and predicted what this day would be," said Neville. "It was eloquent, permeated with deep feeling. The guys rarely shared personal feelings with each other."[20]

On this day, he did. And what Marlowe had written about that cold evening in January 1983, in the solitude and silence of his solo retreat, was not about his hope to make the team, or his individual goals, but his desire for his team to win gold.

"I told them it was the gold," said Marlowe. "That is the one medal that will satisfy the country and the program and the team. It would satisfy us."[21]

As Marlowe spoke, his words evoked memories of their long journey together . . . the sacrifice . . . the delayed careers and families . . . the months of travel away from wives and girlfriends . . . the grind of morning practice, four hours every day . . . the commitment to each other to become the best team they could be. He worked his teammates toward an emotional crescendo, before speaking with certainty, his voice rising in volume.

"And if gold is our destiny . . . ," he said as he looked around the room to make eye contact with every player.

". . . so be it!"[22]

The players erupted with a roar!

"It was perfect," said Neville. "It would have made Lombardi jealous."[23]

Marlowe had set the stage for Neville to deliver the motivational speech of his life, but as Neville looked around the room, he realized that it simply wasn't needed.

"There was nothing more to say," said Neville. "We were ready. . . . At that moment I knew Brazil didn't have a chance."

The players came together for a cheer and made their way down a hallway toward the buzz and excitement.

"On the way out to the arena," recalled Neville, "Pat [Powers] put his arm around my shoulders, whispered in my ear, 'I'm going to have a great match!'"

Marlowe led the team through the tunnel and into the arena. The crowd was already in a frenzy, flags waving everywhere. As the team jogged onto the court, the place turned into a madhouse. The players went through their final warm-ups and took their positions on the court, knowing they faced a team that only three days earlier had beaten them decisively in their home country, in front of their home fans. Tension was high and expectations through the roof, but so, too, was the team's confidence and belief and trust in one another.

The United States jumped to an early lead. The game plan devised by Beal, Neville, and Crabb worked beautifully. The first block of the match, against one of Brazil's best hitters, was delivered by Berzins, the shortest guy on the team. It was a good sign. The jump-spike serve that was so effective for Brazil in pool play was effectively countered by the U.S. blocking scheme. And when the ball did get through, Karch and Berzins handled it nearly flawlessly, passing to Dvorak, who set the ball with precision for Timmons, Powers, Buck, and Karch to kill.

The points piled up for the United States. At one point, the Brazilians spiked the ball toward Buck, scoring an apparent point. The Brazilians started celebrating when the ball bounced off Buck's shoulder high into the air. But Dvorak didn't miss a beat. He calmly tracked it down and set it to Timmons, who spiked it. Side out! It was that kind of game. The United States took the first two games at 15–6.

Yet, despite how well the Americans were playing, Marlowe continued to fret from the bench, apprehensive that something could still go wrong: someone could get hurt or Brazil could get hot.

In the third game the Americans again took a commanding lead. At 14–6, match point, the crowd could taste victory and worked itself into a frenzy, but Brazil put up an effective block, winning back the serve. Brazil then served a jump-spike ace to stay alive.

"It's only [Brazil's] second ace of the night," said Kirk Kilgour, the former National Team player providing color commentary for the match on ABC's national broadcast. "They had eleven the last time these two teams played, and that's the big difference."[24]

"Let's keep in mind that this is a U.S. team that is for real," said Bob Beattie, the play-by-play announcer, as the anticipation built. "They beat the Soviet Union four times in a row in the Soviet Union in May."

"They have to be considered the top team in the world until they play the Soviets and the Soviets prove otherwise," added Kilgour.

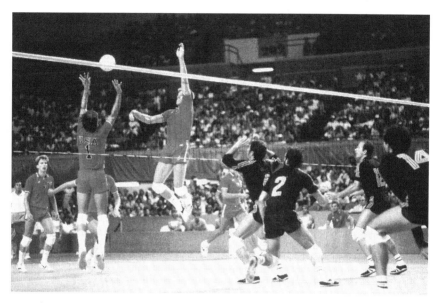

Dvorak setting Timmons from the back row in the gold medal match versus Brazil. The Brazilian defense is clearly out of position and can only look on as "Red" prepares to bring down the hammer. © PHOTO BY BRUCE HAZELTON

On the next play, Dvorak set Powers from the back row, and a player who once had lacked focus delivered a devastating hit, over the top of the Brazilian blockers, winning back the serve.

It was match point again! The coaches wanted Waldie in the back row to serve, so they subbed him in for Powers. The crowd began cheering even more wildly than before. As Waldie prepared to serve, the referee paused the game for a moment while a wet spot on the floor was mopped up. The anticipation only increased.

"The tension was like what you feel in the bottom of the ninth inning in the World Series," recalled Beal.[25]

"The U.S. coach has done a great job preparing this U.S. team after a devastating defeat three days ago," said Kilgour.[26]

Waldie served, and Brazil handled it well, Da Silva making a nice set to one of Brazil's hitters, Rajzman, who scored a decisive hit, thwarting the Americans once again. It brought the crowd down a notch, but only slightly.

On this night, no one feared the return of the "spiral vortex." That was all in the past, what used to happen.

Mario Xando went back to serve for Brazil, "The player they go to for big hits when they are in trouble," said Beattie. Xando went up to deliver a jump spike . . . "And he serves it into the net!"

The crowd went nuts!

"That's the fifteenth serving mistake by Brazil," said Beattie. Brazil was completely thrown off its game. The jump-spike serve, which had been so effective three days earlier, was utterly ineffective.

Now everyone in the stadium rose to their feet.

Timmons walked calmly back for the serve, and he wasted little time. He took a quick dribble, a deep breath, and then launched the ball over the net.

Brazil set up a hit on the outside. But Dvorak, who had once almost abandoned his team, was right where he was supposed to be. He went up and up, arms raised . . . and he blocked the ball to the floor.

It was over.

What came next was complete bedlam. Dvorak jumped around wildly, swinging his arms. Timmons leaped onto the referee stand, pulling himself up before pushing himself off and flying through the air. The other players ran around like crazed inmates in an asylum.

Marlowe and the other players on the bench raced onto the court to celebrate with their teammates. Everywhere were smiles, laughter, and relief.

The team huddled in the middle of the court, hugs and high fives all around. And there, in the middle of the craziness and insanity was Doug Beal. The players put their arms around him and pulled him into the celebration.

Neville looked over and saw Rod Wilde talking to a reporter in the stands. He raced over and said, "You need to get out here, Rod."[27]

"No, I don't think I can," responded Wilde.

"No, you were part of it," said Neville. "You *need* to be out here." Wilde, still in his cast, walked onto the main floor and stood behind the bench, taking it all in.

Beal immediately located Blanchard in the crowd and invited him onto the court to celebrate with the team too.

With millions of Americans watching, the television zoomed in on the players celebrating in the middle of the court. It was hard to tell one from the other. They were just a team.

"That picture tells the story," said Beattie. "The United States has won the gold medal."[28]

Marlowe had special T-shirts made for the occasion, stashed conveniently near the bench, printed with the words "We Did It!" He held one up for the crowd to see, and then he rushed around and gave one to each player and congratulated them.

Then he lifted an American flag over his head, extending both arms, and ran around the court, the Stars and Stripes rippling behind him like a cape.

Someone had the foresight to organize a picture, and the players gathered on the court, their backs to the net, index fingers extended to symbolize the victory. Beal was at the far end of the court talking with friends when he heard his name being shouted out by the players.

Marlowe had stashed an American flag near the bench, and immediately after the United States defeated Brazil in the gold medal match, he unfurled the flag, parading it around the court to raucous cheers from the spectators. SOURCE: USA VOLLEYBALL

The U.S. team celebrating immediately after winning the gold medal match against Brazil. From left to right: Pat Powers, Steve Salmons, partially obstructed, Marlowe, holding the "We Did It!" T-shirt over his head, Paul Sunderland (#4), and Karch Kiraly (#15) with his back turned. © PHOTO BY BRUCE HAZELTON

"Doug, come on, you've got to be in the picture," they pleaded.[29] All three coaches were pulled into the frame, Crabb wearing a Hawaiian lei around his neck, Neville holding up the "We Did It!" T-shirt, and Doug Beal with nothing but a smile, all of them together.

"We were a team," said Beal. "That might have been the best moment of all."[30]

The team gathered for a photo immediately after winning the gold medal match versus Brazil on August 11, 1984. Left to right, standing: Tony Crabb, Bill Neville, Chris Marlowe, Dave Saunders, Craig Buck, Steve Salmons, Steve Timmons, Paul Sunderland, Aldis Berzins, Rich Duwelius, Doug Beal. Knealing, left to right: Karch Kiraly, Pat Powers, Marc Waldie, Dusty Dvorak. © PHOTO BY BRUCE HAZELTON

Epilogue

$\mathcal{A}$fter the victory against Brazil and all the wild celebration subsided, a platform was set up in the middle of the court for the medal ceremony. No one left the arena. The players dashed back into the locker room and quickly changed into those special Levi's medal-winning uniforms they had marveled at earlier.

The athletes from all three medal-winning teams, the United States, Brazil, and Italy, made their way onto the platform. First, the Italian players received the bronze medal and the Brazilian players the silver, and then the American athletes, with Brazil on their right and Italy on their left, each received their long dreamed of gold medal. Bestowing the medals that night were two luminaries of volleyball, Paul Libaud, the first president of the International Volleyball Federation (FIVB), and Ruben Acosta, who was elected his successor at the FIVB Congress held in L.A. just before the Games began. Libaud was president from the founding of the FIVB in 1947 in Paris till 1984, and Acosta was president from 1984 till he resigned in 2008. Their presence that night connected the players to the very founding of the international game.

Each player bowed his head slightly as Libaud and Acosta draped the gold medal over his neck, and for the first time they felt the physical manifestation of their accomplishment, pressing down gently on their chest, near their heart.

The room fell silent as the public address announcer directed the audience toward the flags from the three nations. There was a moment of silence as the players raised their eyes, filled with emotion, toward the American flag.

"Then the house lights went out, the trumpets blared, and the medals came out and the national anthem played," said Beal. "I try not to show my emotions and I'm not usually an emotional guy, but this was too much."

For some players the song delivered tears; for others it brought smiles.

The team on the medal stand shortly after receiving their gold medals. From left to right: Marlowe, Dvorak, Saunders (hidden), Salmons, Duwelius (head), Sunderland, Timmons (hidden), Buck, Waldie (hidden), Berzins (clapping), Powers, and Karch. In the foreground on the left is Paul Libaud, the first president of the International Volleyball Federation (FIVB), and third from the left is Ruben Acosta, elected his successor at the FIVB Congress just before the Games began. The other two people are unidentified.
SOURCE: DOUG BEAL ARCHIVES

"In my mind I had imagined the award ceremony a million times," wrote Marlowe. "It was a little different than I expected because it was happy and joyous, but also a little sad.

"Why? One of the Brazilians, No 12, Rajman [*sic*], broke into tears on the victory stand. And guess who was standing right next to him. Me. Rajman [*sic*] had been a friend of mine since 1975 and is a real classy guy. . . . I actually felt unhappy for him. After all, I had been there before."

What Marlowe felt at that moment was connection. Yes, he was part of the U.S. team, but he now realized that he also was part of something bigger. He was connected not only to the Brazilian team but to all the other Olympians, past and present, the spectators in the arena, and the nation. Even I felt that connection, as I watched the televised coverage that evening, along with millions of others.

"After the ceremony, it was party time!" wrote Marlowe.

The coaches, players, and their ever-growing entourage made their way to the Hyatt Hotel, adjacent to the arena, for the after-party.

"I was walking down from the lobby to the ballroom, where the party was getting set up, and my dad stopped me," said Beal. Coaches aren't awarded Olympic medals. Beal's father, Leonard, knew that, so he secured a set of gold-plated Olympic coins and handed them to his son, saying, "This is the medal that you deserve."

Beal's father was rarely emotional, but he was at that moment. "It was the first time he was really aware of and integrated into my world," said Beal.[1] His father passed away just four years later.

The victory party was epic. Dave Saunders arranged to have three blenders in his room and recruited a couple of buddies to run them, ensuring that the drinks would flow through the night.

"The unofficial party began when Saunders said, 'Gentlemen, start your engines!'" wrote Marlowe.

"Everyone was there, and I mean everyone," noted Marlowe. Jim Coleman was there. Carl McGown was there. Tom Selleck was there. So were all the players and their wives and girlfriends and family members. My parents were there celebrating along with Chuck Johnson. They had come a long, long way from the backyard volleyball games at the married housing complex at the University of Oregon. The entire U.S. volleyball community celebrated that night, wherever they were, players who had only ever played before a handful of friends in near-empty YMCA gyms and who had never sniffed a medal. There was, in Marlowe's words, "Happy people, free booze, a great reason to celebrate . . . what more could you ask for?

"Not only was it a victory for our team, but for American volleyball in general," wrote Marlowe. "William Morgan must be proud, wherever he is."[2]

The players doused Beal with champagne and beer, and he loved it. Suddenly, Beal, the reserved outsider was now the most celebrated coach in the country and the most successful American volleyball coach in the history of the sport. His unpopular decisions were forgotten or forgiven.

"Doug deserves to stand in the sun now," wrote Marlowe. "Beal was the driving force behind our gold medal. For four years he took a lot of criticism about his coaching methods and the way he dealt with players. Well, he showed them!"[3]

The glow from the gold medals lingered. The players took the lessons they learned from their experience on the 1984 gold-medal-winning team and, to varying degrees, applied them to various ventures and career paths they embarked on after the Games. For the rest of their lives, they were Olympians, defined, at least in part, by the gold medals they would cherish forever. In fact, nearly everyone involved in the victory, even those who weren't on the court, took the experience forward.

"These guys are men now," said Neville recently. "We had them when they were boys. They all went on to have tremendous success in life."[4]

After the 1984 Olympics, Karch and a core group of players from the team decided to forego lucrative professional contracts to play in Europe, opting instead to stay with the program and try to win again. Given the Soviet boycott, some critics questioned whether the United States was really the best volleyball team in the world. Beal, his mission accomplished, chose to step down, and in 1985 Marv Dunphy left his position as the head coach of Pepperdine and took over as the men's national team coach. Karch Kiraly, Steve Timmons, Dave Saunders, and Craig Buck became leaders on a team that would eliminate all doubt about whether the 1984 U.S. team was for real. In addition to winning gold at the 1984 Olympics, they went on to win gold medals at the 1985 FIVB World Cup and 1986 FIVB World Championship—the volleyball triple crown—and they won gold at the 1988 Olympics in Seoul, defeating the Soviets in the finals and matching the Soviet's feat of winning consecutive gold medals. Between 1984 and 1988, the U.S. national team never lost a major tournament.

Even many of those who did not make the final roster but nevertheless played a role in the creation of the championship team went on to success. Kirk Kilgour, who was left a quadriplegic after a training accident in Italy, was later voted a charter member of the UCLA Athletics Hall of Fame and joined Bruins legends Kareem Abdul-Jabbar, John Wooden, and Gary Beban as the hall's first inductees. Kilgour was a longtime motivational speaker and hospital volunteer who worked with people with disabilities. "I love life, and I'm not going to waste a minute of it being bitter about it," Kilgour told the *Los Angeles Times* in 1995.[5] He passed away in 2002 at age fifty-four.

Sinjin Smith, who had turned down a chance to play on the national team to pursue other opportunities, went on to become one of the most successful beach volleyball players of all time, winning the Manhattan Open "Kings of the Beach" competition five times. Sinjin partnered with Randy Stoklos on the beach tour, and together they won a remarkable 114 tournaments, the most successful team of all time as measured by wins. Sinjin was a potent force behind the growth of beach volleyball as a sport and the development of the Association of Volleyball Professionals (AVP), the governing body of beach volleyball.

Tim Hovland, who chose to play professionally, continued his career in the Italian league, appearing from 1982 to 1984 for Kappa Sport in Torino before moving to Kutiba Falconara from 1985 to 1987. After 1987, he returned to the United States to play on the AVP beach tour, where he became one of the most popular and recognizable figures in beach volleyball history. "The Hov" was known for his fiery and vocal play, and he won sixty beach tournaments, many with partner Mike Dodd, earning over a million dollars in prize money before retiring in 2000 and being inducted in the Beach Volleyball Hall of Fame.

Mike Blanchard, the last player cut, played in over 225 matches as a member of the U.S. men's national team before he was let go just weeks before the Olympics. After the 1984 Games, he embarked on a career in the health and fitness industry, working as a trainer, coach, and educator before establishing a long and successful practice as a chiropractor. Blanchard passed away in August 2021, shortly before this book was finished.

Rod Wilde, whose broken leg opened the door for Chris Marlowe, remained involved in volleyball as a player and coach. While Marv Dunphy coached the national team, Wilde took over as head coach at Pepperdine from 1985 to 1989. From 1993 to 2000, he was an assistant coach on the U.S. men's national team, which failed to medal at either the 1996 or 2000 Olympics. Today he runs the Wilde4Volleyball Training Academy.

Rich Duwelius, who only began playing volleyball in college, left the national team shortly after the Los Angeles Games. He then worked as a special agent for the U.S. Naval Criminal Investigative Service (NCIS), a federal law enforcement agency under the Department of Defense, where he had a twenty-five-year career. Throughout his career with the Navy, he continued to participate in competitive volleyball on the beach with adult club teams and coached high school teams.

Marc Waldie, who joined the team when it was in Dayton, retired from the national team after the Olympics and moved with his wife back to Wichita, Kansas, but he continued to play with competitive club teams, where he won several first-place finishes at both USVBA Open Team Tournaments and USVBA Masters Tournaments. Outside of volleyball, Waldie has a successful and fulfilling career in real estate development, involved in everything from building houses to designing wood trusses and, more recently, the drawing and permitting of residential remodel designs.

Pat Powers, who returned to the team just before Outward Bound, remained on the national team, where he was a member for the 1985 World Cup and the 1986 World Championships, helping the team complete the "triple crown." After retiring from the indoor game, he competed professionally on the beach from 1986 to 1996, collecting thirteen victories. In 1997 he was hired as the head coach of USC men's volleyball, where he won over 100 matches and twice came within one victory of the NCAA Final Four. Today Powers runs VB Clinics, conducting youth volleyball camps across the country.

Aldis Berzins, who was Karch's partner in the two-man service receive, went on to become an assistant coach to the U.S. women's national team for the 1996 Olympics in Atlanta, where they fell to Cuba in the quarterfinals. From 2001 to 2015, Berzins served as senior director of sports development and coaching education for Special Olympics. Currently, he is the head volleyball coach at Stevenson University in Maryland.

Paul Sunderland, who was the only California player to move to Dayton and stay the entire time, retired from volleyball after winning the gold medal and started a career in broadcasting. In his very first assignment, Sunderland was paired with Marlowe, announcing the 1985 men's NCAA volleyball regionals. Eventually, Sunderland branched out into basketball, and from 2002 to 2005 he was the play-by-play announcer for the Los Angeles Lakers. He continues to announce for NBC, Universal Sports, and ESPN. Sunderland has been the indoor volleyball play-by-play announcer for NBC's Olympic coverage for every Olympics starting in 1992 Barcelona. At the 2021 Olympics in Tokyo, Sunderland announced the gold medal match in which the USA women, coached by Karch Kiraly, defeated Brazil for their first ever gold medal.

Craig Buck, who so effortlessly scaled the cliffs of Chippean Rocks on Outward Bound, remained with the U.S. national team, where in 1985 he was reunited with Marv Dunphy, his college coach from Pepperdine. Buck was named the 1990 Male Volleyball Player of the Year by the U.S. Olympic Committee and was a three-time All-American at the USA Nationals, earning MVP honors in 1987. Buck played professionally in France and Italy from 1988 to 1991 and was named an Italian League All-Star in 1991. From 1991 to 1997, Buck played in the Pro Four-Man Tour, where he earned All-League honors for six years and was named MVP in 1996. In 2015 Buck was severely injured in a bicycle accident near his home in Santa Barbara. Some wondered whether he would walk or talk again, but he has made an amazing recovery. In May 2017 Buck was an inductee with the inaugural Southern California Indoor Volleyball Hall of Fame class, which also included Karch Kiraly, Steve Timmons, and Marv Dunphy. After walking to the podium with the help of Dunphy, he gave a brief speech, expressing gratitude to both Beal and Dunphy, saying, "Without their support, I never would have achieved this."

Steve Salmons, who recovered from a back injury to become a key player on the 1984 team, continued to play for the national team for several more years and was one of the core members of the team that won all three legs of the "triple crown." After retiring from volleyball, he embarked on a career in real estate and today is the owner and president of Commercial Property Services, a real estate firm in San Diego.

Dusty Dvorak, who almost left the team during Outward Bound, remained with the national team after the Olympics, and was critical in helping the U.S. win the 1985 World Cup and 1986 World Championship—the coveted "triple crown." Eventually he did move on from the national team to play professionally in Italy, where his teams won three European Cup Championships. In 1990 he reunited with Doug Beal who coached him at Mediolanum Gonzaga of Milan, which won the 1990 Club World Championship. He returned to the United States in 1993 and joined the Bud Light four-man beach tour, where he was a perennial All-League selection and won the league title in 1993. After retiring from volleyball, Dvorak also went on to a successful career in real estate.

Steve Timmons was named MVP of the 1984 Olympic tournament, quite an accomplishment for a player whose status on the team was uncertain just six months prior. In 1985 Timmons cofounded Redsand Beachwear, an action sports clothing and lifestyle brand he eventually sold in 2016. Timmons left the U.S. national team after winning his second indoor gold medal at the 1988 Olympics in Seoul and pursued a professional career, playing for Il Messagero of Ravenna, Italy, where he was reunited with Karch Kiraly and together they led the squad to a 24–0 record, a division title in 1990, and the Club World Championship in 1991. But the Olympics were too much of a draw for Timmons, and he returned to the national team for the 1992 Games in Barcelona, collecting a bronze medal to become the first American male to win three Olympic medals in indoor volleyball. From 1990 to 1993 Timmons was married to basketball executive Jeanie Buss, daughter of Los Angeles Lakers owner Jerry Buss. He is a member of both the U.S. Volleyball Association and International Volleyball Halls of Fame. Today he is an assistant volleyball coach for the women's team at San Diego State.

After the Olympics Tony Crabb moved back to Hawaii with his family. As a longtime member of the Outrigger Club in Honolulu, he has been a mainstay as a youth volleyball coach and recruiting talent to the Outrigger Club Junior Volleyball program, winning national championships at the AAU Junior National Tournament with the Boys 12 and Under in 1990 and 1991 and second place with the Boys 14s in 1992.

After the Olympics, Bill Neville returned to Bozeman and resumed his position as head coach for the women's team at Montana State University. In 1987 Neville became the national director of coaching education for USA Volleyball and wrote the book *Coaching Volleyball Successfully*. In 1989 he returned to coaching to become the U.S. men's national coach, and from 1991 to 2000 he was the head coach of University of Washington women's volleyball, where he led the team to three NCAA tournament appearances, including a trip to the round of sixteen in 1997. More recently Bill ran and operated Nevillizms Volleyball Training Facility before retiring in 2016.

Chris Marlowe retired from volleyball shortly after the 1984 Games to take another run at an acting career. The leading roles never materialized, but he found himself increasingly in demand as a volleyball announcer. One of his first big breaks was becoming the play-by-play announcer for Prime Ticket, covering volleyball events, where he was paired up with Paul Sunderland as the color analyst. From the late 1980s and through the 1990s, Marlowe was the primary announcer for the AVP Beach Volleyball Tour.

In the early 1990s, Prime Ticket asked Marlowe to call other sports, including basketball, and he became the play-by-play announcer for UCLA basketball. Marlowe's talent behind the mic caught the attention of the NBA, and in 2004 he became the play-by-play announcer for the Denver Nuggets, a role he fills today. Marlowe also continues to call volleyball games during the summer and is a veteran of five consecutive Olympic telecasts on NBC, starting with calling play-by-play for NBC's coverage of beach volleyball in 2004 and, most recently, at the 2020 Games in Tokyo.

Karch Kiraly retired from the national team after helping the United States win a second consecutive gold medal at the 1988 Olympics in Seoul. From 1990 to 1992, Karch played professionally in Europe, where he won the Club World Championship and MVP award with his Italian team, Il Messaggero.

In 1992 Karch embarked on a successful career in beach volleyball, where he won 148 tournaments, becoming the winningest player in the sport's history, nine more than Sinjin Smith. At the 1996 Games in Atlanta, beach volleyball debuted as an Olympic sport, and Karch along with his partner, Kent Steffes, won the gold medal. Kiraly is the only player, man or woman, who has won Olympic gold medals in both indoor and beach volleyball.

At the turn of the century, FIVB designated Karch as the greatest male player of the twentieth century. In 2012 he became the coach of the U.S. women's national team, which won a bronze medal at the 2016 Olympics in Rio de Janiero. He continued as head coach in the next quadrennial, and at the 2020 Tokyo Games (held in 2021), he coached the U.S. women's national volleyball team to its first ever Olympic gold medal.

Doug Beal was elevated to national team director in 1985, where he oversaw both the men's and women's national programs. From 1990 to 1992, he coached Mediolanum Gonzaga in Milan, Italy, and from 1992 to 1997 he served as special assistant to the CEO of USA Volleyball, before he returned for a second stint as the men's national team coach from 1997 to 2004. In 2005 he was hired as the CEO of USA Volleyball, and under his leadership Hugh McCutcheon coached the U.S. men's national team to their third gold medal at the 2008 summer Olympics in Beijing. During Beal's tenure as CEO, USA Volleyball's budget grew from $8.4 million to $32 million, staff grew from 39 to 90, two training centers were established—the Indoor National Training Center in Anaheim, CA, and the Beach Volleyball Training Center in Torrance, CA—and USA athletes achieved extraordinary success in volleyball at the Olympic games in 2008, 2012, and 2016.

Beal retired from USA Volleyball in 2017 and currently serves as the board chair for USA Surfing, which gives his former players, whom he banned from playing on the beach, a good laugh. Beal has long been a driving force of volleyball both in the United States and internationally and is recognized by many as the single most influential person in volleyball in the world.

"I don't think you can even put a measure on the impact Doug has had on our sport as part of some groundbreaking changes," said Karch Kiraly. "He and Bill Neville, and the rest of his staff guided us in a way to where we could have Olympic success in 1984 that we had never had before."[6]

The former Australia men's national coach Roberto Santilli is one of many volleyball figures to recognize the impact Beal made on volleyball not just in the United States but in the world. "For sure Doug was the most innovative coach of the last century. He completely changed the way that a team was organized. He introduced the concept of specialization into the game. After he won the Olympic Games in 1984, the entire volleyball world started to look at the 'American System' as the real deal. They really changed volleyball."[7]

Marv Dunphy said of Beal that "where our sport is today, in the United States and in the world, is due to Doug Beal. His work ethic, creativity and courage earned respect from every aspect and every level of sport. Whenever I was with him, I knew I was in the presence of greatness."[8]

I set out to write a story about a team, but in many ways, I ended up writing a story about leadership as demonstrated by Doug Beal. As I interviewed team members, player after player expressed gratitude for Beal and everything he did to prepare the team for success. The players didn't always understand why Beal did what he did at the time, but looking back on it from a span of thirty or forty years, there is no question he got more out of this team than anyone thought possible.

Dusty Dvorak, the player he clashed with more than perhaps any other, said it best: "Instead of head volleyball coach, he could have been a Wall Street hedge fund manager or a Fortune 50 CEO. We were very fortunate to have him."[9]

Beal feels fortunate as well. "Our whole program, and many of our problems, can be explained very simply," he said. "We developed a program to make our men's team the best in the world. To do that we had to adhere to a philosophy and a set of principles that were the foundation of our program. Any individual who couldn't conform was expendable, but the philosophy, and rules, were not. When players wanted to train under an alternate set of criteria, we frequently got rid of them. We stuck to our principles and succeeded."

Those treasured gold medals are proof of that.

Team psychologist Chuck Johnson continued his teaching career as a professor at Chico State University, where he taught in the School of Education, and remained great friends with Don Murray as the pair worked together on many projects outside of volleyball.

"Don [Murray] and Chuck [Johnson] helped us understand," said Beal. "Success is a journey; it is not a single point in time. For sure, successful athletes talk about winning, but it is not always about just winning."[10]

"Working with Doug Beal and USA Volleyball was an opportunity of a lifetime," said my father. "I got to see how a world-class team comes together and plays at the highest level. And it validated everything we set out to do way back in 1974. Build trust, enhance communication, specialize talent, clarify roles, establish feedback, set goals, improve the culture, foster innovation . . . all of it."

My father, Don Murray, passed away in May 2021, just as I was finishing the first draft of this book. He always considered his work with the U.S. men's volleyball team one of the great achievements in his career. Later, Marv Dunphy heavily relied on my father and Chuck Johnson as he coached the 1988 U.S. team to a gold medal. Then, for several years, my father wasn't as involved with the volleyball team before receiving a call a few weeks before the 1996 Olympics in Atlanta. The team was facing some challenges, and he and Johnson were brought in at the last minute to try to help improve the culture, but it was too late as the team never got out of the preliminary round. When Beal became the coach again in 1997, my father and Johnson reengaged with the team and played an integral role.

After 1984, the bulk of my dad's professional work focused heavily on helping private companies develop what he called a "high performing team culture." He used many of the same tools and methods he first pioneered with the U.S men's volleyball team.

Not long after the Los Angeles Games, my father started working with Nike, a little athletic shoe company in Beaverton, Oregon, where he became good friends with Nike's CEO and founder, Phil Knight. His work with the elite athletes on the U.S. men's volleyball team helped him relate to the executive team at Nike, many of whom were former elite athletes themselves. He helped Knight build a world-class team to take on Adidas and the global athletic footwear and apparel markets. He would stand in front of Knight and his team at Nike's annual executive leadership retreat and pose the same questions he had to the U.S. volleyball team, asking, "What is the mission and vision of this organization?" and "What ground rules can we adopt to ensure we are a high-performing team?" Just as the volleyball players once did, the executives would scribble answers on note cards that my father would post on the wall for everyone to see.

Today I carry on the legacy of my father's work. The methods and tools I use to help corporations build a high-performing team culture are the same practices my father used with Knight and his leadership team and, before that, Beal and his players on the U.S. men's volleyball team.

I'm always amazed that the same timeless principles of leadership and high-performing teams apply whether it's an athletic team, a business team, or even a military team. The story of the 1984 U.S. men's volleyball team contains lessons we can all use.

Over the course of their journey, the players learned that every team member has value and that everyone has a role to play, no matter how big or small. They learned to stay calm under pressure and believe in one another, especially when things didn't go their way. They learned to be resilient and to care for one another. They learned to listen to their own crazy ideas, and they weren't afraid to look foolish. They learned that when mistakes happen the important thing is to support one another and stay dedicated to the team. They learned that even extremely talented players, if unwilling to make sacrifices and place the success of the team above themselves, must leave; the team is stronger without them. And, most significantly, they learned that extraordinary things can happen when individuals believe and trust in one another and commit themselves to a shared purpose.

These lessons not only propelled the 1984 U.S. volleyball team to the gold medal, but they also helped the players achieve success in their lives beyond sports, in their families and private lives, their businesses, and their communities.

And these are lessons we can all use to become better teammates, better leaders, and better human beings. When that happens, each of us, in our way, might make gold our destiny.

Notes

INTRODUCTION

1. Chuck Johnson, interview with author, May 27, 2021.

CHAPTER 1

1. Bill Neville, interview with author, June 17, 2021.
2. Doug Beal, *Spike!* (San Diego, CA: Avant Books, 1985), 67.
3. James F. Smith, "More Than a Drink: Yerba Mate: Argentina's Cultural Rite," *Los Angeles Times*, August 10, 1988.
4. Beal, *Spike!*, 20.
5. Doug Beal, interview with author, August 18, 2021.
6. Beal, *Spike!*, 13.
7. Bill Neville, interview with author, August 7, 2017.
8. Bill Neville, interview with author, August 7, 2017.
9. Bill Neville, interview with author, August 7, 2017.
10. Doug Beal, interview with author, February 27, 2021.
11. Bill Neville, interview with author, August 7, 2017.

CHAPTER 2

1. "The Volleyball Story," FIVB.org, https://www.fivb.com/en/volleyball/thegame_glossary/history, accessed July 1, 2021.
2. Bill Neville, interview with author, July 1, 2021.
3. "1962 All-MIVA," Midwestern Intercollegiate Volleyball Association, https://mivavolleyball.com/sports/2021/1/8/MVB_0108212210.aspx, accessed July 1, 2021.
4. Bill Neville, interview with author, July 1, 2021.

5. Bill Neville, interview with author, July 1, 2021.

6. Bill Neville, interview with author, August 7, 2017.

7. Bill Neville, interview with author, August 7, 2017.

CHAPTER 3

1. "1970 FIVB Volleyball Men's World Championships," Wikipedia, https://en.wikipedia.org/wiki/1970_FIVB_Volleyball_Men%27s_World_Championship, accessed July 1, 2021.

2. Barry McDermott, "Ringing Bells and Spiking Dream," *Sports Illustrated*, June 4, 1973.

3. Don Murray, Charles L. R. Johnson Jr., and Carl McGown, "Training and Team Building with the United States Olympic Volleyball," 1974.

4. Murray, Johnson, and McGown, "Training and Team Building"; Don Murray, interview with author, November 25, 2018.

5. Murray, Johnson, and McGown, "Training and Team Building."

6. Murray, Johnson, and McGown, "Training and Team Building."

7. Murray, Johnson, and McGown, "Training and Team Building."

CHAPTER 4

1. Sam Wood's most famous film, *For Whom the Bell Tolls*, was nominated for Best Picture in 1943.

2. Ray Ripton, "Palisades High Coach Marvin Decides to Call It Quits," *Los Angeles Times*, April 25, 1991.

3. John Maffei, "Students Once Fell Hard for Marlowe, Aztecs Volleyball," *San Diego Union-Tribune*, February 11, 2014.

4. John Maffei, interview with author, January 9, 2021.

5. John Maffei, "The 52: One Big Lovefest for the Aztecs," *San Diego Union-Tribune*, March 19, 2016.

6. John Maffei, interview with author, January 9, 2021.

7. John Maffei, "The 52: One Big Lovefest for the Aztecs," *San Diego Union-Tribune*, March 19, 2016.

8. Joe Jares, "The Big Cy Wasn't One Bit Shy," *Sports Illustrated*, May 23, 1977, 88.

9. Beal, *Spike!*, 62.

10. Greg Noble, "Back to Back Winters of 1976–77 and 1977–78 Were Coldest and Snowiest," *From the Vault*, WCPO Cincinnati, January 14, 2016, http://www.wcpo.com/news/our-community/from-the-vault/from-the-vault-back-to-back-winters-of-1976-77-and-1977-78-were-coldest-snowiest.

11. Rich Duwelius, interview with author, February 2, 2021.

12. Rich Duwelius, interview with author, February 2, 2021.

13. Marc Waldie, interview with author, March 15, 2021.

14. Tom Hoffarth, "Chris Marlowe Keeps His Feet in the Sand and the Heart of a Lion," *InsideSoCal*, August 22, 2015, https://web.archive.org/web/20170812211419/ http://www.insidesocal.com/tomhoffarth/2015/08/22/sunday-media-q-and-a-chris -marlowe-keeps-his-feet-in-the-sand-and-the-heart-of-the-lion/.

15. Beal, *Spike!*, 29.

16. Beal, *Spike!*, 29.

17. Beal, *Spike!*, 31.

18. Doug Beal, interview with author, October 4, 2017.

CHAPTER 5

1. Karch Kiraly, "Episode 45—Karch Kiraly (Uninterrupted)," *Sports Stories with Denny Lennon*, YouTube, August 5, 2020, https://www.youtube.com/watch? v=SU8SgQHU53k.

2. Laszlo Kiraly, "Karch Kiraly in 1988—Volleyball History," *Volleyball 1 on 1 Videos*, YouTube, September 28, 2012, https://www.youtube.com/watch?v=JUAqkk1B6hg.

3. VBM Staff, "From Volleyball Magazine in 1990: An In-Depth Profile of Karch Kiraly," *Volleyball Monthly*, June 12, 2020.

4. Karch Kiraly, "Karch Kiraly in 1988."

5. Karch Kiraly, "Episode 45."

6. Karch Kiraly, interview with author, October 2018.

7. Kiraly, "Episode 45."

8. Kiraly, "Episode 45."

9. Karch Kiraly, interview with author, October 2018.

10. Kiraly, "Episode 45."

11. Karch Kiraly, "Karch Kiraly in 1988."

12. Kiraly, "Episode 45."

13. Kiraly, "Episode 45."

14. VBM Staff, "From Volleyball Magazine in 1990."

15. Kiraly, "Episode 45."

16. Kiraly, interview with author, January 17 and 23, 2018.

17. Kiraly, "Episode 45."

18. Kiraly, interview with author, January 17 and 23, 2018.

19. Kiraly, interview with author, January 17 and 23, 2018.

20. Kiraly, interview with author, January 17 and 23, 2018.

21. Dusty Dvorak, interview with author, March 25, 2021.

22. Kiraly, "Episode 45."

23. Kiraly, "Episode 45."

24. Kiraly, "Episode 45."

25. Kiraly, "Episode 45."

26. Beal, *Spike!*, 20.

CHAPTER 6

1. Beal, *Spike!*, 34.
2. Beal, *Spike!*, 63.
3. Doug Beal, interview with author, October 4, 2017.
4. Bill Neville, interview with author, August 7, 2017.
5. Beal, *Spike!*, 63.
6. Beal, *Spike!*, 64.
7. Beal, *Spike!*, 64.
8. Beal, *Spike!*, 33.
9. Beal, *Spike!*, 33.
10. Beal, *Spike!*, 33.
11. Tim Hovland, interview with author, November 23, 2020.
12. Marc Waldie, interview with author, March 15, 2021.
13. Tim Hovland, interview with author, November 23, 2020.
14. Steve Salmons, interview with author, December 11, 2020.
15. Marc Waldie, interview with author, March 15, 2021.
16. Doug Beal, interview with author, October 4, 2017.
17. Beal, *Spike!*, 33.
18. Beal, *Spike!*, 33.
19. Beal, *Spike!*, 38, 12.
20. Marc Waldie, interview with author, March 15, 2021.
21. Bill Neville, interview with author, August 7, 2017.
22. Marc Waldie, interview with author, March 15, 2021.
23. Beal, *Spike!*, 12.
24. Beal, *Spike!*, 36.
25. Beal, *Spike!*, 36, 37.
26. Steve Fiffer, "Olympic Profile: Paul Sunderland; Respect, at Last, for U.S. Volleyball," *New York Times*, May 27, 1984.

CHAPTER 7

1. Kiraly, "Episode 45."
2. Kiraly, "Episode 45."
3. Dusty Dvorak, interview with author, March 25, 2021.
4. Kiraly, "Episode 45."
5. Doug Beal, interview with author, March 18, 2021.
6. Dusty Dvorak, interview with author, March 25, 2021.
7. Doug Beal, interview with author, March 18, 2021.
8. Doug Beal, interview with author, March 18, 2021.
9. Gordon Smith, "Men's Volleyball Aims for Olympics from San Diego," *San Diego Reader*, August 18, 1983.
10. Tim Hovland, interview with author, November 23, 2020.

11. Beal, *Spike!*, 41.
12. Beal, *Spike!*, 41.
13. Paul Sunderland, interview with author, June 29, 2017.
14. Kiraly, "Episode 45."
15. Smith, "Men's Volleyball Aims for Olympics."
16. Smith, "Men's Volleyball Aims for Olympics."
17. Beal, *Spike!*, 12.
18. Beal, *Spike!*, 12.
19. Smith, "Men's Volleyball Aims for Olympics."
20. Bill Neville, interview with author, August 7, 2017.
21. Bill Neville, interview with author, August 7, 2017.
22. Bill Neville, interview with author, August 7, 2017.
23. Dave Saunders, interview with author, March 10, 2021.
24. Aldis Berzins, interview with author, February 6, 2021.
25. Aldis Berzins, interview with author, February 6, 2021.
26. Beal, *Spike!*, 43.

CHAPTER 8

1. Beal, *Spike!*, 19.
2. Beal, *Spike!*, 46.
3. Kiraly, "Episode 45."
4. Beal, *Spike!*, 48.
5. Bill Neville, interview with author, August 7, 2017.
6. Tim Hovland, interview with author, November 23, 2020.
7. Beal, *Spike!*, 49.
8. Beal, *Spike!*, 14.
9. Beal, *Spike!*, 14.
10. Chris Marlowe, interview with author, September 20, 2017.
11. The letter no longer exists.
12. Rod Wilde, interview with author, November 24, 2020.
13. Smith, "Men's Volleyball Aims for Olympics."
14. Doug Beal, interview with author, March 18, 2021.
15. Karch Kiraly, interview with author, November 30, 2020.

CHAPTER 9

1. Don Murray, interview with author, November 25, 2018.
2. Beal, *Spike!*, 42.
3. Beal, *Spike!*, 42.
4. Details of meeting discussion from Don Murray, interview with author, November 25, 2018; Don Murray and Charles L. R. Johnson Jr., "Social-Psychological

Consultation with USA Men's Volleyball Team," Report for Team Workshop, September 14, 1982.

5. Beal, *Spike!*, 72.

6. Don Murray and Chuck Johnson, "Memo to U.S.A. Volleyball Team Coaches," October 4, 1982.

7. Charles Stetson, "An Essay on Kurt Hahn, Founder of Outward Bound," Kurt Hahn.org, February 2017, https://www.kurthahn.org/wp-content/uploads/2017/02/2017-stet.pdf.

8. Outward Bound, "Our Story," https://www.outwardbound.net/our-story/, accessed July 1, 2021.

9. Bill Neville, letter to Outward Bound, June 26, 1981.

10. Paul Sunderland, interview with author, July 29, 2017.

11. Beal, *Spike!*, 74.

12. Beal, *Spike!*, 74.

13. Chris Marlowe, interview with author, September 20, 2017.

14. Beal, *Spike!*, 74.

15. Paul Sunderland, interview with author, July 29, 2017. The player was Jay Hanseth.

16. Bill Neville, interview with author, July 29, 2021.

17. Bill Neville, interview with author, July 29, 2021.

18. Beal, *Spike!*, 74.

19. Aldis Berzins, interview with author, February 6, 2021.

20. Beal, *Spike!*, 74.

21. Randy Udall, "Striving for Gold—Medal That Is: An Account of the Outward Bound Course Taken in January 1983 by the US Men's Olympic Volleyball Team," Outward Bound.

22. Peter O'Neil, "USA Men's Volleyball Course Report," January 1983.

23. Don Murray and Chuck Johnson, "Memo to U.S.A. Volleyball Team Coaches," October 4, 1982.

24. Doug Beal, interview with author, April 25, 2021.

25. Beal, *Spike!*, 49.

26. Tim Hovland, interview with author, November 23, 2020.

27. Beal, *Spike!*, 49.

28. Chris Marlowe, interview with author, September 20, 2017.

CHAPTER 10

1. Rod Wilde, interview with author, February 7, 2021.

2. "Snow Survey Reveals High Moisture Content," *San Juan Record*, January 1983.

3. Doug Beal, interview with author, March 30, 2021.

4. Eddie Young, interview with author, June 28, 2021.

5. Udall, "Striving for Gold."

6. Marc Waldie, interview with author, March 15, 2021.

7. Udall, "Striving for Gold."

8. Bill Neville, interview with author, August 7, 2017.

9. Dave Saunders, interview with author, March 10, 2021.

10. Chris Marlowe, interview with author, October 3, 2017.

11. Chris Marlowe, interview with author, October 3, 2017.

12. Chris Marlowe, interview with author, October 3, 2017.

13. Bruce McAlister, "United States Volleyball Team versus the Elements," *Stars in Motion*, Spring 1983.

14. Peter O'Neil, "USA Men's Volleyball Team Course Report, January 7–27, 1983," Colorado Outward Bound School.

15. O'Neil, "USA Men's Volleyball Team Course Report."

16. Bill Neville, interview with author, August 7, 2017.

17. Bill Neville, interview with author, August 7, 2017.

18. Bill Neville, interview with author, August 7, 2017.

19. Bill Neville, interview with author, August 7, 2017.

20. Udall, "Striving for Gold."

21. Beal, *Spike!*, 76.

22. Chris Marlowe, interview with author, October 3, 2017.

23. Udall, "Striving for Gold."

24. Beal, *Spike!*, 77.

25. Steve Timmons, interview with author, December 3, 2020.

26. Chris Marlowe, interview with author, October 3, 2017.

27. Udall, "Striving for Gold."

28. Aldis Berzins, interview with author, February 6, 2021.

29. Beal, *Spike!*, 77.

CHAPTER 11

1. Dusty Dvorak, interview with author, March 25, 2021.

2. O'Neil, "USA Men's Volleyball Team Course Report."

3. Chris Marlowe, interview with author, September 22, 2017.

4. Bill Neville, interview with author, August 7, 2017.

5. Dusty Dvorak, interview with author, March 25, 2021.

6. Dusty Dvorak, interview with author, March 25, 2021.

7. Bill Neville, interview with author, January 25, 2018.

8. Bill Neville, interview with author, January 25, 2018.

9. Doug Beal, interview with author, March 30, 2021.

10. Beal, *Spike!*, 76.

11. Doug Beal, interview with author, March 30, 2021.

12. David Saunders, interview with author, March 10, 2021.

13. O'Neil, "USA Men's Volleyball Team Course Report."

14. Udall, "Striving for Gold."

15. Chris Marlowe, interview with author, September 22, 2017.

16. Chris Marlowe, interview with author, September 22, 2017.

17. Mark Waldie, interview with author, March 15, 2021.

18. Doug Beal, interview with author, April 22, 2021.

19. Bill Neville, interview with author, April 5, 2021.

20. Doug Beal, interview with author, April 22, 2021.

21. Chuck Johnson, interview with author, May 27, 2021.

22. Bill Neville, interview with author, April 5, 2021.

23. Chuck Johnson, interview with author, May 27, 2021. Neville was referencing the well-known Robert Frost poem, which goes on: "Two roads diverged in a wood, and I— / I took the one less traveled by, / And that has made all the difference."

24. Bill Neville, interview with author, April 5, 2021.

25. Chris Marlowe, interview with author, September 20, 2017.

26. David Saunders, interview with author, March 10, 2021.

27. Aldis Berzins, interview with author, February 6, 2021.

28. Bill Neville, interview with author, January 25, 2018.

CHAPTER 12

1. Smith, "Men's Volleyball Aims for Olympics."

2. Bill Neville, interview with author, August 7, 2017.

3. Doug Beal, interview with author, October 4, 2017.

4. Bill Neville, interview with author, August 7, 2017.

5. Bill Neville, interview with author, August 7, 2017.

6. Bill Neville, interview with author, August 7, 2017.

7. Bill Neville, interview with author, August 7, 2017.

8. Bill Neville, interview with author, August 7, 2017.

9. Bill Neville, interview with author, August 7, 2017.

10. Doug Beal, interview with author, October 4, 2017.

11. Bill Neville, interview with author, April 5, 2021.

12. Chris Marlowe, interview with author, September 22, 2017.

13. Bill Neville, interview with author, April 5, 2021.

14. Beal, *Spike!*, 81.

15. Bill Neville, interview with author, April 22, 2021.

16. Smith, "Men's Volleyball Aims for Olympics."

17. Chris Marlowe, interview with author, September 22, 2017.

18. Beal, *Spike!*, 83.

19. Chris Marlowe, interview with author, September 22, 2017.

20. Bill Neville, interview with author, April 5, 2021.

21. Bill Neville, interview with author, April 5, 2021.

22. Steve Timmons, interview with the author, December 3, 2020.

23. Smith, "Men's Volleyball Aims for Olympics."

24. Bill Neville, interview with author, August 7, 2017.

25. Smith, "Men's Volleyball Aims for Olympics."

CHAPTER 13

1. Bill Neville, interview with author, August 7, 2017.
2. Chris Marlowe, interview with author, September 22, 2017.
3. Beal, *Spike!*, 16.
4. USA Volleyball, "Players," *Countdown to Los Angeles*, 1983.
5. Karch Kiraly, interview with author, January 23, 2018.
6. Steve Timmons, interview with author, December 3, 2020.
7. Steve Timmons, interview with author, December 3, 2020.
8. Bill Neville, interview with author, June 9, 2021.
9. Chris Marlowe, interview with author, September 22, 2017.
10. Doug Beal, interview with author, June 4, 2021.
11. Chris Marlowe, interview with author, September 22, 2017.
12. Karch Kiraly, interview with author, January 23, 2018.
13. Steve Timmons, interview with author, December 3, 2020.
14. Chris Marlowe, interview with author, September 22, 2017.
15. Chris Marlowe, interview with author, September 22, 2017.
16. Karch Kiraly, interview with author, January 23, 2018.
17. *Sidronio Henrique,* "Doug Beal, the Man Who Reinvented Volleyball," *At Home on the Court*, Mark Lebedew website, October 19, 2014, https://marklebedew.com/2014/10/19/doug-beal-the-man-who-reinvented-volleyball/.
18. Beal, *Spike!*, 125.
19. Kiraly, "Episode 45."
20. John F. Burns, "Moscow Will Keep Its Team from Los Angeles Olympics," *New York Times*, May 9, 1984.
21. Doug Beal, interview with author, June 4, 2021.
22. Beal, *Spike!*, 125.
23. Beal, *Spike!*, 126.
24. Bill Neville, interview with author, August 7, 2017.
25. Bill Neville, interview with author, August 7, 2017.
26. The player was Alexsander Sorokolet.
27. Gary Klein, "At 33, Wilde Revisits Olympic Dream," *Los Angeles Times*, November 17, 1989.
28. Rod Wilde, interview with author, November 24, 2020.
29. Bill Neville, interview with author, June 9, 2021.
30. Chris Marlowe, interview with author, September 22, 2017.
31. Chris Marlowe, interview with author, September 22, 2017.
32. Steve Timmons, interview with the author, December 3, 2020.

CHAPTER 14

1. Chris Marlowe, interview with author, September 20, 2017.
2. Doug Beal, interview with author, June 7, 2021.

3. Marc Waldie, interview with author, March 15, 2021.
4. Bill Neville, interview with author, April 5, 2021.
5. Doug Beal, interview with author, June 7, 2021.
6. Bill Neville, interview with author, August 7, 2017.
7. Chris Marlowe, interview with author, September 20, 2017.
8. Steve Timmons, interview with author, December 3, 2020.
9. Doug Beal, interview with author, May 3, 2021.
10. Don Murray, interview with author, November 25, 2018.
11. Chris Marlowe, interview with author, September 20, 2017.
12. Karch Kiraly, interview with author, January 23, 2018.
13. Bill Neville, interview with author, June 14, 2021.
14. Karch Kiraly, interview with author, January 23, 2018.
15. Chris Marlowe, interview with author, September 20, 2017.
16. Karch Kiraly, interview with author, January 23, 2018.
17. Chris Marlowe, interview with author, September 20, 2017.
18. Bill Neville, interview with author, June 14, 2021.
19. Doug Beal, interview with author, June 7, 2021.
20. Karch Kiraly, interview with author, January 23, 2018.
21. Karch Kiraly, interview with author, January 23, 2018.
22. Doug Beal, interview with author, June 7, 2021.
23. Karch Kiraly, interview with author, January 23, 2018.
24. Karch Kiraly, interview with author, January 23, 2018.
25. Doug Beal, interview with author, June 7, 2021.
26. Karch Kiraly, interview with author, January 23, 2018.
27. Chris Marlowe, interview with author, September 20, 2017.
28. Bill Neville, interview with author, June 14, 2021.
29. Chris Marlowe, interview with author, September 20, 2017.
30. Karch Kiraly, interview with author, January 23, 2018.
31. Chuck Johnson, interview with author, May 27, 2021.

CHAPTER 15

1. Chris Marlowe, "'84 Olympic Diary, Marlowe Chronicles the USA's Golden Moment," *Volleyball Monthly*, August 1984.
2. Beal, *Spike!*, 134.
3. Beal, *Spike!*, 135.
4. Marlowe, "'84 Olympic Diary."
5. Doug Beal, interview with author, June 14, 2021.
6. Doug Beal, interview with author, June 14, 2021.
7. Doug Beal, interview with author, June 14, 2021.
8. Marlowe, "'84 Olympic Diary."
9. Marlowe, "'84 Olympic Diary."
10. Chris Marlowe, "'84 Olympic Diary, in Part II, Marlowe Tells How a Dream Came True," *Volleyball Monthly*, August 1984.

11. Steve Timmons, interview with the author, December 3, 2020.
12. Marlowe, "'84 Olympic Diary, in Part II."

CHAPTER 16

1. Beal, *Spike!*, 4.
2. Beal, *Spike!*, 4.
3. Marlowe, "'84 Olympic Diary, in Part II."
4. Bill Neville, interview with author, June 14, 2021.
5. Marlowe, "'84 Olympic Diary, in Part II."
6. Marlowe, "'84 Olympic Diary, in Part II."
7. Doug Beal, interview with author, June 14, 2014.
8. Doug Beal, interview with author, June 14, 2014.
9. Marlowe, "'84 Olympic Diary, in Part II."
10. Beal, *Spike!*, 138.
11. Beal, *Spike!*, 40.
12. Beal, *Spike!*, 138.
13. Beal, *Spike!*, 40.
14. Doug Beal, interview with author, June 14, 2021.
15. Bill Neville, interview with author, June 14, 2021.
16. Bill Neville, interview with author, June 14, 2021.
17. Marlowe, "'84 Olympic Diary, in Part II."
18. Bill Neville, interview with author, June 14, 2021.
19. Bill Neville, interview with author, June 14, 2021.
20. Bill Neville, interview with author, June 14, 2021.
21. Chris Marlowe, interview with author, August 24, 2021.
22. Aldis Berzins, interview with author, February 6, 2021.
23. Bill Neville, interview with author, June 14, 2021.
24. ABC Olympic Broadcast, "Olympics—1984 Los Angeles—Volleyball—Men's Finals—USA vs Brazil & in Studio Player Interview," YouTube.com, April 4, 2016, https://www.youtube.com/watch?v=rwn3QIa2aeM.
25. Beal, *Spike!*, 2.
26. ABC Olympic Broadcast, "Men's Finals."
27. Rod Wilde, interview with author, November 24, 2020.
28. ABC Olympic Broadcast, "Men's Finals."
29. Beal, *Spike!*, 2.
30. Beal, *Spike!*, 2.

EPILOGUE

1. Doug Beal, interview with author, June 14, 2021.
2. Marlowe, "'84 Olympic Diary, in Part II."
3. Marlowe, "'84 Olympic Diary, in Part II."

4. Bill Neville, interview with author, August 17, 2017.

5. Mike Bresnahan, "Kirk Kilgour, 54, Volleyball Standout," *Los Angeles Times*, July 12, 2002.

6. Zuzanna Dulnik and Ekaterina Semenova, "Volleyball's View of a Legend," Game in Focus, *Volleyverse*, accessed February 18, 2016.

7. Dulnik and Semenova, "Volleyball's View of a Legend."

8. Dulnik and Semenova, "Volleyball's View of a Legend."

9. Dusty Dvorak, interview with author, March 25, 2021.

10. Doug Beal, interview with author, October 4, 2017.

Index

About the Author

Sean Murray is the founder of RealTime Performance, a consultancy dedicated to helping organizations develop leaders and build high-performing cultures. He also hosts *The Good Life Podcast* and writes regularly at the *RealTime Performance Blog*. Sean delivers workshops, courses, and keynote speeches on leadership, team building, and how to create a high-performing culture. He lives in Seattle with his wife and two children.

To learn more about introducing the timeless principles of leadership and team success to your organization, visit www.real timeperformance.com.